PRUDE

PRUDE

How the Sex-Obsessed

Culture

Damages Girls

(And America, Too!)

Carol Platt Liebau

CENTER
STREET

New York Boston Nashville

Center Street
Hachette Book Group USA
237 Park Avenue
New York, NY 10017

Visit our Web site at www.centerstreet.com.

Center Street is a division of Hachette Book Group USA, Inc. The Center
Street name and logo are trademarks of Hachette Book Group USA, Inc.
Book design by Fearn Cutler deVicq
Printed in the United States of America

First Edition: November 2007
10 9 8 7 6 5 4 3 2

Library of Congress Cataloging-in-Publication Data
Liebau, Carol Platt.
Prude : how the sex-obsessed culture damages girls (and America too!)
/ Carol Platt Liebau.—1st ed.
p. cm.
ISBN-13: 978-1-59995-683-1
ISBN-10: 1-59995-683-7
1. Mass media and teenagers—United States. 2. Teenage girls—United
States—Attitudes. 3. Teenage girls—Sexual behavior—United States.
4. Teenage girls—United States—Social conditions. 5. Popular culture—
United States. I. Title.

HQ799.2.M352L54 2007
306.70835'20973—dc22   2007006724

For my mother, Jo Ann Haynes Platt,
whose lifelong love and encouragement convinced me
that my opinions were interesting and important.
(Now everyone else is paying
the price!)

For my father, Daniel Wall Platt, M.D.,
who always offered the paternal love and approval
that means the world to every girl.

And, of course,

For my husband, Jack,
truly a companion in joy,
a comfort in sorrow,
and the man of my dreams.

ACKNOWLEDGMENTS

So many wonderful people to thank, so little time.

The entire team at Center Street Books—particularly Rolf Zettersten and my editor Chris Park, along with Sarah Sper—made the writing and editing process a pleasure. If everyone had the opportunity to work with such gracious and talented people there would be more great books and many, many, happy authors.

I am grateful also to Ann Reyes Robbins, who fulfilled all my research requests amid a very busy and challenging schedule. Thanks also go to my agent, Craig Wiley, for his efforts on my behalf.

National Review's Kate O'Beirne took time at the inception of this project to offer helpful guidance and advice. The content of the book benefited greatly from the expertise of Dr. Drew Pinsky, Dr. Adria O'Donnell, Dr. Thomas Lickona, Dr. Melissa Johnson, and Elayne Bennett, president and founder of the Best Friends Foundation. Liz Fisher, Emily Limbaugh, Sherif Girgis, and Cassandra DeBenedetto were likewise generous with their time and their insights.

With the help of Dr. Eddie Newman of the Pasadena Unified School District, I was able to interview participants in the "Baby, Let's Wait" program. Young women at Blair High School, Pasadena High School, Flintridge Prep, and Polytechnic School also shared their thoughts and observations. Special thanks to Mary

Institute/St. Louis Country Day School for making both middle and upper school students available on short notice—and for the thirteen happy years I spent there.

My experience as a Lincoln Fellow at the Claremont Institute was of enormous value in completing the book. The faculty, the program, and the other fellows played an invaluable role in stimulating my thinking about its final chapters (and much else).

A host of friends also assisted along the way. At various times, Lauren Boeschenstein Gundlach and Robert Zafft reviewed portions of the manuscript, while Jennifer Zelaya and Phyllis Wilburn provided practical advice. I am grateful to them all—as well as to Carole Cleveland Peterson, who both helped with the book in various ways and guided me through the only project even more important than this one.

Like so many others, I am particularly indebted to Hugh Hewitt for his wise counsel and kind encouragement, which have always seemed to come when they're most needed.

Finally, my mother-in-law, Charlene Liebau, offered useful suggestions and my father-in-law, F. Jack Liebau, Sr., was enthusiastic even before he knew any of the specifics! I relied, as always, on the support of my older brother, Drew. The thoughts of my sister-in-law, Mariela, were likewise remarkably helpful—and, of course, I'm glad to be able to fulfill my twin brother, Brett's, confident and long-held expectation that sometime, someday, I would, indeed, write a book.

CONTENTS

1 The New Scarlet Letter   1

2 Defining Decency Down   15

3 Hooked In, Hooked Up   35

4 Between the Covers   59

5 Truly the "Boob" Tube   81

6 Aural Sex   113

7 Barely There   133

8 Paying the Piper: The Toll on Young
    Girls and the Cost to America   151

9 Do-Me Feminists and
    Doom-Me Feminism   173

10 From Liberty to Licentiousness   197

11 Stemming the Tide   215

12 Proudly, a Prude   229

    Notes   251

PRUDE

1

THE NEW SCARLET LETTER

ourteen-year-old Jennifer awakens well in time for school. As she dresses, pairing a cropped top with a trendy miniskirt, she listens to a popular radio station where the male–female morning team is discussing whether more men "go" for women's breasts, legs, or buttocks. On the school bus, the new rumor is that Amy gave Mike a blow job after the party last Saturday night. In her homeroom, her teacher is annoyed—a used condom has been found in the hall.

After school, Jennifer and her friends head to the mall. They check out the stores, including the provocative window display at Victoria's Secret, and try on clothes—camisoles styled like lingerie, short shorts, tight pants—designed to showcase their figures. They pick up the "hot" new novel Rainbow Party—about a group of fifteen-year-olds who plan to attend a sex party, and the newest Gossip Girl book (the one where high school senior Vanessa juggles sex with two different guys and her friend Blair sleeps with a young English lord).

Back at home, Jennifer is about to start her homework, but decides to check in at MySpace.com and get the latest dish at

CosmoGirl.com, where she encounters the question: "Are you a lesbian or bisexual and have a romantic story about you and your girlfriend? Tell us your love story and it could get picked for the magazine!"

As she types on her computer, the stereo's playing a hit song, and Jennifer sings along with a hit from one of her favorite groups, the Pussycat Dolls: "Don't cha wish your girlfriend was hot like me? Don't cha wish your girlfriend was a freak like me?"

Better get down to work, she decides. That way, she'll finish everything in time to watch Laguna Beach. *Although Talan has confessed his love to Taylor, he's hooked up with Kristin (again)—that's the one who outraged her sort-of boyfriend, Stephen, in Season 1 by dancing provocatively on a table during a coed Mexican vacation (even though, at the time, Stephen cheered her on, calling, "You look so good—keep dancing on the bar, slut!"). Jennifer doesn't want to miss tonight's episode—*everybody *will be talking about it tomorrow at school.*

⌒∞⌒

In some ways, the first decade of the twenty-first century might seem like an odd time to focus on the challenges confronting adolescent girls.

By most measures, young women in America have never had it better. Their professional options are limitless—they can become anything from an astronaut to a zoologist. No longer need girls think twice before pursuing graduate degrees; females constituted a majority of the nation's law students by 2000,[1] and in 2003, for the first time, the majority of applicants to US medical schools were women.[2] Even the choice to stay home and work as a wife and mother now earns some well-deserved and long-overdue respect.

At school, girls are outpacing their male counterparts by most measures. They are half as likely as boys either to be diagnosed with learning disabilities or placed in special education classes.[3] The advantage girls enjoy over boys on reading tests is five times as large as boys' advantage on math—and more girls than boys are enrolled in high-level math and science classes.[4] Girls are less likely to be disciplined, suspended, held back in school, or expelled. They are more likely than boys to graduate from high school, enter college, and graduate from college. In fact, where men represented 58 percent of the undergraduate student body on college campuses thirty years ago, they now constitute only 44 percent.[5]

And American girls are much less likely than their male counterparts to die, commit crimes, or become the victims of them, according to a study of gender-specific trends published in 2005.[6] They are almost half as likely to be binge drinkers, and less likely to succeed in committing suicide.

Given the breathtaking opportunities before them and the magnificent advantages they enjoy, it would seem that American society has treated young girls with enormous generosity. And in many ways, it has.

But not all the changes in recent years have been to the good. Today, American girls are forced to navigate a minefield more challenging, difficult, and pressure-filled than ever before when it comes to one vital topic: sex. With a frequency that would have been unimaginable even two decades ago, newspapers run stories of girls giving boys oral sex on school buses, in classrooms, at parties. Magazines feature stories of pansexuality among New York teens.[7] Gossip sheets report that many of the celebrities idolized by adolescent girls are wearing clothes and engaging in behavior so vulgar that it once would have destroyed their careers. Lyrics to popular music contain unspeakably coarse and often derogatory references to sex in general, and to women in particular—and young girls sing along without a second thought. Pornography pops up, unbidden, on the Internet. Stores such as Victoria's Secret and restaurants like Hooters capitalize on an implicit message that being sexy at all times is a female imperative.

Fifty years ago, in an era of poodle skirts and bobby socks—or even twenty years ago, well after 1967's summer of love—few would have predicted the scope of the transformation of young girls' lives. How did this happen?

The Sexualizing of America

Certainly, cultural Cassandras have wrung their hands about the moral disintegration of youth before—not just in Victorian or Puritan times, but during the Middle Ages and even back in the days of the Greek philosophers. With any significant cultural change, especially concerning something as personal and powerful as sex, there are bound to be those in any age who will fiercely object and confidently predict disaster. So it's a fair question: What's so different now?

Perhaps the most noteworthy aspect of the sexual revolution over the last half century is the rapidity and the scope of the changes. A report from researchers at San Diego State University, which analyzed 530 studies spanning five decades and involved more than 250,000 young people between the ages of twelve and twenty-seven, offers a glimpse into the magnitude of the transformation in both sexual behavior and attitudes.[8]

Between 1943 and 1999, even as life expectancy rose, the age of first intercourse dropped from nineteen to fifteen for females. During the same period, the percentage of sexually active young women rose from 13 to 47 percent. And between 1969 and 1993, the percentage of female teenagers and young adults having oral sex skyrocketed from 42 to 71 percent.

But perhaps the most dramatic phenomenon was the revolution in young women's beliefs about premarital sex. Only 12 percent approved of it in 1943; by 1999, 73 percent did.

One of the authors of the report noted that "Baby Boomers were having sex for the first time in college, but [the current generation] started having sex in high school; there's been a major shift there."[9] Reflecting on the changes, she observed that women's sexual behaviors had been much more affected by cultural influences than men's.

In fact, over the last forty years the United States has indeed experienced an incremental but aggressive sexualizing of its culture—until today there exists a status quo in which almost everything seems focused on what's going on below the waist. Sex has become virtually unavoidable in every context; the public square—from the airwaves to billboards to newspapers—is saturated with it.

Sometimes it seems that sexiness has become the most important measuring stick for determining what is worthy of public interest; being "sexy," as most celebrities would attest, has become the ultimate accolade. *Everything* is about "sexy," from shades of lipstick and eye shadow to hair, as evidenced by the advent of products like the Big Sexy Hair grooming line.

Nor is the sexiness craze limited to fashion and beauty items—it pops up in some unlikely places. Food, apparently, is sexy[10]—and so are some of the chefs who prepare it, according to the press.[11] Cars can be sexy, too—*Road & Travel* magazine featured a "2004 Sexy Car Buyer's Guide" (extolling "sensuous hunks of gorgeous metal").[12] Even cameras can apparently experience their own moments of sexiness—one ardent admirer of a Samsung Digimax wrote a piece designed to change the mind of "[w]hoever said cameras could never be sexy."[13]

And even though politics has long been known as "show business for ugly people," it hasn't remained immune to the cultural obsession with sex. Even some political activists have adopted the vocabulary of suggestiveness. In the heat of the 2004 elections, a group called Votergasm called on its members to pledge not only to vote in the election, but to have sex with another voter as well. Similarly, members of F the Vote sought to defeat George W. Bush by inviting conservatives to sign a contract pledging not to vote for the president in exchange for sex.[14]

Current press coverage of politics and public policy likewise employs sexual imagery. Notably, a *Washington Post* piece discussed the "sexual frisson" precipitated by the wardrobe of Secretary of State Condoleezza Rice.[15] Fashion writer Robin Givhan asserted that "Rice's coat and boots speak of sex and power," alluded to "the erotic nature of high heels," and went on to exclaim, "Dominatrix!"

In 2002, CNN also resorted to the language of the bedroom in an effort to lure viewers to Paula Zahn's morning news program.[16] The promo included a picture of Zahn as PROVOCATIVE and SEXY flashed across the screen and a voice-over asked, "Where can you find a morning news anchor who's provocative, super-smart, [and] oh yeah, just a little sexy?" In conjunction with the word *sexy*, viewers heard the sound of a zipper opening. The ad was pulled only after Zahn herself and some CNN executives objected.

In fact, behavior that would once have been the occasion for shame is touted in the mainstream press as a harmless diversion. Consider the coverage of Jessica Cutler, the Capitol Hill intern who published a Web log discussing her sexual exploits with six different men. *The Washington Post* covered the story in glowing detail, and when its reporter last caught up with Cutler, she was writing a book, preparing to appear in the pages of *Playboy* magazine, and enjoying the innumerable small perks of minor celebrity, such as tables at trendy Washington nightclubs.

When even *60 Minutes*—the epitome of the stodgy, old-line television newsmagazine—devotes an entire hour to the world of pornography, it's clear that sex talk has become an integral part of Americans' daily experience.

It's certainly become part of the American vocabulary. Even the word *sucks*—as in something or someone *sucks*—frequently used even by the most affluent and educated, locates its origin in oral sex. As Lee Siegel pointed out in *The New Republic,* "Considering how many times 'sucks' is used in print, in conversation, and online now, the entire country is evoking the act of fellatio on a continuous basis."[17]

⟡

From all of this, one message emerges: *Sex is everywhere: Everyone's doing it, and that's just the way it is.* This message is disseminated to young girls through almost every element of their lives. One journalist who shadowed a twelve-year-old girl estimated that she had been exposed to about 280 sexy images in the course of a day.[18]

In short, today's girl world has become saturated with sex. Even girls standing only at the threshold of adolescence are forced to absorb information, confront issues, and handle situations that, in past generations, would have presented themselves much later in their lives, if at all.

The Impact on Young Girls

Somehow, as some segments of American society have been reveling in the ubiquity of sex, the very real psychological, emotional, and physical impact on young girls of giving too much, too soon has been discounted.

This relentless emphasis on sex has eroded the standards by which young women have traditionally been able to win appreciation and recognition for something more than their sexiness. In a culture that celebrates Paris Hilton, thong underwear, and songs like "My Humps" (wherein the female singer extols the sexual magnetism of her breasts and buttocks)—there's scant recognition or respect for female modesty or achievement that isn't coupled with sex appeal.

In fact, living in an overly sexualized culture takes a very real toll on girls. The emphasis on sexiness, revealing fashions, and the overvaluing of physical appeal creates pressure to measure up to bone-slim models or celebrities—and leads to unrealistic expectations among young women about how their own bodies should actually look. And although unwed mothers were treated with deplorable cruelty all too often in the past, today's nearly universal acceptance of premarital sex has effectively sanctioned a life decision that can have a severely negative impact on the futures of the unwed mothers, the children they bear, and the society that, too often, must support both.[19]

Along with the ongoing threat of unwanted pregnancy or sexually transmitted diseases, a growing body of research confirms that sexual activity may be detrimental to young girls' emotional and psychological well-being as well. In fact, giving too much, too soon has been associated with an increased risk of suicide and a greater incidence of depression. There are good reasons to believe that the psychological and spiritual costs to girls of living in a sex-saturated society can't be calculated in physical or economic terms alone.

Why It's Happened

Several long-standing social trends account, in part, for the current public obsession with sex. They include radical feminism, which insists that true female liberation encompasses sexual license and that chastity is nothing more than the dead relic of a patriarchal culture's twisted efforts to control female sexuality. The emphasis on sexual self-expression rather than sexual self-restraint, as well as the triumph of moral relativism, likewise has contributed in part to the culture's sexualization.

And all this has occurred even as the privatization of religion and its disappearance from the public square have deprived American youth of a once widely respected and understood moral foundation for chastity. Finally, too many parents have been reluctant to criticize current trends in sexual attitudes and mores, lest they be accused of being judgmental or—worse yet—hypocrites for denouncing youthful sexual behavior in which they themselves might once have engaged.

Letting Girls Down

In a world where being judgmental sometimes seems to have become the only behavior that elicits nearly universal condemnation, many Americans understandably find it difficult to challenge the gratuitous coarseness and mindless vulgarity that surrounds young girls at virtually every moment.

But by acceding to the rampant sexualizing of its culture, America has been letting its young girls down. When it comes to sexual matters, the discussion has shifted. Young girls now hear a great deal about ethically neutral health issues, but almost nothing that would suggest that sex is a matter that implicates personal morality and—yes—even religious values.

Over time, that results in an erosion of the kind of modest behavior encouraged in the past. As Elayne Bennett, president and founder of a character and chastity program based in Washington, DC, points out, "When society keeps giving a message that (a) you won't get pregnant and (b) that society doesn't condemn you [for engaging in promiscuous sexual activity], it really wears down some of the healthy and correct hesitancy on the part of . . . young girls."

Over the past several decades, American society has instituted welcome reforms to ensure equal opportunity for women in the workplace. But even as barriers to female professional advancement have fallen, so, too, have many of the traditional social conventions that protected girls by supporting those who abstained from sex until maturity and/or marriage. Too many of us have forgotten that traditions now scorned as hopelessly retrograde—like requiring boys to come to their dates' house and meet their parents before their first date—existed for a reason. On the individual level, they were intended to send the message that a girl's parents were actively aware of and concerned about what she was doing (and with whom) when she left the house; from the boy's side, it signaled a willingness to assume responsibility for the safety and well-being of the girl whose company he sought. Collectively, such customs indicated that American society expected behavior from young people that combined sexual restraint, on the one hand, with respectful (even chivalrous) treatment of women, on the other.

In this more liberated age, it's fashionable to deride the conformity and inhibition that conventions about male–female behavior sometimes engendered. But this much can be said for the old order: Through its clear expectation of sexual modesty and self-control, society emphasized that chastity was valuable and honorable. Ironically, many of the customs that today are dismissed as limiting were actually empowering, because they offered young women a way to resist unwelcome sexual activity without themselves being labeled as cruel, frigid, or uninviting. Ultimately, the status quo provided reinforcement for girls who were making choices that would protect them from heartbreak, loss of self-respect, pregnancy, and sexually transmitted disease—and which, not incidentally, minimized the chances that the state would need to step in and support, financially or otherwise, the upbringing of a child.

The contrast with current mores couldn't be greater. Now the girls who refuse to accede to a boy's demands for sex are no longer backed by a social consensus that honors chastity, even in the breach. Instead, every social pressure pushes young girls *toward* sexual experimentation—and sends the message that the sexually inexperienced are uncool, abnormal, or hopelessly undesirable. That matters, because what teens understand to be socially acceptable is an important influence on their decisions about whether to have sex themselves.[20]

Ultimately, it's as if the sex-saturated culture were a giant tsunami rolling toward young girls—with only their parents, clergy, and some teachers standing between them and the overpowering force of the wave. And even those supports have been eroded over time as parents, churches, and schools have, perhaps unwittingly, ceded much of their authority when it comes to the management of adolescent sexuality. Too often, the sex lives of young girls are seen as a matter exclusively for the young girls themselves—and, then, when necessary, for the public health, social services, and justice systems (whether to provide treatment for sexually transmitted diseases, offer government aid for the babies of teen mothers, or enforce child support decrees against unmarried fathers). When cultural trends combine to discourage parental and clergy guidance and influence over girls' sexual decision making—and replace them with role models and pressures that encourage girls to "just do it"—it's hard not to conclude that somewhere, something has gone terribly wrong.

❧

In a world threatened by life-or-death issues like terrorism, the hypersexualization of American society, though regrettable, hardly seems to constitute an urgent problem. But while attention is focused on the most pressing issues of the day, cultural shifts of potentially immense and lasting significance, both positive and negative, can occur virtually unnoticed. For example, even as the nation focused on winning World War II, the conflict also subtly facilitated both greater interaction among America's social classes and races, and more sexual license. Or to take a frivolous example: Hillary Clinton's 1993 health care plan may be dead, but the pantsuits she popularized during her tenure as first lady have become a staple of the female wardrobe.

In truth, the state of the culture matters to all of us—it's like the air we breathe. We're rarely conscious of it, but we rely upon it constantly, and its quality affects all of us, individually and collectively, far more than we realize. When it's polluted or corrupted, there's no meaningful refuge for anyone.

Over time, there's been a gradual but dramatic shift in the culture when it comes to sex. There's been a sea change in how American society understands, evaluates, and transmits values about sexual morality.

Even our language is revealing. Once, *slut* was one of the most derogatory and insulting epithets that could be hurled at any woman—accusing her, in effect, of lacking the self-respect to be discriminating in bestowing her sexual favors. In today's world, however, both the term itself and the sexual promiscuity it signifies are embraced—as a headline in Salon.com urged, "Be a Slut! Be a Slut! Be a Slut!"[21] Fashion sensation Tom Ford asked gossip columnist Liz Smith, "What's wrong with sluts? If sluttiness is what you like, what's wrong with that? Why do we think being a slut's bad? Sluttiness is just a lot of freedom."[22] Not surprisingly, even young girls have come to embrace the concept—to the point that the epithet has become a widely accepted, affectionate term of familiarity among girlfriends.[23]

But even as the virtues of sluttiness are celebrated, the tolerance and affirmation extended toward the sexually promiscuous slut by elite culture hardly extend to her antithesis—the chaste prude. As Cassandra DeBenedetto, a Princeton student instrumental in founding a pro-chastity group on campus, puts it, "Many people associate chastity with being a prude. They assume I'm afraid of men, really ugly, antisocial, and overly intellectual. As a matter of fact, I have a boyfriend, I'm told I'm relatively attractive, I like to socialize and have fun, and while I enjoy learning, I am far from overly intellectual."

Prude derives from the old French *prude-femme,* meaning "a good or virtuous woman," but perhaps it's no surprise that its connotation is no longer positive. Today, as almost every girl knows, the term is "often used to judge someone as sexually conservative and no fun."[24]

That, at least, is how the online resource produced by Columbia University's Health Promotion Program defined *prude* in response to a question from a self-described "thirteen-year-old clueless girl." Being sexually conservative is, apparently, tantamount to being considered no fun, at least in the judgment of Columbia University's online health counselor.

And it seems that attitude has spread. Another girl wrote in for advice on the Web site gURL.com, asking, "How can I become less of a prude?" She was advised, "If you really listen to your own desire you may be able to learn and to understand it better so that taking more action will come more easily, although the first steps might still be a bit scary." In other words, becoming sexually active is the best way to get over being a prude. Likewise, an eighth-grade girl at a Midwestern private school admitted, "Our grade is relatively prude compared to what I've heard about in other schools"[25]—in a tone that made it clear she was hardly indulging in self-congratulation. "We are just not as sexually active as the people who are non-prude," she confessed.

Like the concept of chastity itself, it seems that *prude*—derived from a term that used to denote honor and virtue—has almost become a badge of shame. Apparently, scarlet letters still exist in American life. But ironically, it's now the chaste who must wear them.

CHAPTER 2

DEFINING DECENCY DOWN

Both casual and more serious relationships include many of the same sexual behaviors; [teens] are just as likely to agree that oral sex and intercourse are part of an exclusive dating relationship as a casual "hook-up." Teens were more likely to say kissing and touching define a dating relationship, as compared to more "casual" ones—perhaps signaling that young people consider these to be more intimate behaviors.

SexSmarts survey, July 2002[1]

Those who have seen the 1990 film *Pretty Woman*—about a streetwalker who meets and ultimately marries a business mogul—may recall the advice that the pretty young prostitute played by Julia Roberts receives from a more seasoned colleague: Never, ever kiss a client on the mouth. Kissing, she's told, is infinitely more intimate than the sex acts for which a prostitute is paid, and doing it is a sign that a relationship has moved beyond business into the realm of romance.

Apparently, many of America's teenagers have, in essence, performed the same social and moral calculation. It seems that kissing and touching have become the indicia of intimacy, whereas oral sex and intercourse are deemed appropriate for casual and dating relationships alike.

But anyone who is shocked at the results of the survey above hasn't been following the news. Reports of promiscuous middle school and teen sexual behavior have appeared in the press and elsewhere with notable and troubling frequency.

The first widely publicized account of rampant young teen sexuality in recent years came from Georgia and was covered extensively in a 1999 PBS *Frontline* broadcast called "The Lost Children of Rockdale County."[2] After a widespread outbreak of syphilis, the community learned that girls, some as young as thirteen, had been engaging in group sex with boys and girls alike. Some fourteen-year-old girls—described as "normal, everyday, regular kids"—had "twenty, thirty, forty, fifty, or a hundred sex partners," according to a nurse at the county's public health department. She noted, "These girls were not just having regular intercourse, they were having every kind of possible sexual act you could do."

A professor at the Emory University School of Public Health, in whom some of the Rockdale County youth had confided, noted, "The only type of group sex that I did not hear about . . . was group sex just between guys." Through the broadcast, Americans were exposed to terms such as *the sandwich*— one girl engaging in several simultaneous sex acts with several partners. They also learned about *riding the train* (or *running a train*[3]), an expression referring to different variations on group and serial sex.

The shock created by "The Lost Children of Rockdale County" was intensified by the fact that, as the broadcast noted, Rockdale County was hardly the type of community that would seem to breed stereotypically disaffected, sexually audacious young people. Eighty-five percent of county youth reportedly went on to higher education after high school; test scores were some of the highest in Georgia, and athletic and drama programs received high marks.

But the 1999 PBS broadcast turned out to be just the most dramatic early example of a growing phenomenon—oral sex and intercourse among young people outside the context of intimate relationships (or, in some cases, any relationship at all). In fact, at around the same time, *The Washington Post* reported on a parents' meeting at an Arlington, Virginia, middle school, convened to discuss the fact that approximately a dozen girls and two or three boys—all thirteen and fourteen years old—had been engaging in oral sex at parties and in local parks.[4]

Nor have these been isolated incidents. Sexual activity has infected middle school with a vengeance. Middle school girls in Michigan encountered a "girl with her hand down her boyfriend's pants" on the school bus;[5] another girl at the same school masturbated a boy during math class. The newspaper account also alluded to "weekend nights in a local movie theater when classmates masturbated their boyfriends while moviegoers looked at the screen ahead."[6]

Other accounts include reports of a twelve-year-old girl and a fourteen-year-old boy having oral sex in a classroom in Dallas,[7] oral sex being performed in a bathroom and in the gym bleachers in a Syracuse, New York, middle school,[8] and a fourteen-year-old providing oral sex behind an elementary school near Detroit.[9] In 2003, a thirteen-year-old was suspended for having performed oral sex while on a school bus in Beaver County, Pennsylvania;[10] young people in Ligonier Valley, Pennsylvania, engaged in the same behavior.[11] In March, 2007, two fifth graders in Spearsville, Louisiana, reportedly had sex on a classroom floor and two others fondled each other when the class was left unattended.[12] And one suburban teacher in

New Jersey told a health trainer about the Touchdown Club, in which cheerleaders reportedly promised oral sex to any football players, including those as young as the eighth grade, who scored for the home team.[13]

Similar reports have issued from high schools. In Jacksonville, Florida, a sixteen-year-old girl was paid by an eighteen-year-old boy to perform oral sex on an underaged boy—which she did, under a table in a large class of students.[14] Newspapers have reported that students have engaged in oral sex in a high school auditorium, a high school gym,[15] a school parking lot, and school bathrooms.[16] Administrators at a public school in Southern California were shocked to learn that a female student was offering blow jobs on the school roof for five dollars. And in 2006, a ninth-grade coach was indicted in southwestern Texas for having overseen the Koochie Kissing Klick, which provided freshman and sophomore girls to athletes for sexual favors.[17] Upon investigation, nearly all the students interviewed by the local paper about the "3K Club" knew what it was, and laughed when they were asked about it.

One of the most dramatic media narratives about teen sex in recent years has focused on a piece of jewelry. In spring and fall 2004, a spate of nationwide newspapers—from New York[18] to Philadelphia[19] to Washington, DC,[20] to Gainesville, Florida,[21] to Cleveland[22] to St. Louis[23] to Dallas[24]—reported that girls in junior high and high school were wearing plastic "jelly" bracelets as a way to signal which sex acts the wearer was willing to perform.[25]

Accounts described a game called Snap, where ripping one of the jelly bracelets from a girl's arms would constitute a "coupon" for a particular sex act, depending on the color of the bracelet. Each colored band signified a different practice, with red signaling a lap dance, green meaning sex outdoors, black for intercourse, and blue for oral sex. Although the reports were hotly disputed by some teens, at least one eleven-year-old girl went on the record acknowledging the practice.[26]

Of course, sexual activity is hardly restricted to school hours—if anything, it occurs more frequently at parties.[27] A ninth grader at a California public school confided, "[Sexual activity] happens after dances, after parties, after social events period. Most of the time, there's somebody whose parents aren't home, or the parents don't really care or the parents are asleep or something, and everybody who wants to do something goes over to that person's house and they have sex or do whatever they want."[28] Not surprisingly, alcohol and parental absence play a prominent role in enabling sexual experimentation. In a typical admission, a public school freshman conceded, "When there's a party and there's no parents, people get really drunk and go ahead and do it with guys."

Not surprisingly, word about the sexual encounters gets around. A senior at a Midwestern private school said, "After the weekend, you'll come to school and it will be, like, 'So-and-so hooked up with so-and-so' . . . I guess it makes people who do it want to do it more." And the gossip is especially intense in the lower grades, often among the younger girls. One seventeen-year-old noted that she hears the gossip at volleyball practice: "You hear 'I was with a guy' or something. It happens a lot with younger classes; they *do* talk about it, because they don't know *not* to talk about it."[29] Another stated that talking about one's sexual exploits "is the cool thing to do in, like, eighth grade . . . and they'll be telling everybody."[30]

What's less clear is how the hookup culture is satisfying for girls. A senior at a Midwestern high school referenced a friend who regularly engages in hookups with boys she'd like to date. "She'll hope to pursue the relationship, but usually the guy will turn her down because it's just a onetime hookup," she reported.[31]

Sex by the Numbers

Although statistics, without more, offer scant insight into the depth of the problem, they do provide some information about the prevalence of particular sexual practices.

Sexual Intercourse

Reliable figures suggest that many girls are having sex early. The National Survey for Family Growth, taken in 2002, found that 53 percent of girls between fifteen and nineteen (and 38.7 percent of those between fifteen and seventeen) had had intercourse.[32] According to the Centers for Disease Control's 2005 Youth Risk Behavior Surveillance study,[33] only 3.7 percent of female high school students had sexual intercourse before the age of thirteen (although, according to the 2002 National Survey for Family Growth, fully 13 percent of never-married female teens had sexual intercourse before age fifteen[34]).

As of 2005, again according to the CDC,[35] 45.7 percent of high school girls had engaged in intercourse. Broken down by grade, 29.3 percent of ninth-grade girls had had sex, as well as 44.0 percent of tenth-grade girls, 52.1 percent of eleventh-grade girls, and a whopping 62.4 percent of twelfth-grade girls. What's more, 20.2 percent of twelfth-grade girls have slept with four or more persons during their life, along with 14.2 percent of eleventh-grade girls, 9.7 percent of tenth-grade girls, and 5.7 percent of freshman girls.

Obviously, taboos against premarital teen sex have significantly eroded, at least for a sizable percentage of teens. In fact, 61 percent of girls aged fifteen through nineteen agreed or strongly agreed that it was all right for unmarried eighteen-year-olds to have sex if they have strong affection for each other; 31 percent believed it was acceptable for sixteen-year-olds.[36] And a *Seventeen* magazine/SexEtc. survey found that for 38 percent of participants, simply being in a relationship where both partners had said "I love you"[37] was enough for them to feel comfortable having sex.

In some cases, girls not only believe that losing their virginity at an early age is unobjectionable—in fact, they're positively eager to do so. One fourteen-year-old freshman said, "I have a friend—a really close one—and she thinks she's ready [for sex]. Her boyfriend is my cousin, and I know what he wants from her . . . He just wants sex. But she thinks she's ready. I told her she needs to wait a little longer, like, see if he's really in it for you or for the sex. But she says she doesn't care. She just wants to lose it, to get it over with."[38]

Oral Sex

While oral sex is hardly the ubiquitous phenomenon that the most lurid media reports would suggest, it's surprisingly common. According to the National Survey of Family Growth, of girls between the ages of fifteen and nineteen generally, fully 54.3 percent have engaged in oral sex, with 43.6 percent having performed it on a partner and 49.6 percent having received it.[39] And 42 percent of girls between fifteen and seventeen (ninth through eleventh grades) have participated in oral sex, with 30 percent having given oral sex to a male and 38 percent having received it.[40]

It's more difficult to ascertain the percentage of younger teens participating in oral sex because of impediments to obtaining the relevant data. However, a 2002 study of adolescents younger than fifteen found that while 11 percent of girls between the ages of twelve and fifteen had performed oral sex, an even higher number—17 percent—had had it performed on them.[41] And about two-thirds of the 70 percent of teens between thirteen and sixteen who knew what oral sex was reported that they knew at least a few thirteen- or fourteen-year-olds who were having oral sex.[42] The study likewise found that rates of participation in oral sex rose dramatically at the ages of fourteen and, especially, fifteen.[43]

It seems clear that the incidence of oral sex has risen appreciably over the last decade. A team of researchers compared 1994 medical records of twelve- to twenty-five-year-olds with records of the same age group in 2004. Over that decade, the prevalence of self-reported oral sex in the past ninety days more than doubled among females (from 14 to 33 percent) and doubled among males (16 to 32 percent).[44]

What's most remarkable is the extent to which young people are now participating in oral sex while declining to have intercourse. According to the 2002 National Survey of Family Growth, 18 percent of girls aged fifteen through seventeen (and 35 percent of those eighteen and nineteen) reported participating in oral sex without having engaged in vaginal sex.[45] Similarly, a 2005 study of ninth graders (fourteen- and fifteen-year-olds) in *Pediatrics* found that more of the girls had engaged in oral sex than in intercourse—20 percent versus 14 percent.[46] And 32 percent of the girls said they intended to have oral sex in the next six months, compared with 26 percent who intended to have intercourse in the same period.[47] The *American Journal of Health Behavior* likewise reported that of those younger than fifteen who had experienced oral sex, fully 21 percent had *not* engaged in sexual intercourse.[48]

So what's behind this new trend?

The New Emphasis on Oral Sex

Over the last twenty years or so, young people have formed perceptions about oral sex that differ greatly from those of their elders. Once, oral sex was considered to be an act even more intimate than that of intercourse—"beyond getting a home run"[49]—reserved solely for close, safe, trusting relationships.

Today, however, oral sex is largely seen as a safer, easier, less messy, and more impersonal precursor to or substitute for vaginal intercourse. As one fourteen-year-old girl told Katie Couric on *The Today Show*, "First [base] would be like kissing; second base would be like making out; third would be, like oral sex."[50] In short, for many girls and boys alike, oral sex has become "no big deal."

Dr. Melissa Johnson, clinical psychologist and founder and president of the Institute for Girls' Development, offers an explanation for the increased popularity of oral and anal sex, noting that they are "ways for kids to be sexual, and if they don't have sufficient information, to think those are safe ways to have sex. I've heard girls say, 'I can't get pregnant having oral sex. I can't get pregnant having anal sex.'"

It's likewise been theorized that perhaps girls choose to engage in oral sex rather than intercourse because they believe that they control oral sex, whereas boys control intercourse.[51] But in a study of ninth-grade adolescents in *The Journal of Adolescent Medicine*, control issues didn't even come up. Rather, the five top reasons girls provided for engaging in oral sex were: to improve a relationship (24.8 percent); for pleasure (19 percent); for popularity or reputational reasons (17.4 percent); out of curiosity or for the experience (12.4 percent); and only then because they perceived less risk with oral rather than vaginal sex (9.8 percent).[52] A 2005 NBC News/*People* magazine poll found that although 21 percent of teens aged thirteen through sixteen reported having oral sex for the first time to be more popular or accepted, fully 76 percent reported that they did so because the other person wanted to.[53]

In fact, Dr. Adria O'Donnell, a clinical and consulting psychologist whose practice focuses on young girls, believes that girls provide oral sex just to please their male counterparts. "They avoid conflicts with their boyfriends or their male friends by just giving in," O'Donnell says. "Girls want to please, and if it makes the boys happy, they will give them a blow job." She adds, "But they will tell you they did it because it's no big deal."

In a poll of a thousand teens between the ages of thirteen and sixteen conducted by NBC News in 2005, 40 percent of the sexually active young people reported that they have had oral sex at least once to avoid having intercourse; 68 percent also said that they did it to avoid pregnancy.[54] A 2003 Kaiser Family Foundation study likewise found that 33 percent of girls aged fifteen through seventeen had had oral sex to avoid having intercourse.[55] And the 2005 study of ninth-grade adolescents in *Pediatrics* revealed that all the ninth graders—male and female—perceived a reduced chance of contracting STDs from oral (as compared with vaginal) sex,[56] and believed that they were less likely to get a bad reputation, get into trouble, feel bad about themselves, or feel guilty about having oral sex.[57]

What's most interesting is that young teens seem to believe that having oral sex is both more common in and more acceptable for their age group than intercourse—whether in the context of a dating relationship or not. In the *Pediatrics* study of ninth graders, girls reported that engaging in intercourse at their age was *more* against their ethical beliefs than participating in oral sex.[58]

Perhaps that's because a significant number of the young teens engaging in oral sex don't actually consider it to be "sex." Dr. O'Donnell reports that "Girls say, 'It was kind of gross, but it's not that big of a deal. He was happy afterward and I'm still a virgin.' They see it as a win–win."

In a 2003 survey of teens aged fifteen through seventeen conducted for the Kaiser Family Foundation and *Seventeen* magazine, 52 percent of girls either strongly or somewhat agreed that one could have oral sex and remain a virgin.[59] Even so, there's evidence that girls take oral sex somewhat more seriously than boys do. A 2003 Kaiser Family Foundation study found that 38 percent of girls aged fifteen through seventeen—versus 54 percent of boys the same age—believed that "oral sex is not as big of a deal as sexual intercourse."[60]

But such reservations don't necessarily mean that girls are refraining from oral sex. In a *Seventeen* survey, 28 percent of participants reported that they felt comfortable having oral sex with a guy so long as they were exclusively boyfriend–girlfriend.[61] As a fifth-grade girl told *U.S. News & World Report,* "[N]ow, it's like everyone's at least having oral sex. Freshmen might wait up to a year, sophomores wait, at most, a couple of months."[62]

In some circles, oral sex is common enough that the girls who *aren't* doing it feel like oddballs. A freshman at a Southern California public high school recalled how uncomfortable she'd felt the year before, walking home with two of her friends as they were talking about having performed and received oral sex. "I had just got past regular kissing a boy," she said. "I felt kind of out of place, like I did want to lie and say I had done things I hadn't, but I just thought about it and I didn't. I just got quiet."[63]

What It Means

Certainly, some of the recent news about sexual activity among young people is welcome, including the fact that the percentage of ninth- through twelfth-grade students claiming to have had sex with four or more partners has fallen,[64] as well as the decrease in the number of girls who have had sex before the age of thirteen.[65] But self-congratulation is somewhat premature, in light of still-high rates of sexual activity, the apparent popularity of oral sex, and the fact that 31 percent of sexually active

American girls become pregnant at least once before they reach the age of 20.[66]

A 1970s Single Bar

Overall, perhaps what's most troubling is an increasing tendency among adolescents to divorce sexual activity from committed relationships in particular, and from any concept of traditional morality in general. As a Long Island psychologist told *The New York Times*, "Before, the dialogue was, 'I love you and care for you, so let's experiment.' Now, the dialogue is 'This is safe and fun and OK, and you have nothing to worry about.' "[67]

Many teens have come to see sex generally as nothing more than another form of recreation—an activity that requires no more emotional commitment than, say, that required of a tennis partner. And like tennis, as developmental psychologist and professor of education Dr. Thomas Lickona observes, "Sex is a recreational sport."

In fact, a 2005 NBC poll reported that fully half of the adolescents having oral sex or intercourse had done so in a casual relationship.[68] Indeed, the practice of engaging in some kind of sexual activity outside the context of any relationship or romantic attraction has become common enough that a term has been coined to describe it: *hooking up*. In its "2006 Hookup Survey," *Seventeen* magazine canvassed ten thousand of its readers and found that 30 percent had hooked up with someone they had just met that day, while 64 percent had hooked up with someone they considered just a friend.[69]

One senior at a Midwestern high school tried to explain the appeal of the hookup. She noted, "[Hookups] will be random. That's why people want to do it. You'll go out to a party not knowing what's going to happen and . . . something happens but you don't expect it."[70]

In fact, hooking up with a friend is part of an arrangement popularly known as "friends with benefits" (or "buddy-sex"[71])—a system that, according to some girls and boys, allows them to integrate sexual activity into their busy lives.[72] Under the friends-with-benefits system, a couple may engage in some sexual activity from time to time, with the explicit understanding that no particular commitment is either expected or implied. Certainly the emotional dangers of such a system are rife, chief among them that one partner will develop feelings for the other, then be hurt by a lack of reciprocation. As Dr. Drew Pinsky, host of the television and syndicated radio program *Loveline,* put it, "Friends with benefits is always a catastrophe, because we're human beings and somebody always gets involved—not always the woman—but *somebody*."

There's also the potential for exploitation. Girls are far more likely than boys to believe that improving a relationship is a reason to engage in oral sex.[73] What's not clear is whether the hoped-for improvement was the enhancement of an already existing relationship or a transition from a casual to a dating relationship.

It does seem that at least some girls use hooking up as a method for initiating a relationship—but with limited success. A senior at a Midwestern high school summarized the situation as follows: "[T]here are a lot of girls who are, like, 'Well, I want a boyfriend,' and they have fantasies about the perfect relationship with boys. They'll do stupid things to get that, like hooking up, and then they end up unsatisfied, and I really think it makes them even worse sometimes."[74] Another noted, "Kids will get together and hook up on the weekends, and sometimes they'll end up being a couple and sometimes they'll not. And sometimes, they'll hook up on the weekends and not mean to, and it's kind of awkward afterward."

Social science researchers have estimated that more than

one-third (37.7 percent) of sexually active teens have had sexual intercourse with someone they were not dating.[75] And that study doesn't take oral sex into account. Given that some teens engage in oral sex without intercourse (and that teens consider oral sex to be less important or intimate than intercourse, and therefore may not report it as conscientiously[76]), the figure for all forms of uncommitted sexual activity is likely to be even higher.

Perhaps it's no wonder the teenage sexual world has been compared to the stereotypical 1970s-era singles bar.[77]

The Ubiquity of Sex

The significant number of young girls engaging in oral sex and intercourse both drives and reflects the saturation of teen culture with sex. It seems that sex is almost always in the air, one way or another.

Certainly, from time immemorial, young people have been curious about sex—and it's long been a frequent topic of schoolyard chatter for some. But today, whether or not they've been targets of them, almost all young girls are familiar with crude sexual come-ons that would have been unthinkable even twenty years ago. Many report being solicited by their male classmates with questions like "When are you going to give me head?"[78]

A freshman at a Southern California high school says, "A lot of guys like to see if they can get you to do it [have oral sex], so they just push and push." She adds, "They will just straight up tell you. And sometimes it's kind of disrespectful. They say, 'Hey, when are you going to let me hit it?' or worse stuff. Or they'll come by and hit you, like, on the butt. And when they give you a hug . . . it'll be a little more than a hug. Some will come up and say, 'Oh you, you're thick,' 'cause like, boys like big butts and big breasts."[79]

Even so, crude and graphic sex talk isn't coming just from the boys. A cavalier attitude toward sex likewise permeates girls' conversations and behavior. One Washington, DC, suburban commuter was startled to find three young girls playfully flinging condoms at one another on the train.[80] And even middle school girls—many of whom, in fact, haven't ever engaged in oral sex—talk about it, discuss what might taste good on a partner's penis, swap tips on oral sex technique, and debate swallowing versus spitting out a partner's ejaculate. Girls likewise toss around hitherto arcane terms like *tossed salad*—an expression that entered the vernacular around 2004, when it was discussed on *Oprah*.[81] A high school freshman observed, "A lot of girls think it's really attractive to talk kind of smutty in front of guys."[82]

Given all this, it's hardly surprising that 77 percent of girls aged fifteen through seventeen surveyed in 2003 believed that teens were more likely to have sex than teens were ten years ago.[83] Both the frequency and the frankness of sexual discussions make sex seem even more ubiquitous than it already is.

Even teachers and administrators have expressed surprise at the vulgarity of the conversations taking place in school halls.[84] And the objectionable behavior isn't limited just to talking. One female high school student said, "On my way to class every period, I see about three couples at least somewhere in a corner doing something. Most of the time they're just kissing and rubbing on each other . . . [but] the teachers don't really say anything."

It's not ultimately clear exactly what motivates girls to engage in sexual activity. One study of ninth graders found that, in relationships, girls ranked intimacy as a significantly more important goal than either social status or sexual pleasure.[85] But they had much lower expectations than boys that having sex would serve any of their relationship goals, which researchers speculated might be more effectively met through behaviors that aren't overtly sexual as much as romantic, like hand-holding.[86]

It may be that the widespread acceptance of teen sex and the sexualized atmosphere within teen culture itself combine to impose added pressure on girls to engage in sexual activity. A study of tenth graders found that teens who reported that they engaged in oral sex and intercourse were more likely to be perceived as popular by their peers.[87] As the researchers noted, "These results indicate either that sexually active adolescents enjoy higher status among peers or perhaps that popular adolescents feel more pressured or inclined to report that there [sic] are sexually active."[88] One senior at a Midwestern high school observed, "If you say [about a friend] that 'she hooked up with him'—and he's really popular—then . . . people will see that as a sign of [her] popularity."[89]

Popular or not, in one 2002 survey, the overwhelming majority of girls between fifteen and seventeen reported "a lot" of pressure or "some" pressure from boys to have sex, and that it's common for girls to "lose their boyfriends because they won't have sex."[90] More than 90 percent of girls responding to a different survey agreed that "girls are often pressured to have sex before they are ready."[91] Perhaps not surprisingly in light of these figures, a Kaiser Family Foundation study reported that fully 31 percent of girls between fifteen and seventeen reported that they had done something sexual they really didn't want to do.[92]

It's worth noting, however, that sexual pressure isn't imposed exclusively by boys; girls themselves may be contributing to the "everyone does it" atmosphere. In fact, a survey of fifteen- through seventeen-year-olds found that more than half of the girls responding said that there was a lot of or some pressure from other girls to engage in sex.[93]

There may even be internal pressure to engage in sexual behavior. Increasingly, girls define sexual activity as part of what it means to be a typical teen. One senior at a private Midwestern high school said, "Sometimes you want to feel like you're part of the high school thing—that if you don't do this, this, and this, then you're not the typical high schooler." She recounted a story about a friend (whom she characterized as a "very, very good girl") who got "wasted" and then engaged in some kind of sexual behavior. Discussing the experience, her friend told her, "It was weird, because I'm not the typical high schooler, and for once, I wanted to feel and do what the typical high schooler should be doing . . . I just wanted to have it over and do something normal."

Obviously, there's something significantly amiss with the way that teens are defining what's typical and normal.

Pushing the Envelope: Sexual Experimentation

With so many sexual taboos having been effectively dismantled, perhaps it's no surprise that sexual experimentation doesn't carry the kind of stigma it used to, especially for young girls. Previously unacceptable sexual behavior, like same-sex relationships, is increasingly common, and at younger ages.[94]

Washington Post reporter Laura Sessions Slepp identified a new phenomenon at a Washington, DC–area high school: an increasing resistance on the part of high school girls to defining their sexual identities as either straight or gay.[95] Some high school girls instead choose to experiment publicly with same-sex relationships without classifying themselves as gay, instead coining terms such as *gayish*. The enterprise seemed to represent an effort to defy any categorization of their sexuality.[96]

Likewise, in February 2006 *New York* magazine reported on the exploits of a group of mainstream students at a Manhattan high school—identified as the "bi clique," closer in the high school hierarchy to the cool kids than to the nerds—who engaged in sexual activity with partners regardless of gender.[97] The piece noted that girls (and boys) were defining themselves in new terms, some of which they had invented: "polysexual, ambisexual, pansexual, pansensual, polyfide, bicurious, bi-queer, metroflexible, heteroflexible, heterosexual with lesbian tendencies—or . . . 'just sexual.' "[98] At parties, the piece reported, teens "make the rounds" (a reference to hooking up with partners of both sexes).[99]

Taken together, all this seems to suggest that even as more young girls forge sexual identities at younger ages, they're increasingly resistant to any effort to categorize them. But these arrangements are scarcely evidence of some new biological imperative on the part of middle and high school girls. Rather, they suggest a youthful desire to rebel against the status quo and push the envelope—a formidable task in an era where there are ever fewer boundaries to transgress. It may be that engaging in simple heterosexual oral or vaginal sex has become so widely expected, some young people are seeking new ways to dramatize their sexual open-mindedness or availability.

Emily Limbaugh, who visits high schools across the entire St. Louis region as coordinator of the Best Choice sexual education program, observes, "It's 'cool' to be bisexual. One girl made out with her girlfriend in front of me, just to push the envelope. Just for the shock value. It's not that they actually enjoy it—they just want to put on a show for guys because it gets them attention."[100]

Ironically, perhaps the most profound type of rebellion is adhering to the older, traditional norm of premarital virginity, which, in many circles, is increasingly perceived as being somewhat freakish. Three girls in Rockdale County, Georgia, who had remained virgins reported being isolated by their peers and even harassed for their decision. When asked about girls who had decided to abstain until marriage, another sexually active girl answered, "It's not going to happen."[101] Sadly, many girls believe that "[W]aiting to have sex is a nice idea but nobody really does."[102]

HOOKED IN, HOOKED UP

When girls have orgasms, do they also eject a liquid,
  like guys?
I faked orgasms with my bf [boyfriend].
Can a gynecologist tell if you're a virgin?
How can I be less of a prude?

Sample sex questions on gURL.com[1]

Any hot ass girls want to chat on yahoo im [instant message] me

MySpace teen chat room

Of all the myriad forms of new, sophisticated communications technology, the Internet is certainly the most significant. In fact, as author and radio talk-show host Hugh Hewitt has pointed out, the Internet may well be one of the most significant revolutions in communication since the printing press.[2] Certainly the Web allows users to access and consume an almost infinite variety of content. What's more, it offers a cheap, easy way for ordinary Americans to create content themselves: Blogs, home pages, and the like allow almost anyone to write and design for a public audience.

In an average day, more than half of all young people use a computer for recreational purposes,[3] and teens spend about seven hours per week online.[4] Not surprisingly, teen girls are avid users of the Internet, both as content consumers and content creators. In fact, fully 88 percent of girls between twelve and seventeen go on to the Internet.[5]

In contrast with boys, who often use the Web for entertainment and online purchasing, girls are primarily "social surfers."[6] Online, they are most likely to send or read e-mail (93 percent).[7] They'll also visit Web sites about movies, TV shows, music groups, or sports stars (88 percent), or look for health, dieting, and fitness information (37 percent).[8]

Girls between fifteen and seventeen are the most likely of all teens to research a "health topic that's hard to talk about" (such as sex) online; 34 percent will do so, compared with only 18 percent of boys the same age.[9] Even as early as 2001, more than half (51 percent) of all girls between fifteen and seventeen who had access to the Internet had, at some point, looked up information on a sexual health topic.[10] Girls also place a higher priority on being able to access Internet information on a range of health topics than do boys.[11]

The fact that so many girls go online—and that a fair percentage of them go there to find information about deeply intimate issues like sex—makes the Web a powerful influence in the lives and development of teen girls. So it's worth taking a look at some of what they're finding online.

Accessing Information: What's Available on the Web

Researchers have noted the easy accessibility and low cost of online health information. The Internet does, indeed, "provide . . . a level of confidentiality that could particularly appeal to teens, especially for embarrassing or controversial inquiries."[12] And certainly, there are responsible sites that will provide accurate information to teen girls who are simply seeking medical advice. Yet those sites may likewise offer facts that far exceed in specificity and theme what young people have traditionally learned from their parents or in sex ed class—and more often than not, the information is completely devoid of any overarching religious, moral, or ethical context.

Sites for Teen Girls

WebMD is one of the most respected medical sites on the Internet. Although it is not targeted explicitly at teens, it is well-known to Web-surfers of all ages as a reliable source on a variety of topics. There, a search of the word *sex* recently provided, as the top three results, an article on "information for a better sex life," a bulletin that one in five teens have reportedly tried oral sex, and an update on "Romance After 60."[13] While this information may be helpful, pertinent, and appropriate for adults, it's hardly the kind of reading that was readily accessible to teens in the pre-Internet era.

The Planned Parenthood site does include a section aimed at young people. In the "teen health" section teens can read about topics including "How do you know when you're ready for sex?" "Is abstinence right for you now?" "Birth control choices for teens," and "Sex—safer and satisfying."[14] The site does include one link reading "Teen sex? It's okay to say 'no way' "—along with other potentially useful information, such as links to ar-

ticles about what happens during a visit to the gynecologist and
the symptoms of testicular cancer. And no doubt the facts are
accurate. But they're rendered without reference to morals or
ethics. There's no "right"—it's all just a matter of "what's right
for you." Whether or not to have sex is presented as just another
choice, much like whether to purchase a Britney Spears album or
one by Christina Aguilera.

In fact, the Planned Parenthood site offers a carefully neutral
moral review of the pros and cons of an extensive variety of sexual activities. In the "Outercourse" section (linked from "Birth
Control"), readers learn about what Planned Parenthood considers the "lower-risk forms of outercourse," including "erotic
massage" (where "couples touch and rub each other's sex organs
using their hands, bodies, or mouths") and body rubbing/frot-
tage.[15] As for masturbation, the site helpfully informs young
readers that "Partners can masturbate alone, together, or watch
each other." In fact, the site contains such an extensive menu of
sexual activity that it's hard to tell whether it's intended to serve
as an information clearinghouse or a how-to manual.

In conjunction with its main site, Planned Parenthood spon-
sors Teenwire, specifically aimed at teen girls. Along with
providing opportunities to "fight for reproductive rights" and
information about the nearest Planned Parenthood clinic, the
site includes an "ask the experts" section, featuring questions
like, "Is it safe to keep having sex with my girlfriend after I ejaculate in the condom?" and "When a guy has a condom and comes,
does he have to put on a new condom?" (No and yes.) All advice
is offered with an air of moral equivalence—one response even
noted that a young correspondent might not have menstruated
despite a negative pregnancy test because she has "a menstrual
cycle that hasn't become regular yet."[16] Apparently, there is no
age so tender that sex is deemed to be just plain wrong.

Elsewhere, sex and sexual decision making are even more

lightly treated. On the Sex, Etc. Web site (www.sexetc.org)—a site "for teens, by teens!" run under the auspices of Rutgers University—one feature story, written by an eighteen-year-old, was titled "Friends with Benefits: The Perfect Solution or Risky Ventures?" The piece begins:

> *Is it OK for two close friends to have some sexual fun together, safe and secure in the comfort of each other's familiar arms? Or will sex ruin the friendship? These are questions lots of teens struggle with, as many of us shy away from steady relationships, but still like to have a little physical affection every once in awhile.*[17]

The author concluded that "Many teens ultimately say that a 'friends with benefits' relationship really depends on how close the bond between the two friends is, how mature they are, and how well they deal with the situation."[18] In other words, it may be okay for teens to engage in sexual activity without a romantic attachment, as long as they can "deal with it." Hardly the kind of peer guidance most parents would want for their children.

A poll question from the site reads as follows: "Your boyfriend/girlfriend forgets to bring a condom and you're thinking about having sex. You say . . ." The statement is followed not by any advice, but rather by a selection of choices, some far more responsible than others.[19] What's remarkable isn't the array of choices in the poll, however; it's the underlying assumption, reflected also in the "friends with benefits" feature, that teen sex isn't just acceptable, but ubiquitous.

In fact, Sex, Etc. isn't afraid to proselytize, albeit indirectly. A piece on the site by a sixteen-year-old female writer is called "Abstinence Is Foolproof? Think Again!"[20] The author argues that, like other forms of birth control, abstinence can "fail" and as a result, teens can become pregnant if they haven't been taught how to use contraception properly. (What she doesn't consider is that when abstinence "fails," it's because it's not being practiced. The same isn't necessarily true for birth control.)

At the article's conclusion, there's an editor's note referring readers to the Sex, Etc. "Take Action Center" if they "would like to make sure that [their] school gets all the facts about sexual health." At the "Take Action Center," teens are offered the opportunity to "learn more about the movement for honest sex ed in the US and start acting up for change." Whatever "acting up" on behalf of "honest sex ed" means, it certainly doesn't seem to indicate any agenda supporting teen sexual restraint.

Another site, gURL.com, describes itself as a place "committed to discussing issues that affect the lives of girls age 13 and up in a nonjudgmental, personal way."[21] (Heaven forbid that judgment be exercised anywhere!) It notes, "Our content deals frankly with sexuality, emotions, body image, etc.,"[22] and even warns parents that it "contains mature content."[23] Of course, that last warning would be more helpful if parents were capable of monitoring their daughters' every move on the Internet.

In any case, the site lives up to its billing, and is nothing if not graphic when it comes to the discussion of sex. Questions for the site's advice guru include "How do I tell my mom I want birth control?" to "I can hear my parents have sex," "Am I allergic to condoms?," and "Can a penis be too big?"[24]

Along with the information about eating disorders and how to register to vote on gURL.com, "girls age 13 and up" can access information on dry humping, fingering, oral sex, anal sex, and wet dreams.[25] There's the clichéd one-link nod to abstinence, too—a discussion that predictably concludes by reminding readers, "Whether or not you choose to be abstinent, how long you decide to abstain, and how you define it, is completely up to you."[26] Again, no judgment here—and no guidance, either.

Sex is referenced even more casually elsewhere. According to

Nielsen/NetRatings,[27] in June 2005 the site visited most by US teen girls was MemeGen.net, which lets users create quizzes or tests that are compatible with their blogs or online journals. As of July 2006, listed among the most popular quizzes were the following: "What's your sexual position?" "Would anyone want to bang you?" "What makes you sexy?" and "Your stripper info."[28] At Flooble.com, another site popular with teen girls according to Nielsen/NetRatings,[29] there's a "gay quiz" that asks participants about a variety of personal matters, including whether they've ever had "lesbian sex with another girl" or done "it with another guy." After taking the quiz, visitors can obtain HTML code that allows them to broadcast their sexual orientation on their Web sites.[30] And polls on the MisterPoll.com site include questions about "when you first had sex (girls only!)," "oral," "guys who have been raped," "honest porn poll," "sex and nudity in public," and "who's on top."[31]

Not surprisingly, the Web sites attached to popular teen girl magazines mirror the more provocative content of the magazines themselves, even seeking content for upcoming issues. In February 2006, CosmoGirl.com posted the following request: "Girlfriend Stories: Are you a lesbian or bi-sexual and have a romantic story about you and your girlfriend? Tell us your love story and it could get picked for the magazine!"[32] Topics on the "SexSmarts" portion of the *Seventeen* Web site include "Can Minors Get Birth Control all on Their Own?"[33] "The Lowdown on Hooking Up,"[34] "What's Your Sexual Orientation,"[35] and "How to Deal with a Pregnancy Scare."[36] (Like a lone voice in the wilderness, one sensible piece "debunking myths about going all the way"[37] reminds girls they don't *have* to have sex.)

Ultimately, much of the sex advice dished out on sites intended for young girls is factually sound—as far as it goes. But it doesn't go far enough. There's little that would really convey to a young girl the potentially life-changing seriousness of a decision to have sex, even as she's besieged by messages (like gratuitous sexual quizzes) suggesting that "everyone's doing it."

To the extent that teen girl sites attempt to dissuade their readers from having sex, it's only because of the potential physical ramifications (becoming pregnant or infected with an STD), or very occasionally the emotional ones ("getting hurt"). The sites virtually never make determinations about the ethical, moral, or religious aspects of teen sex—even though most Americans would surely agree that it's never right, or even acceptable, for girls between the ages of twelve and seventeen to be conducting the active sex lives that many of the sites apparently presume they have.

Pornography on the Web

Sexual content accessible to young girls on the Internet is hardly restricted to the sites intended for them. Far from it. Even as the Internet has offered numerous educational opportunities, it has likewise resulted in a tremendous number of young girls (and boys, too) being inadvertently exposed to pornography and other adult sexual media—subjects and images that used to be almost impossible for them to access.

The Internet, as anyone who's been online knows, is rife with pornography. In 2007, there were 4.2 million pornographic Web sites (12 percent of all Web sites), 68 million daily pornographic search engine requests (25 percent of all requests), and 2.5 billion daily pornographic e-mails.[38] Not surprisingly, the Internet is significantly reducing the age at which girls and boys alike are first exposed to sexually explicit or pornographic material.[39] A 2002 study for the London School of Economics found that 90 percent of those between the ages of eight and sixteen had, in fact, been exposed to pornography online.[40] And in 2004, *The Washington Post* reported that pornographic sites had eleven million visitors younger than eighteen every week.[41]

A significant portion of the exposure to sexually explicit images online is involuntary. More than a third of the teens who are online report having received a link to sexually explicit content; 24 percent report having received sexual content four times or more.[42] Not surprisingly, it makes some girls uncomfortable. As one thirteen-year-old told a researcher, "I think these sites were put on the Web to corrupt society."[43]

In fact, it's not difficult to access a pornographic site by accident. Some use Web addresses that are common misspellings of popular words, or innocuous-sounding sites that many visitors are likely to seek for nonsexual purposes. For many years, www .whitehouse.com offered inappropriate content to all those who had typed the wrong suffix as they searched for the page about the president's residence (www.whitehouse.gov).[44]

Nonsexual searches likewise can yield a variety of pornographic links. The top results for a Google search of "teen girls" recently included an offer for pictures of "31 fresh hot girls every day," images of "young girls naked," and a site for "hardcore movies of teen girls."[45] (A search for " 'teen girls' and 'sexy clothes' " yielded even more risqué results.[46])

Ultimately, it's nearly impossible for young girls—or Americans generally—to avoid Internet porn. A prominent 2003 study found that 25 percent of American youths between ten and seventeen who were regular Internet users had experienced one or more unwanted exposures to sexual pictures just in the past year.[47]

Even though most of the ten- to seventeen-year-olds reported no ill effects from being accidentally confronted with pornography, fully 24 percent reported being very or extremely upset, with 21 percent likewise experiencing embarrassment.[48] And 19 percent reported the manifestation of at least one stress symptom—experiencing it "more than a little"—in the day immediately following the exposure.[49] In a report from the Girl Scout

Institute, one participant, aged fourteen, analogized accidentally accessing pornography to "a car crash. You want to look away but you can't."[50]

Although the 2003 study found that the involuntary exposures happened to both genders equally,[51] research from the Kaiser Family Foundation reported that girls were much more likely than their male counterparts to report being "very upset" as a result of stumbling on online porn (35 versus 6 percent).[52] This result is consistent with an earlier study in which college students recalled their emotional response to a significant experience with a sexually themed medium, such as a sexual film or video.[53] Negative emotions (disgust, shock, surprise, and embarrassment) were the most commonly named responses to the exposure by participants of both genders, but females were even more likely than males to respond negatively—crying and feeling sad.[54]

Describing the results, that study's authors noted the "feelings of vulnerability engendered by sexual media in teenage girls and young women."[55] It's a safe bet that negative feelings and outcomes are even more frequent in a brave new online world where the raunchiest pictures imaginable are little more than a mouse click away.

Communicating: Interaction on the Web

Even as the Internet allows teen girls to access a variety of information—often the kind they'd be embarrassed to seek in less anonymous settings—it offers them an opportunity to create content of their own. "Cool" sites like www.uthtv.com, in fact, offer a place for teens to contribute "youth created video, audio, image and word."

Fully 57 percent of the teens who are online generate some kind of online content[56]—working on blogs, posting personal

Web pages, or sharing photos, stories, and artwork online. In fact, girls between fifteen and seventeen are the most likely to blog (25 percent),[57] the most likely to read others' blogs (53 percent),[58] and the most likely to create and share "self-authored content" such as artwork, stories, or photos (38 percent).[59]

One of the Internet's distinguishing characteristics is the unparalleled opportunity it presents for teens to communicate and connect with others. A study of seventh and tenth graders found that they spent about forty minutes daily sending instant messages, and about twenty-two minutes on e-mail.[60]

While most of those they're communicating with online are acquaintances made offline (82 percent of IM partners are friends or best friends[61]), teens also have significant exposure to new people through the Internet: 54 percent of online teens report having communicated with someone they've never met using IM, and 32 percent have done so weekly.[62] Often, teens meet new people online either through using message boards or in chat rooms.[63] And given the ubiquity of sexual content in teen life generally, perhaps it's no surprise that teen chat rooms and message boards often feature a broad range of sexual content.[64]

Teen Message Boards

Both on message boards and in chat rooms, teens identify themselves through screen names that they select (also known as nicknames or "nicks").[65] "Nicks" can range from the innocent, like "Tinkerbell," to the raunchier "The One N Only Sex Goddess" or even "your little pimpette" (all real-life examples from a popular teen site). Nearly 20 percent of girls who are online have more than four online identities.[66]

Message boards are areas in which those interested in a particular topic can post public questions or comments about it, and then monitor responses from others that are likewise posted publicly for anyone to read. Many teen boards are devoted to innocuous topics like fitness, world affairs, school, sports, music, and television. But for those who are interested or even just curious, graphic sexual content can easily be accessed on message boards. In fact, the section devoted to "Teen Issues" on TeenSpot. com[67] offers a link to "Sex Questions: Should I? What if? How do I? What can I? Ask anything you want about sex!"

On a typical visit to the sex questions board, girls can find other teens advising their peers about a wide range of matters. Just one board, one day, featured topics ranging from anal masturbation ("I'm a straight guy, and I have tried anal masturbation a few times and I'm just wondering, is there any chance that by just using a couple of fingertips . . . that i may be stretching the muscles irreversibly?")[68] to sexual positions ("when you girls 'ride' the guy, exactly how do u sit or lay? i've tried and it's not going very well")[69] to a question directed to "guys" about "fingering and porn" ("what do you want to see when you watch a girl fingering herself?")[70] to an inquiry about how to deflower a virgin.[71]

In fact, the content of the TeenSpot "Sex Questions" board is consistent with a 2004 study of a teen issues board and a teen sexual health board. Researchers noticed a "focus on sexuality" generally, and reported that the sexual board was more popular than the one devoted to teen issues.[72] Not surprisingly, questions about sexual techniques prompted great interest, as did interpersonal aspects of sex.[73] Interestingly, on the teen sexual health board, pregnancy and birth control questions were the least frequently viewed.[74]

The apparent anonymity afforded by the Internet may well account for both the emphasis on sex itself and the unusually graphic nature of the questions. Even a cursory review of teen sex message boards confirms that they aren't being used primarily for the health information that can be obtained more reliably from other sources or even provided at school, but rather for the kind of intimate advice that in an earlier day might have been solicited only in the darkest hallways of the roughest schools—if there.

Teen Chat Rooms

Chat rooms are much more interactive than message boards. Any number of users can exchange messages, and several topics may be discussed simultaneously by different (but sometimes overlapping) groups of people, with text scrolling up the screen as the conversation progresses. The written conversation tends to mimic spontaneous speech, and teens have adopted a number of strategies—including the use of acronyms, numbers, and distinctive scripts—to create what researchers have called "the emerging language of chat."[75]

Chat rooms are popular with teens—by 2005, 45 percent had used them to communicate with someone they'd never met.[76] In fact, a variety of wholesome chat rooms exist—Yahoo!, for example, has rooms devoted to different religious beliefs, finance, politics, entertainment, and other topics.

But for young girls who are naturally interested in boys and in flirting, chat rooms, coupled with the recent explosion of social networking sites like MySpace, Xanga, and Facebook, also provide a hitherto unimagined method for interacting with the opposite sex. Some girls have reported that they feel more confident and less shy talking to boys online because the boys can't see them;[77] researchers have even theorized that "the relative anonymity and absence of bodies on the Internet may liberate women from an often subordinate position."[78]

If that's true, it's worth noting that the liberation is taking some pretty strange forms. The kind of superficial interactions facilitated by chat seem like natural precursors to hookups—that is, no-strings sexual encounters, devoid of any sort of romantic interest or commitment.[79] Indeed, the relative anonymity of the

Web seems to elicit quite provocative online behavior on the part of some girls.

Through numerous visits over time, the chat room reserved for teens on the popular MySpace.com site featured online dialogue from girls and boys alike that was saturated with sexual allusions and general vulgarity. In fact, the bulk of the content of the teen chat seemed to consist of invitations to chat privately via instant message, presumably about matters of a sexual nature. In the course of five minutes on a Saturday afternoon, the following come-ons appeared from boys and girls alike:

"Any hot hornie girls want to chat press 451"
"Hot guys who want to talk press 222"
"hornie ass chic waitin fer action"
"You are a slut you got monkey tits bet you fucked everyone"
"Horny guys press 123"
"Any hot horny guys want to talk to 2 horny bitches press 1223"
"I have a 9 in dick any woman live in va can have it"
"I'm getting wet wanna help me message me"

There were plenty of explicit offers and solicitations from teens of both sexes to "cyber"—that is, to engage in cybersex, a practice in which participants simulate sex while sending each other graphic instant messages or images. And "cybering" does seem to be a popular practice—at least judging by a Dutch survey, which found that 25 percent of boys and 20 percent of girls in the Netherlands had engaged in it.[80] An American survey of thirteen-through eighteen-year-olds revealed that 27 percent had talked online about sex with someone they had never met in person.[81] That's a significant statistic, as the ability to engage in deeply intimate sexual conversation with a stranger only reinforces a mentality in which sexual activity is little more than another form of recreation—one that doesn't necessarily require face-to-face contact, much less a committed relationship.

In fact, just entering a chat room with a "nick" indicating that one is a female makes it easy to garner a slew of uninvited sexual invitations and solicitations (a result consistent with similar experiments conducted by academic researchers[82]). Research published in 2001 reported that 19 percent of the study's participants (youth between the ages of ten and seventeen) had received at least one sexual solicitation over the course of the previous year,[83] and 89 percent of solicitations made of youths take place in chat rooms.[84] Given the more recent explosion in Web sites and chat rooms, it seems likely that girls currently would be receiving such messages much more frequently. Even lurking in the rooms (reading the messages without participating) is enough to provide quite an education in the practice of sexual come-ons, most of them crudely graphic.

Over on Yahoo!, simply signing up for an identifier in order to participate in chat rooms—and then heading to the "flirting" room—can result in an onslaught of instant messages offering links to free nude pictures. Showing up online with a "nick" like "GoddessC90" in one chat room devoted to "flirting" and another reserved for "20's love" and then entering a relatively neutral greeting ("What's up? I'm lonely" or "What's up? I'm bored") was, at least on several occasions, sufficient to receive an immediate invitation to chat more intimately via instant message. Some of the solicited interactions were for little more than small talk, but for most it became clear quite quickly that "cybering" was on the agenda.[85]

Yahoo!, MySpace, and other chat services try to ensure that those participating are of an appropriate age—for example, on MySpace, the service limits a sixteen-year-old to the teen chat room (though, as noted above, the age restriction doesn't necessarily mean that the dialogue will be innocent), and in 2005

Yahoo! closed its chat rooms to anyone under eighteen. Of course, all those safeguards are contingent on girls reporting their ages honestly. Those who are willing to misrepresent or manipulate their identities significantly can do so undetected—and then, on Yahoo! alone, access gay and lesbian chat rooms, the "pick up bar," or even a chat room for those who are "married and flirting."

For whatever purpose, it's clear that a significant number of teens are, in fact, misreporting their identities online. The Kaiser Family Foundation found that 31 percent of seventh through twelfth graders have pretended to be older than they are in order to access a Web site.[86] In a survey conducted for the Polly Klaas Foundation, more teen girls than boys reported having lied online about their age (50 versus 38 percent).[87] And in a study of seventh and tenth graders, half of the participants admitted to having pretended to be someone else on the Internet "a couple of times" or more,[88] most pretending to be older.[89]

Certainly some teens may adopt another identity as a way to avoid divulging personal information on the Internet. But the ability to "become" another person can have less wholesome effects as well. The fact that screen "nicks" render a user anonymous promotes a sense that there are no consequences for behavior that would be deemed inappropriate elsewhere. This, of course, means that some users will behave badly. In a 2001 study, 30 percent of girls aged thirteen through eighteen reported that they had been sexually harassed in a chat room.[90]

What's more, the anonymity means that girls themselves may, with a false sense of security, engage in risky or risqué behavior that they wouldn't dream of in real life. For many teen girls, the Internet may well seem like a "fantasyland where the innocent can be sexy, the obedient can be naughty, and even the meek can swear with the best of them."[91] But the result, in many cases, is a race to the bottom in terms of the sexual content of online discourse—and a greater susceptibility to the very real dangers that the Internet can pose for the naive or unwary.

Personal Web Pages

Social networking sites are extremely popular with teens. In fact, 61 percent of teens between thirteen and seventeen have posted a personal profile on sites like MySpace, Friendster, or Xanga.[92] The best known, MySpace—which was ranked the number one US Web site in July 2006, according to Internet tracking firm Hitwise[93]—boasts about fifty million users[94] who set up their own "profiles" (Web pages), which include information like name, birthday, address, school, and interests. While the pages of those identifying themselves as sixteen or over are public, the profiles of those under sixteen are set to "private" by MySpace; even so, they can be made available to all those who e-mail the proprietor and ask to be accepted as a "friend." Once the would-be visitor is accepted as a friend (and many strangers are, with minimal questioning), all information posted on the page becomes accessible, and the page's proprietor can receive notes from their "friends"—which, some parents have found, are filled with salacious content.[95]

Most young girls post profiles on MySpace simply to make friends and socialize. But given that personal Web pages are a vehicle for self-expression, it's not surprising that some teen girls lard their pages with sexual content. Suggestive photographs on MySpace sites are not unusual—with some so explicit that two teen girls were arrested in spring 2006 on a charge of child pornography for the pictures of themselves on their Web pages.[96]

Teen "cam girls" likewise boast Web pages of their own.[97] Cam girls establish Web sites that they update using a Web camera, some with live video and others with still pictures, featuring a slew of more or less scantily clad images. The cam girls allow viewers to take a good look at them (often in a variety of provocative poses), and in return many seek gifts, often establishing registries that will allow their fans to send presents.[98]

The popularity of amateur cam girls may have peaked in 2001 and 2002—a large chunk of the market has been absorbed by professional pornography—but many teen girls continue to use Web cams nonetheless. In fact, after a boy has asked a girl to "cyber" (that is, to engage in cybersex), it's not unusual for him next to ask if she has a Web cam that she's willing to turn on.

The Risks

Certainly teens are aware of the risks that careless online behavior can entail. Nearly one in eight have learned that someone they've communicated with online was an adult pretending to be younger,[99] 56 percent say they've been asked personal questions online,[100] and 19 percent report that they've known a friend who has been asked or harassed about sex online by a stranger.[101]

What's more, they're reminded frequently of the dangers that lurk online. Magazines such as *Seventeen* run articles that combine a sex angle with warnings, like the October 2004 piece "She Had an Online Stalker."[102] The media has reported vigorously on numerous instances of pedophiles arranging face-to-face meetings with children and teens through online chat. In particular, NBC's *Dateline* made a great splash when it wired a house with hidden cameras and used the services of an online vigilante group to lure predators there under the pretext that there were children or young teens home alone.[103] And in spring 2006, papers recorded instances of pedophiles contacting or attempting to contact girls between thirteen and fifteen through MySpace. com, everywhere from Laguna Beach, California,[104] to Connecticut,[105] Wisconsin,[106] Honolulu, Hawaii,[107] Massachusetts,[108] and suburban Chicago.[109]

Despite the cautionary tales, however, fully 42 percent of online teens report that they've posted personal information on the

Internet so that others can contact them.[110] Some teens' pages go so far as to include lengthy surveys that spell out their proprietors' likes and dislikes in detail—information that's priceless for a pedophile trying to forge a bond with a potential target.[111] And girls engage in riskier online behavior than boys. More teen girls than boys have posted online profiles (56 versus 37 percent), more girls have shared personal information with someone they've never met in person (37 versus 26 percent), and more have been asked about sexual topics (33 versus 18 percent).

Girls likewise are more likely than boys to form close online relationships (16 versus 12 percent), with girls between fourteen and seventeen being twice as likely as those aged ten through thirteen to do so.[112] Nearly 30 percent of teens generally have talked about meeting someone they've encountered only on the Internet; 27 percent report having a friend who's actually met someone they knew only from the Web; and 21 percent say that someone they knew only from the Internet had asked to meet them.[113]

Clearly, the sexualization so pervasive elsewhere in American culture is found along the information superhighway as well—and it's made doubly dangerous by the Internet's capacity to connect strangers, constrained only by their own honesty, in a medium that allows them to remain largely anonymous.

What It Means

New technology has made it infinitely easier for young people to be in touch without their parents being aware of it. "Even my really good girls are able to sneak out of the house," says Dr. Adria O'Donnell, a clinical and consulting psychologist whose primary focus is on adolescent girls. "They have computers so they can IM each other, and cell phones so they can text—'meet me in the park.' They can arrange meetings because they are in contact all the time. Underground communication has allowed kids access."

Lowering Social Inhibitions

It's not hard to understand how the use of instant messaging allows teens to set up hookups easily and serves as a system by which their friends can alert them if parents are trying to locate them—all without their parents' knowledge. Because instant messaging on the computer and cell phone text messaging involve neither face-to-face nor even voice-to-voice communication, it can lower social inhibitions generally, leading teens to engage in behavior (from cyberbullying to sexual banter) that they might otherwise avoid.

When it comes to the Internet, teen girls are both consumers of online content and prolific creators of it. Even as they are exposed to a variety of sexual material, some may also be contributing to the sexualized environment through the content they provide. That, in itself, is a warning sign that too many young women are learning all too well the lessons a sexualized culture is teaching them.

Dr. O'Donnell observes, "Girls on the Internet can type and play with their sexual energy—girls are re-creating themselves over and over. They can say sexy things on the Internet and not know the charge it has. They can throw it out there and it could be a sixteen-year-old boy or a forty-year old man [responding], and it doesn't matter."

Learning About Sex from Strangers

Perhaps most significantly, the advent of the Internet means that, for the most part, adults have lost almost all control both over what even the youngest teens can learn about sexuality—and who's teaching them. There's simply no denying that teens can access a range and depth of sexual information (accurate or not) that was once unavailable to those their age. Given the widespread accessibility of Internet access—at home, at school, at libraries, at friends' houses—even the most stringent filtering system isn't likely to be a wholly effective response.

Certainly, parents may not object to their children being able to find some information about sex; many may, in fact, approve of their daughters accessing accurate facts on responsible sites. Teens themselves express discomfort about discussing sex with doctors, both because they're embarrassed and because of the potential for disclosure to their parents.[114] So girls are likely to appreciate being able to obtain information about sensitive matters without the difficulty of confronting someone face-to-face or locating a book on the relevant topic.

But teens—and their parents—should at least acknowledge that, by turning to the Web instead of a responsible adult, they're relying on sources that aren't accountable, and that have little personal stake in a particular teen's health and well-being. Like other media, the Internet doesn't necessarily answer questions about sex with messages that represent safe and healthy choices.[115]

In fact, what's most remarkable about the overwhelming majority of sexual advice and information on the Internet is how it's presented: without reference to the moral, ethical, or religious considerations that are more likely to inform the exchange of similar information in less anonymous forums.

None of this, of course, even takes into account the ramifications of many teens' exposure to online porn at a relatively tender age when their impressions of sex are still being shaped. Not surprisingly, experts have noted that voluntary and involuntary exposure to porn may affect attitudes about sex;[116] indeed, "the evidence indicates that pornography and related sexual media can influence sexual violence, the sexual attitudes, moral values, and sexual activity of children and youth."[117] And the effects can be pernicious—exposure to pornography as a child has been found to be significantly related both to rape fantasies and to rape-supportive beliefs (trivializing/normalizing rape, or blaming the victim) in female adults.[118]

What's more, the images affect teens' conceptions of sex and intimate relationships. Pornography teaches boys that girls are little more than fungible sex objects. And even as it presents unrealistic expectations about sex and relationships for young boys, porn sets unattainable (and often undesirable) standards for girls when it comes both to appearance and behavior. Neither phenomenon is wholesome, or healthy for teens' future relationships.

Teens themselves seem instinctively to understand the dangers of easily accessed online porn. A 2001 report by the Kaiser Family Foundation found that 57 percent of fifteen- through seventeen-year-olds and 65 percent of fifteen- through twenty-four-year-olds believe that exposure to online pornography could seriously impact those under eighteen, and 59 percent agree (32 percent strongly) that seeing porn on the Internet encourages adolescents to have sex before they're ready.[119] Being exposed to dysfunctional fantasies or sexual scenarios (images of rape or bestiality, for example) early in the developmental process may even affect a young person's lifelong sexual interests or proclivities.[120] And for older adolescents, such exposure can feed "obsessional fantasies," even prompting them to seek people with whom to experiment.[121]

When it comes to interactive forums such as chat rooms and message boards, emotionally immature young girls (and boys, too) are likely to be poorly equipped to understand and process a lot of the information with which they're confronted. Particularly in chat rooms, teens are exposed to material that one expert characterized as "a not-so-virtual sexual come-on, which the teen may not have been seeking and may not be developmentally or psychologically prepared for."[122]

In at least some teen chat rooms, the discussion of sexuality is public, linked to strangers, and completely devoid of any sense of relationship.[123] Research, coupled with personal experience, indicates a focus on physical acts rather than their emotional meaning—often involving the degradation of women.[124] It's hard to escape the conclusion that frequent exposure to such material could be damaging to any teen's development of a healthy, responsible sense of sexuality.

Finally, even as it introduces infinite educational and creative potential into the lives of teen girls, the Internet allows those who are so inclined to orchestrate a virtual sex life with strangers, unbeknownst to their parents, while they sit alone in their bedrooms. And more is at stake than the obvious physical risks that can result from a girl deciding to pursue an online relationship in real life.

In fact, the false sense of anonymity and security that the Internet engenders may convince girls that engaging in a variety of virtual sexual activities, ranging from cybersex to provocative Web cam displays, is essentially harmless. Dr. Adria O'Donnell notes, "[Girls] can try [their sexuality] out on the Internet. It's almost 'try before you buy.' They think, 'I can talk sexy and it has zero ramifications.' "

And of course, that's not always the truth, as many parents realize. As of 2005, 54 percent of parents with teens online reported that there was a filter on their home computer;[125] other research has shown that young people report they are 40 percent less likely to be involuntarily exposed to sexual content when filtering software was being used.[126]

Taking measures to prevent exposure to inappropriate material is an important first step—but so, perhaps, is the increasing recognition that careless online behavior can ultimately damage girls' developing sense of self and sexual identity. Provocative behavior can be harmful for girls not just physically but also, in some instances, emotionally and psychologically. In an era when sex acts or sexy pictures can be recorded on cell phones with cameras, as well as by video and digital cameras,[127] seemingly harmless "misbehavior" may well result in embarrassment, shame, and regret in years to come.

CHAPTER 4

BETWEEN THE COVERS

Press one for a maid. Press two for the chef. Unfortunately, there was no "Press three for a hot guy," but that could be taken care of on her own. And soon. She hadn't been about to lose her virginity to some five-foot-nothing Amazonian warrior with brown teeth. But she was sure she could find just the right American warrior prince to do the manly deed.

The Nannies, by Melody Mayer

These reflections from Lydia, one of the approximately fifteen- or sixteen-year-old protagonists of *The Nannies,* are emblematic of a relatively new genre of fiction aimed at young teen girls. Drugs and alcohol surface in the plots, but all too often the main focus is sex: who's having it, who's not, who wants to, who did and was disappointed by it. The overarching theme is that sexual activity on the part of teen girls is normal, acceptable, and even expected.

Young adult fiction has become one of the book industry's most profitable areas. Sales for books directed at those twelve and older have increased 23 percent since 1999, while adult sales during the same period decreased approximately 1 percent.[1] In 2004, even without the release of a new installment in the *Harry Potter* series, revenue in the genre of young adult fiction was approximately $410 million.[2] Notably, sexually charged young adult fiction is the fastest-growing segment of publishing—and young girls are its biggest consumers.[3]

Although girls continue to read longtime classics like *Little Women* and newer ones like the *Harry Potter* series, contemporary young adult fiction is larded with sexual themes to an astounding degree. Those who came of age giggling with their classmates over the single, relatively tame sex scene in a contraband copy of Judy Blume's *Forever*—once the most risqué teen-oriented book available—would hardly recognize much of today's young adult fiction. Not only is sex between teenagers treated as a given, but teachers routinely display sexual interest in their students. Parents are on the periphery of the action—when they're present at all. And traditional morality plays a minimal role in sexual decision making.

The pervasive sexuality in recent young adult books recently came to public attention with the release of the novel *Rainbow Party* by Paul Ruditis. Reviewed by *Publishers Weekly* and the *School Library Journal* as appropriate for those fourteen (ninth grade) and up, the story centers on two girls planning a "rainbow party": Several girls wear different shades of lipstick, then perform oral sex on a group of boys, thereby leaving each with a "rainbow" around his penis at the party's conclusion. In the novel, the party never comes off; the story concludes with a gonorrhea outbreak extending to thirty-nine sophomores, including one of the party planners.

Even so, *Rainbow Party* is no morality tale. It introduces young readers to the concept of a party featuring an oral sex round robin, and is populated by characters guided by nothing larger than what feels right to them. Along with its primary girl-on-boy blow job plot, *Rainbow Party* also features homosexual sex in a school bathroom, a girl receiving oral sex for the first time (in her mother's bedroom), and raunchy dialogue: "*'I've got Gin so wrapped around my dick that she's usually begging for it,'* Hunter said."[4]

Author Paul Ruditis has insisted that he "just wanted to present an issue kids are dealing with,"[5] expressing hope that "parents and children or teachers and students can open a topic of conversation through it."[6] But titillation seems to have been a more important selling point than education, at least in the book's original marketing plan. Until booksellers complained, the novel's bound galleys included the tagline: "Don't you want to know what really goes down?"[7]

Not surprisingly, some schools, libraries, and bookstores declined to carry *Rainbow Party*.[8] The vice president and editorial director of the company that published the novel told *Newsday* that the controversy had occurred "because adults don't want to believe that teens are having sex."[9] But although the sheer outrageousness of its plot attracted widespread notice, *Rainbow Party* is hardly unique in its preoccupation with sex.

In fact, today's young adult fiction leaves no sexual aberration unexplored. *Teach Me* by R. A. Nelson, reviewed by the *School Library Journal* for grades nine and up (fourteen years and older), gives a whole new meaning to the term *high school sweetheart*. Nine, a high school senior, embarks on a tempestuous affair with her thirty-five-year-old English teacher. As the teacher kisses her, Nine confides that she "didn't know he'd taste this sweet" as "his tongue touches [hers], gentle, alive."[10]

The relationship quickly progresses to the bedroom (conveniently, the affair isn't fully consummated until the evening of

Nine's eighteenth birthday, presumably to avoid the ugly specter of statutory rape). There, as the novel breathlessly recounts, the teacher is "kissing [her] everywhere, squeezing [her], running his fingers over places no one else has touched."[11] The teacher even refers to marrying her at the end of her sophomore year in college—until he breaks off the liaison unexpectedly to marry another woman.

Stung to the core, Nine crashes the wedding, where she presents the bride with a box containing her newly extracted wisdom tooth. While the teacher-lover and his new wife are on their honeymoon, Nine breaks into his apartment, smearing the bedsheets with raspberry jam. Obsessed with heartbreak and rage, she likewise steals the teacher's suitcase from the baggage carousel when he's returning from his honeymoon, eavesdrops at his house, and engages in other unsavory activities.

By the book's end, Nine has also stolen a pistol, been suspended for physically assaulting another teacher, and shown up at the ex-lover's off-campus poetry reading, where she shoots a paintball gun at him. Near the book's end, her best friend has a concussion, broken wrist, and ten stitches in his head—as a result of being trapped in a flash flood with Nine as they pursue the teacher by car.

Even so, the heroine suffers no long-term repercussions from her behavior—and the teacher is ultimately portrayed fairly sympathetically. He rescues Nine and her friend from the flood, and, it turns out, he married because his other girl-friend (now wife) had become pregnant with his child before he met Nine.

Although *Teach Me* doesn't glamorize student–teacher affairs, it certainly romanticizes them. The novel doesn't stint in describing Nine's heartbreak, but its plot unfolds in florid, pretentious prose that suggests that her over-the-top, even illegal behavior is part of a magnificent obsession. It encourages young girls to fantasize about their teachers as sexual objects, thereby ripening them for exploitation by real-life classroom Lotharios. And it breaks down the long-standing taboo on relationships between teachers and pupils by removing both the love affairs and the concealment of them from the realm of the unfathomable.

Sex-hungry teachers also emerge in *Nothing Can Keep Us Together,* the eighth installment of the fantastically successful *Gossip Girl* series. There, a female teacher has a "serious crush"[12] on her student, one of the male protagonists. And Serena, another of the book's main characters, learns that "the only cool young male teacher" at her school is attracted to her when they're alone in the darkroom, where he confesses that he's been "watching" her since the seventh grade before asking for a kiss.[13]

And that's the least of the *Gossip Girl* action. At one point in the same book, Serena also shoplifts—although she's so appealing that the guard declines to arrest her. She's also having sex with Nate (in the formal gown department of Barneys department store), who himself regularly smokes pot and steals Viagra from his lacrosse coach.

During exams at Serena and Blair's all-girl school, readers learn, the students "cheat all the time" and protagonists "Blair and Serena were no exception."[14] In passing, we learn that the school's headmistress is a lesbian; after graduation, which involves "[h]alf an hour of shaking parents' hands and offering a few lame anecdotes about their sweet intelligent daughters," she would be "off to Woodstock for the summer to watch Vonda weed their heirloom tomato collection wearing only the red embroidered halter top [she] had bought for her at the craft fair last weekend."[15]

Other characters in the book include quirky Vanessa, who

enjoys frequent, loud sex both with her boyfriend, Aaron, and (unbeknownst to him) with her former boyfriend, Dan, whose younger sister, Jenny, has appeared "semiclothed" on the Internet and in fashion magazines. At one point, Jenny is offered an Ecstasy tablet by students at a boarding school she's visiting—it turns out to have been a teacher's. Ultimately, she presents it to Serena's boyfriend, Nate (who was once with Blair), before they enjoy a torrid encounter in the handicapped stall of a men's room. Jenny notes that she "loved the idea she was using Nate, and the fact that he *wanted* her to use him gave her even more of a thrill"[16] (emphasis in the original).

The novel ends on a note of lesbian chic. *Nothing Can Keep Us Together* concludes as Blair asks guests at her graduation party if they want to "see something really cool"—after which she and Serena engage in a lingering kiss.[17]

Even with its undeniably racy plot, "Product Details" on Amazon.com presents the reading level for this book as "Young Adult." And although the editorial review from the American Library Association on the site states that the book is for those in grades ten through twelve (ages fifteen through eighteen), it describes the book in largely favorable terms, characterizing it as "[u]napologetically lightweight and glamorous and filled with snarky, humorous asides" (like the one about the lesbian headmistress, no doubt).

The attitudes, practices, and usages being popularized through the *Gossip Girls* series might be less worrisome if the books were relatively obscure. But they're not. As of July 2005, the *Gossip Girl* books had sold 2.2 million copies in the United States alone, in an age when most books for those twelve and up sell fewer than 20,000.[18] The three *Gossip Girl* installments immediately preceding *Nothing Can Keep Us Together* debuted at number one on *The New York Times*' children's best-seller list.[19] News reports indicate that the *Gossip Girl* books are being "devoured" by thirteen-year-olds.[20] And their success has only encouraged the development of similar series—including *The Clique, The A-List,* and *The It Girl* series.

Not surprisingly, the author, Cecily von Ziegesar, has branched out. The first installment of her new series, *The It Girl,* follows a familiar template. There, Jenny (she of the bathroom encounter with Nate in the *Gossip Girl* series) embarks on life at her new boarding school. The plot revolves around whether Jenny will take the fall for one of her two new roommates when the girl and her boyfriend are discovered one night by a teacher on the point of having sex in the room Jenny shares with her (while Jenny is present, trying to sleep).

Predictably, given the conventions of the genre, Jenny's other roommate is involved with a teacher; their relationship progresses almost to the point of sex (even though she's been engaging in phone sex with her boyfriend at another school). One of the novel's secondary characters is nicknamed Pony because "everybody has taken a ride."[21] Casual vulgarity, presented as sexual sophistication, is the order of the day.

Both von Ziegesar and R. A. Nelson, the author of *Teach Me,* adamantly defend their work. The former has argued that the characters in the *Gossip Girl* series are "wealthy, they party a lot, but they're also, in a sense, just like every other teenager."[22] According to von Ziegesar, her books "are less shocking than what kids are seeing in movies and in magazines and on television" because "there is no graphic sex."[23]

And in fact, the sex scenes in von Ziegesar's books aren't described in particular detail. But graphic depictions of sex in the context of marriage would be more wholesome than the scenarios she dreams up, filled with protagonists who glamorize shoplifting and cheating, and where drug use and casual sex of all sorts become the hallmarks of worldly-wise allure.

Nelson, like von Ziegesar, asserts that his work "fills an important niche in moving the readers to a higher level of maturity."[24] What he doesn't explain is how a story about a young woman who behaves in a bizarrely immature fashion—and suffers no lasting repercussions from her affair with a teacher or her actions thereafter—actually meets that objective. If anything, *Teach Me* invites young girls vicariously to experience a liaison with a teacher, and then justifies criminal behavior in the wake of a breakup.

Today's racy teen fiction is the literary equivalent of cotton candy laced with arsenic. It substitutes cheap thrills for sound and memorable characters and plotlines, offering nothing of substance to nourish girls' minds or uplift their souls. The enduring lessons and healthy role models that provide guidance and inspiration for girls confronting the eternal challenges of adolescence are entirely absent—and moral relativism rules.

In the novel *The Virginity Club,* focusing on a competition for a scholarship requiring "purity of the soul and body" (thus allowing the entire book's plot to be driven by sex, or the lack thereof), three of the four main female characters are or become sexually active. One chooses to remain a virgin. The latter wins the fellowship; even so, the other three fortuitously end up healthy and happy at the colleges of their choosing. The message: Any sexual choice is as good as any other—to each her own.

Parents appalled by the behaviors and attitudes glamorized in racy young adult fiction will find little institutional support for efforts to limit girls' exposure to even the most outrageous novels. The American Library Association, which bills itself as "the oldest and largest library association in the world," has declined to criticize such books on the grounds that the novels encourage teens to read.[25]

The argument, of course, is specious—a little like contending that young girls must be offered a steady diet of Twinkies and Cheetos so that they'll continue to eat. In fact, the printed fare that is made available to young girls not only helps form their attitudes (which, in turn, inform their behavior) but also shapes their tastes in reading. After the cheap titillation and sexual intrigue of modern teen fiction, the quaint (but timeless) dilemmas and old-fashioned morality of many of the classics seem both irrelevant and tame. For some young girls, encountering works of more literary merit becomes a bit like being asked to sample a wholesome meal of meat loaf and potatoes after subsisting on a steady diet of deep-fried Snickers and cherry Kool-Aid.

In a poll of teen reading habits, 67 percent of girls said that they like to read about "people or characters who are a lot like me."[26] Clearly, they are looking for characters with whom they can identify and situations to which they can relate. It's unfortunate that so many of the characters they meet between the covers of the books aimed at them are girls who would be deemed a bad influence, if they actually existed.

⌒∞⌒

In the second volume of *Little Women,* the professor who eventually becomes Jo's husband, Mr. Bhaer, offers his opinion of the "sensation stories" of the era (some of which Jo has, in fact, authored): "They ha[ve] no right to put poison in the sugar-plum, and let the small ones eat it. No; they should think a little, and sweep mud in the streets before they do this thing."

Precisely.

Magazines

"All About Hookups"
"Terrifying Sex Stories"
"She Had Sex with Her Daughter's Friends"
"I Got an STD"

Features in *Seventeen* magazine, June 2006

In many respects, the magazines targeted at girls mimic young adult fiction—featuring titillating, sensational pieces that treat teen sex as a given and highlight some of its most salacious aspects. Predictably, boy–girl relationships are viewed almost exclusively through a sexual prism.[27]

The relationship between girls and magazines is one of perceived mutual benefit. Girls are faithful magazine consumers, representing a significant portion of the market for women's magazines generally.[28] It's been estimated that 77 percent of teen girls read fashion and beauty magazines.[29]

Conversely, magazines play an important role in the lives of young girls. As a Kaiser Family Foundation study pointed out, magazines are seen by teens as trusted advisers when it comes to matters pertaining to their personal lives.[30] Extensive interviews with twelve- and thirteen-year-old girls indicated that they depended on the advice contained in the magazines about how to behave in relationships with males.[31] And a 2003 focus group revealed that 42 percent of girls aged twelve through fifteen relied on magazines to keep abreast of current trends— almost as high a percentage as those depending on their friends (45 percent).[32]

Two of the most popular magazines are *Seventeen* and *Cosmo GIRL!* (the "younger sister" to *Cosmopolitan*).[33] The former, long an industry leader,[34] decided to adopt a racier tone in 2004 in an attempt to attract older teens (seventeen and up),[35] although judging from the age of the girls referenced in many of its stories, it still likewise strives to appeal to a younger audience. *Cosmo GIRL!*, one of the most successful of the teen magazines,[36] is marketed to girls between the ages of thirteen and fifteen.[37] Not surprisingly, however, many of the teen magazines are, in fact, being read even by younger tween girls as well.[38]

Some of the content is relatively innocuous teen fare, with

stories about lip gloss, parties, and how to be popular. But 18 percent of magazine articles pertain either to sex, sexually transmitted diseases, pregnancy, contraception, or abortion.[39] That's a greater percentage than articles devoted to career, school, nutrition, music, or sociopolitical ideas. And even a random sampling of popular magazines reveals that much of the information is presented in a flip, value-neutral tone.

Cosmo GIRL! carried a piece on its regular "Guys Confess" page titled: "Bust-ed! They Can't Seem to Stop Staring, so We Got Guys to 'Fess Up About Their Breast Intentions."[40] Accompanying a picture of a boy holding two big melons (captioned "You two are *such* great listeners!") were quotes, including this one from "Jacob, 16, Perrysburg OH": "I'm not going to lie . . . I'm definitely a boob man. I get caught staring all the time, but I look away quickly and walk away. If there were no boobs in the world, I'd be bored." In contrast, "Sam, 20, Lakewood OH" opined: "Girls obsess about breasts too much. I'm more into butts . . ." Obviously, the fact that teen boys are examining the bodies of their female counterparts hardly comes as a shock. Even so, is this kind of objectification something that a magazine aimed at teen girls should be emphasizing, and implicitly condoning?

The same principle holds true when it comes to boys discussing their sexual exploits with girls—everyone knows it happens, but should it really be presented as expected and acceptable behavior? In another issue of *Cosmo GIRL!*, the "Guys Confess" page focused on whether boys are "dishing" about their "romantic" activities with girls.[41] One ("Alex, 17, San Jose CA") responded, "Guys talk about girls like we talk about sports: We give highlights about what she was good at, how she compares to other girls we've hooked up with, and how hot she is on a scale of 1 to 10." Another ("Dan, 20, Cleveland OH") reported that "Most of my friends just want to know if the girl is hot and I'm happy." Obviously, the magazine never even hints that kiss-and-tell behavior has long been considered contemptible among honorable men—or suggests that there's anything wrong with rating girls as if they were circus performers. Nor is it likely to promote much respect for teen boys on the part of their female peers.

A different regular *Cosmo GIRL!* feature, "Love Stories," highlights "The Crazy Things You've Done in the Name of Love!" In one issue, a teen correspondent discussed an encounter at her new all-girl school: "I didn't even ask if she was a lesbian—I just went over and grabbed her hand and gave it a soft kiss. At first, she looked at me funny—like she thought I was crazy—but then she started to smile. I can't believe that I found the girl of my dreams the first five minutes I was in a new school!"[42] Another featured story ended with a less fortuitous outcome, however. The correspondent met a "hot guy who was sleek and had a good tan," but, it's revealed, she "didn't know he was bisexual. I was so into him until one day he said, 'Look at that guy's butt. It is so tight.' "[43] Such vignettes hardly provide girls with examples of constructive preoccupations or behavior that's worthy of emulation. Nor are many of the other topics highlighted by the magazine—including features such as "Who's Your Girl Crush,"[44] "I Was a Teen Prostitute,"[45] and "TV Star Turned Porn Star"[46]—any more wholesome.

Cosmo GIRL! featured even racier content with the results of its Global Love Survey.[47] The US girls polled were sixteen, and readers learned that 39 percent of American respondents had engaged in oral sex (compared, for example, with 65 percent of the seventeen-year-olds surveyed in the Czech Republic and 34 percent of the fifteen-year-olds in the United Kingdom); that American respondents lost their virginity at the average age of fifteen, and that 32 percent of them had "experimented with someone of the same sex." One can hardly blame the average teen for concluding that American girls are "backward" about sex when compared with their more experienced global peers—but it's worth asking whether that's an inference most parents in the United States would want their daughters to draw.

Cosmo GIRL! makes it clear that it's not attempting to appeal to the sexually modest. The same issue as the Global Love Survey also included a health feature, "10 Questions You Can't Ask Anyone."[48] It was preceded by a sassy little disclaimer—"PSSST! If you're offended by sex talk, skip this story!" The article itself entertained questions like "Can you get pregnant if a guy fingers you with sperm on his hand?" and "If a lesbian couple uses dildos and vibrators, could either of them get an STD?" and "Are hand jobs and oral sex safer than sex?" In contrast with the many parents who presumably lace discussions of sex with allusions to morality or values, the magazine insisted that "we're here to answer your questions accurately, honestly, and without judgment." The clear suggestion? That teen girls being fingered, playing with dildos and vibrators, and indulging in hand jobs and oral sex is simply to be expected. Exercising judgment, on the other hand—that would be *wrong*.

Traditional morality in general seems somewhat hard to find in the *Cosmo GIRL!* world. In a piece reminiscent of teen novels' obsession with teacher–student affairs, the magazine also included a feature titled "I Had an Affair with My Coach."[49] The story recounted that "one afternoon, we were kissing as usual, when suddenly, he pulled down my pants and underwear, got on his knees, and said, 'Now for my specialty.' Then he gave me oral sex." The piece goes on to report that the young girl tried to lose her virginity to her coach, but that once, "it hurt too much" and that, another time, "[the coach] couldn't keep his erection." Like the teen fiction focusing on student–teacher affairs, it normalizes what is neither normal nor desirable behavior, encourages young women to see their teachers as sex objects rather than authority figures, and glamorizes inappropriate, unhealthy, and often exploitative relationships.

Cosmo GIRL! also includes celebrity coverage—not always for the better, given the attitudes and behavior of some of the celebrities who are profiled. In honor of April Fools' Day, it offered a tongue-in-cheek interview with Chris and Steve-o, stars of MTV's program *The Wildboyz*. Chris confided that if he were an animal, he'd be a hyena, because "the females have these rad mock penises!" Steve-o described his "turn-ons" as "Really, *really* hot chicks who really, *really* want me."[50] The cover of a March 2001 edition likewise assured readers about "The Real Jessica Simpson: She's No Prude"—obviously, that's a very good thing, to judge from *Cosmo GIRL!*'s coverage.

Even relatively innocuous stories are run with suggestive headlines, including a quiz asking "What Kind of Sexy Are You?" Other examples include "Guys' Secret V-Day Wishes (You'll Be Shocked!)"—as it turned out, boys were seeking innocent tokens of affection—and "Embarrassing Hookup Moments" (which involved only kissing). Even so, the headlines keep the titillation factor high and the sexual allusions constant.

⚬∞⚬

Like *Cosmo GIRL!*, *Seventeen* features graphic question and answer columns about sex that reinforce, above all, an impression that teen sex is common and normal. "L. S." wrote: "My friend and I—she's 12 and I'm 13—want to have sex with our boyfriends. We'd use condoms. Is it okay for us to do it?"[51] Although the response sought gently to dissuade the thirteen-year-old—noting even that "it's illegal to have sex if you're under 16"—the response was hardly the unequivocal "No!" that would signify the utter inappropriateness of such a course of action. The other two questions were: "Can you get an STD from being fingered?"

and "Before my boyfriend has an orgasm, he pulls out, ejaculates, wipes himself off, and then we continue to have sex. Can I get pregnant this way?" From a slew of such questions, it's hard for an average teen reader *not* to conclude that "everybody" is engaged in some kind of sexual activity.

In another issue,[52] one graphic inquiry came from "Anonymous," who was worried about being pregnant because "Me and my boyfriend had sex about three weeks ago, and he wasn't wearing a condom. He didn't come inside me," the fifteen-year-old wrote, "but I'm still worried." A seventeen-year-old was concerned about "some small white bumps around the tip of my boyfriend's penis," and another seventeen-year-old confided, "The other day my friend and I were messing around in the car. He didn't have a condom, so he wanted to have anal sex . . ." She, too, wondered if she could become pregnant as a result of engaging in sexual activity with her "friend."

The magazine provides sexual advice as well—although it's always carefully "non-judgmental" and unleavened by traditional moral guidance. In a health item about sexual pressure, *Seventeen* ran an item about a seventeen-year-old who was challenged to perform oral sex in truth or dare, and then counseled readers to "talk with your clothes on."[53] A survey of fourteen thousand boys and girls aged thirteen through twenty-one about "safe sex" asked, "Do You Trust Him Too Much?"[54] Readers were told that they could "receive confidential testing" at a local clinic they could locate through Planned Parenthood. *Seventeen* also ran "Stop! Read This Before You Have Sex."[55] Although abstinence was mentioned as one option and readers were urged to talk to their parents, they were also advised on how to obtain a referral to a gynecologist (either through their regular doctors or through Planned Parenthood), presumably without their parents' knowledge or consent.

Like many of the magazines aimed at girls, *Seventeen* purports to offer insights into teen male behavior—but again, references to any sort of sexual morality (or self-restraint) are few and far between, and little of the information presented is likely to enhance a girl's respect for her male counterparts. In a health feature on "Guys' Love & Sex Secrets"—which surveyed "more than 5,000 guys ages 13 through 21,"[56] "Keya, 17" of New York insisted, "The need for sex gets really strong in high school—and guys get fickle. Like, one day you like one girl, and the next day, you hook up with a new girl. It's like sexual ADD." Readers learned that 20 percent of respondents had engaged in anal sex, while 59 percent of them hadn't used a condom while doing so; 54 percent had had vaginal sex, and 52 percent had performed oral sex, while 59 percent had received it.

Seventeen regularly polls boys for its "Guy Talk" column, but rarely publishes results that would make parents proud. On the subject of why boys liked dating younger girls,[57] one respondent noted that "Younger girls just put out way faster and easier. You don't have to try hard to get into their pants because they aren't that experienced . . ." Another "Guy Talk" item purported to explain why "your guy might cheat."[58] There, twenty-year-old Brandon recounted an experience in his junior year of high school where "another girl" had tried to seduce him by inviting him over and greeting him in her cheerleader uniform. "Soon we were making out; she even took off her top," he recalled. Whatever value there is to acquainting girls with the thought processes of teen boys is undermined by the relatively consistent portrayal of young men as body-ogling sex hounds.

Even so, in true equal-opportunity spirit, *Seventeen* makes it clear that girls can be sexual aggressors, too. One piece focuses on the chagrin of a college junior (who had "done everything sexually except have intercourse") when her boyfriend declines to have intercourse with her. The article's tagline ran, "Sarah, 21, told Travis she wanted to lose her virginity to him—but he didn't feel the same way. Can their relationship survive his decision?"[59] (Happily for all, it could.) The magazine also included a story about a female college freshman who lost her virginity on a whim,[60] determined not to be the only "loser" who was still a virgin.

Not surprisingly, politics or public affairs are seldom referenced. But when a high school principal prohibited "freak dancing"[61]—a practice that involves "guys dancing behind their dates, grinding their hips against the girls as the girls gyrate back against them"—*Seventeen* presented it as an opportunity for activism. The magazine suggested that those opposed to the ban attend a school board meeting and stress the importance of "expressing yourself at dances."

Given its sexual content, it's not surprising that *Seventeen* was one of the magazines banned from a middle school in 1998.[62] After perusing the magazine, a school superintendent in Long Island concluded that the tone of the magazine's columns on sex, birth control, and the prevention of sexually transmitted disease was at odds with school policy teaching that abstinence constitutes the best way of preventing the spread of STDs.

There's no doubt that *Seventeen* is at odds with any efforts to teach young girls about the importance of sexual restraint—but its approach is subtler than openly advocating teen sex. In fact, *Seventeen*, *Cosmo GIRL!*, and the magazines like them occasionally engage in a pro forma recognition of the possibility (if not the likelihood) of abstinence. But the magazines' preoccupation with sex of all kinds, their question-and-answer columns referencing sexual activity at all ages, and their blasé acceptance of teen sexuality should concern parents and schools alike.

What It Means

Ultimately, it's unlikely that reading a sexually explicit magazine or book will *make* any young girl have sex if she wouldn't do so otherwise. In times past, *some* sexually explicit fiction aimed at teen girls certainly existed. But to the extent such books or magazines were even available, they were outliers. The activities and behaviors described in them were perceived as unusual, even by the girls who gathered to titter over their contents at recess or after lights-out at summer camp; the very act of reading them seemed forbidden. Nor were the fictional characters who engaged in sexual activity likely to emerge from the experience unscathed.

Today, in contrast, books and magazines too often present sexual activity as the preferred pastime of sophisticated, alluring, and glamorous protagonists. Through their reading, young girls become vicariously embroiled in sexual intrigue and are confronted with distasteful issues—such as student–teacher affairs—to which previous generations would never have been exposed. Such exposure is hardly conducive to a healthy, wholesome perspective toward male–female relationships.

In fact, it's tempting to wonder how sex-saturated reading material shapes girls' views about boys in general. The emphasis on sex in teen books and magazines—coupled with a typical teen girl's love of drama—means that plenty of ink will be spilled on the less attractive aspects of adolescent male behavior. The boys who appear in these books and magazines are frequently portrayed as being obsessed with sex. As a result, teen girls not only perceive that their sexiness (and willingness to engage in sexual activity) are central to achieving the coveted objective of attracting male attention, but are vicariously exposed repeatedly to boys who are willing to mislead or exploit girls, all in the pursuit of easy sex.

Certainly, cautionary tales have their place, but the volume and repetition of accounts of adolescent boy crudeness and misbehavior is hardly a recipe for a real-life relationship filled with trust and mutual respect. And too often, books and magazines cloak gratuitous and risqué content in the guise of real-life stories—where, they can claim, they are helping the young girls who are thereby becoming acquainted with a variety of sexual practices and predators.

Even when books and magazines aren't actively encouraging young girls to have sex, titillating material creates the perception that sex is all-important, and that it's everywhere. The more outrageous stories reduce girls' shock at and resistance to even very undesirable sexual behavior (such as having an affair with one's teacher or engaging in a sex party). Over time, a steady diet of sexually charged stories featuring sexually active protagonists makes sex seem common, appropriate (at least between mutually attracted partners), and even integral to teen experience.

Some of this content might have some redeeming social value if, in fact, there were any effort to infuse the stories with traditional concepts of right and wrong. But the sexual issues raised in teen novels and magazines are portrayed and resolved with scant reference to or respect for traditional morality. In the rare instances when religion comes into play, a pose of studied neutrality is the preferred course of the writers. In a feature asking "Does Your Faith Affect Your Love Life?"[63] *Seventeen* quoted an atheist, a Wiccan, and a polytheist along with Muslim, Seventh-day Adventist, Jewish, and Christian girls. Not surprisingly, all had different takes on the question; nowhere was there a sense that any one answer might have more inherent merit than any other.

Similarly, when *Seventeen* ran an article about a twenty-year-old who chose to dress modestly,[64] it noted that "Twenty-year-old Maggie wants guys to notice what's inside—without having to reveal too much of what's outside." The magazine added dubiously, "But is that possible?"

Make no mistake—Maggie hardly arrayed herself in sackcloth and ashes. She was merely "choosing to be different" by wearing "Gap skirts or vintage dresses" and opting for "tankini tops and boy shorts" instead of "skimpy bikinis" (her "technique," the reader is informed, "is to put [her] arms at [her sides] and see where [her] fingers end, buying shorts no higher than that"). The eminently reasonable decision to dress modestly was treated as noteworthy at best—and maybe even freakish.

Likewise in novels, the girls with more restrictive or traditional moral principles are treated as anomalies. Eva, the virgin in *The Virginity Club,* is portrayed as an awkward, unsophisticated girl—nice, perhaps, but hardly charismatic or exciting (at the book's conclusion, she's engaged in her freshman year to her one and only boyfriend). In *Rainbow Party,* Allison, the president of the Celibacy Club (and the only character willing to countenance abstinence openly), is responsible for the school reprimanding a popular teacher who conducted a sex ed class that was "actually interesting and informative."[65] And Benny, a secondary character in *The It Girl,* is contemptuously dismissed as "a prude [who] always blamed it on where she grew up, as if Philly were a different planet where the girls drank whole milk and saved themselves for marriage."[66]

In fact, judging by many of the books and magazines aimed at teen girls, sexual restraint is almost the only behavior that's portrayed as aberrant. Doing what's right becomes a conveniently elastic concept, best understood as doing what's "right for you."

There's no doubt that sexual morality is a difficult topic—and one upon which consensus is elusive. But surely the reading material being marketed to girls between twelve and seventeen could refrain from relying on double entendres and romanticizing, glamorizing, and focusing so heavily on sex of all kinds. Surely girls who choose not to have sex could be portrayed as something more appealing than prudes, shrinking violets, or humorless harpies. And couldn't teen books and magazines work a little harder to define their female characters without reference to their sexual status?

CHAPTER

Truly the "Boob" Tube

Grace: I always thought of myself as a little kinky.

Will: It's okay; I've never been in a three-way.

Grace: Yeah, but you're gay. You have the kinky built in.

Will: Sure, that's why I joined.

Karen: How was the sexcapade? Were you the ham in a
Philharmonic sandwich? Did you roll over Beethoven?

Grace: It was fantastic. There were so many arms and legs
everywhere, Hindus were praying to us.

Will & Grace, "Love Plus One," November 9, 2000

ccording to A. C. Nielsen, *Will & Grace* was one of the top four television shows for twelve- to seventeen-year-old girls during 2005, along with *American Idol, The O.C.,* and *One Tree Hill.*[1] The show centers on the friendship of the two title characters, roommates who dated briefly in college before Will discovered that he was gay. The other main characters include Grace's friend Karen, an inveterate pill popper, and Will's friend Jack, an aspiring entertainer who is also gay.

Will & Grace—along with some of the other programs most

popular with teen girls—may not have been created specifically with twelve- to seventeen-year-old females in mind. Even so, given their enormous popularity among young girls, they're influential. For instance, when teen girls tuned in to *Will & Grace,* they saw a lot. The program contained a good deal of overtly sexy content, including references to oral sex; in one episode, Jack wore an apron reading KISS THE COOK so that the words were directly in front of his genitals. After Grace mentioned the phrase on the apron, Jack replied, "What? Cook? That's an *o*? That doesn't make any sense. Who goes on a date hoping someone will kiss their cook?"[2] Another episode featured two clothed women simulating sex;[3] in another, Grace's boyfriend and Will have drinks at a gay bar, where a waiter asks them, "Who ordered the Penis Colossus?"[4]

In March 2000, KSLX in Salt Lake City wrote NBC to inform the network it didn't intend to run the sitcom any longer because of its heavily sexualized content. The affiliate backed down only under threat of a lawsuit.[5] That month, the program included dialogue like the following:

Jack: I can't pee in public bathrooms.
Will: Why not? You do everything else in them.[6]

Will & Grace is hardly unique. In fact, the granddaddy of heavily sexualized teen television fare was *Dawson's Creek,* which ran between 1998 and 2003. The program focused on four teens: Dawson, Jen, Joey (a girl), and Pacey (a boy). The series began with a bang—in the first season, Pacey (at the age of fifteen) had an affair with a teacher. All of the protagonists had sex during the show's run; the last to do so, Dawson, made up for lost time. Losing his virginity to Jen, he is about to return to his "soul mate" Joey—but has sex with a movie critic instead. The critic informs him that he belongs with Joey. He returns to her and . . . they have sex. It's a grand total of three women in about as many episodes.

Later in the series, Pacey asks his love interest, Audrey, how many lovers she's had. She tells him that the number is twenty-seven. He's shocked (Pacey himself has slept with seven people, viewers learn), especially when Audrey admits that the figure is actually fifty-seven. Once Pacey assures her that he loves her nonetheless, she confesses that she was "testing" him—and the actual number is five. What a relief: Sex with five guys before the age of eighteen almost seems socially backward.

A more recent teen drama, *One Tree Hill,* is similarly laced with plots that assume sexual activity on the part of teenagers. In one episode, a teenage female protagonist holds up a box of condoms in front of her boyfriend and asks, "Don't you think it makes more sense to buy in bulk?" She then shows him a can of whipped cream and adds seductively, "For dessert."[7]

In a different episode, the same character is chatting with her love interest during class, and asks him, "What is your favorite sexual position?"[8] To blow off steam, she and her female friend go shopping and try on sexy lingerie together.[9] Two seasons later, yet another female character attempts to seduce a boy by waiting for him, naked, in the backseat of his car.[10] The show includes dialogue like the following:

> Brooke: Well, I was gonna say, my parents usually close this place down every year, so if you wanted, we could go back to my place and start the party early. We have a Jacuzzi.
>
> Lucas: That sounds tempting, Brooke . . .
>
> Brooke: We have a naked me in a Jacuzzi.
>
> Lucas: Okay. Um, what if I told you there was someone else?
>
> Brooke: Normally, I'd suggest a threesome but I think the person you have in mind is getting back together with her old boyfriend.[11]

The "threesome" theme also emerged on teen girl hit *The O.C.* when its two female protagonists, Summer and Marissa, pretended they were seeking an encounter with another character, Seth, in a hot tub.[12] In fact, the program's pilot featured a party scene with two girls and a boy in a bathtub.[13]

In the teen soap, characters hook up and break up, with sex a constant issue. One installment features Seth, the least sexually experienced male character, receiving a Kama Sutra from a female friend; the episode concludes with all the high-school-aged main characters having sex in their respective houses.[14] In a different episode, trying to explain herself to a surfer with whom she's had casual sex, teen idol Mischa Barton's character confides that, "I found myself doing coke and sleeping with a guy who I'd never had one real conversation with."[15]

The first season of *Desperate Housewives*—winner of the Teen Choice Award in 2005 for "Choice Breakout Show" and one of the five most popular shows among teens in March 2006, despite having been intended for an older demographic—likewise featured two titillating subplots. One housewife conducted an affair with her teenage gardener, while another found she was married to a sexual fetishist. In January 2005, in the midst of its first season, it was the most popular broadcast-network television program with children aged nine through twelve.[16]

Similarly, an episode of *That '70s Show*, which featured teen heartthrob Ashton Kutcher, focused on a character being caught masturbating in his girlfriend's bathroom[17]—after looking at pictures of a friend's mother. Dialogue from the show included the following:

> Donna: I knew he did it, but knowing and seeing are totally different things. It's like you know there are rats in the basement, but . . .

Jackie: But you don't want to see rats wanking themselves in
your bathroom.

In one episode of *Veronica Mars*—marketed as "your typical high school student with one exception: she's a world class
private eye"[18]—Veronica shows up at a young man's house car-
rying cartons of Chinese food. As he opens the door, she coos
seductively, "How about some dim sum—and then some?" Soon
the audience sees her typing in bed on her laptop computer as
the man sleeps next to her.

And an episode of the immensely popular sitcom *Friends*
focused on the characters' obsession with pornographic movies after they discover they're receiving a pay-per-view channel
free.[19] Throughout the show's long run, plotlines covered the active sex lives of all six of the attractive main characters—sometimes with one another. During the show's run, Rachel, played
by tabloid darling Jennifer Aniston, even gave birth to a baby out
of wedlock, conceived during a one-night fling with on-again-
off-again love interest Ross.

Sex and the City, a chronicle of the romantic lives of four
attractive single women living in Manhattan, was likewise extremely popular with girls. Along with the fashion and the
glamorous portrayal of life in the Big Apple, the series included
nudity and plenty of sex talk—subplots featured golden show-
ers,[20] threesomes,[21] vaginal ejaculations,[22] anal sex,[23] the taste of
semen,[24] a character nicknamed Mr. Jungle Pubes,[25] and rim-
ming[26] (otherwise known as analingus). Perhaps it's not surprising that a *MADtv* parody called it "Sluts and the City." An
"edited" version now runs daily on TBS.

Some reality shows also brim with vulgarity. A study conducted by the Parents Television Council found that relation-
ship-based reality series on the networks averaged 3.9 instances
of sexual content per hour.[27] The reality show *Chains of Love*

featured 6.5 instances of sexual content per hour; *Temptation Island 2* showed two men receiving lap dances. The first season of *Joe Millionaire* strongly suggested that one of the female finalists had provided oral sex to "Joe" on a private walk, while *Big Brother 2* showed a male and female contestant showering together. And more recent reality shows are following suit: Even the racy musical group Pussycat Dolls (a burlesque-troupe-turned-musical-act) introduced a reality show focused on finding a new member of the group. The program airs on the CW, a channel where most of the programming is aimed at teens.

Cable reality shows were even more risqué, with an overall rate of sex, foul language, and violence that ran more than three times the broadcast average. Dialogue in *Bands on the Run* included a band member looking at his crotch and remarking, "Well, that thing's not going to suck itself." On *The Real World: Chicago,* as two participants showered together, the female remarked, "I dropped something, and I don't want to bend over, especially when his schlong is in my face." *Flavor of Love,* which focused on twenty women competing for the affections of one-time rapper Flavor Flav, was consistently rated in the top thirty shows for young people aged twelve through seventeen. Along with unspeakable vulgarity (a woman defecated on the stairs in the premiere of Season 2), it seemed clear that the "star" had dismissed a contestant because she revealed that she was saving herself for marriage. In the premiere of *The Real World: Denver,* two housemates hooked up and had sex on their first night in the house. Sexual threesomes figured prominently on commercials for the show, which aired during teen hits such as *Laguna Beach.*

The exposure to sexual content doesn't end with sitcoms, dramas, and reality shows. Fully 54 percent of female adolescents in grades nine through twelve watch talk shows sometimes or every day.[28] Although some talk shows, like *Oprah,* promote responsibility and awareness, the vast majority seek out outlandish subjects. *The Jerry Springer Show,* for example, has entertained topics and guests ranging from extramarital (and intrafamilial) affairs to flamboyantly rebellious and promiscuous teenagers, porn stars, and bestiality. It's worth noting that although talk shows rarely depict sex, sexual talk on television has been found to have the same effect on teens as actual portrayals of sex.[29]

These examples are hardly comprehensive. They're a small but representative sample of the routine vulgarity and sexual suggestiveness in the television content available to young people each day.

The Facts

Given the examples above, perhaps it's hardly surprising to learn that 70 percent of all television shows were found to include some sexual content, with either portrayals of sex or discussion of it.[30] For programs aired in prime time on the major broadcast networks, the percentage of sexual content was even higher: 77 percent.[31] In fact, one study found that "more than one in four of the interactions in the prime-time television diet of young viewers contained statements related to sexuality."[32]

Not only do more television programs contain sexual content, but the ones that do contain sexual overtones have more of them than ever before. One highly regarded study found that the total number of sexual scenes on television has increased by 96 percent since 1998. In other words, the sexual content on television has almost doubled in less than a decade.[33] And the programs most popular with teenagers have an even *higher* number of scenes with sexual content (at 6.7 per hour) than television programs generally.[34]

It's worth noting that the mass media constitutes the main source of information about sex for America's thirteen- through fifteen-year-olds.[35] For teens, many of whom are just learning to navigate opposite-sex relationships (or looking for tips on how to do so), television is offering a blatantly unrealistic view of how much sex is going on, who's doing it, and when.

Television Exposure

To understand the impact of sex-laden television programming, it's important to understand not only how much sex there is on television but also how much television teens are watching.

America's young people live in a television-rich environment.[36] Fully 99 percent of American children between the ages of eight and eighteen live in a home with at least one television, and 97 percent live in a home with a VCR; 82 percent have cable or satellite TV, while 55 percent enjoy premium channels such as HBO.[37] In fact, 73 percent of children between eight and eighteen live in a home with three or more televisions; 53 percent have three or more VCRs. In short, a typical American child is likely to live in a home with three televisions and three VCRs.[38]

All those televisions and VCRs apparently come in handy. As of 2004, children between eleven and fourteen spent an average of three hours and sixteen minutes daily watching television, and forty-six minutes watching videos and DVDs.[39] Those between fifteen and eighteen spent an average of two hours and thirty-six minutes watching TV, and forty-four minutes watching DVDs and videos.[40]

Often, they're watching alone. Of those aged eight through thirteen, 20 percent report that their overall daily TV viewing takes place without siblings, parents, or friends; the number rises to 33 percent among those fourteen through eighteen.[41] Even at night, when parents are home, 32 percent of the eight- to thirteen-year-olds and 38 percent of the fourteen- to eighteen-year-olds watch by themselves.[42] The solitary viewing may be partly explained by the fact that so many young people have televisions in their own bedrooms. As of 2004, 64 percent of girls between the ages of eight and eighteen had a television in their bedrooms; 49 percent likewise had a VCR or DVD player.[43]

Together, all the statistics point to a worrisome trend. Not only is there plenty of risqué content on television, it's also easier than ever before for girls to access it. After all, they're watching television alone and in their bedrooms, away from the inquisitive eyes of parents who can put some of the content into context, or insist that the set be turned off—and at least one study has found that teens watching television away from their families had a rate of intercourse three to six times higher than those who watched with their families.[44] Similarly, a study found that adolescents who discuss television content with their parents have lower rates of intercourse than those who don't,[45] and at least some research indicates that "[a]mong daughters of traditional parents, the incidence of sexual activity is lower when the parents discuss sex and/or television programming with their daughters."[46] So the young girls watching alone may be learning very different lessons from those who have the opportunity to view and discuss television content with their parents.

But it's harder than ever for parents to keep up with what's on television. Along with the wonderful variety that cable brings into each home, it also permits a segmentation of the viewing market. So in contrast with the days when every household had only five or six channels—and the programs being aired were known to adults and teen viewers alike—today the segmentation of the TV market means that *The O.C.* or *Sex and the City* can run for years without even penetrating the awareness of adults. Unlike many of the other agents of socialization—family, school, and church—young people can, in effect, choose what television programs they'll watch. Too often, parents have only a limited idea of what those are.

To some extent, V-chip technology can be useful to parents. With it, they are able to program televisions to block particular programs based on their ratings. Those who have used the V-chip have been pleased with it. According to a Kaiser Family Foundation survey, 61 percent characterized it as "very useful" and 28 percent found it "somewhat useful."[47] It's worth noting, however, that when the study was released, only 15 percent of parents had ever used the technology.

In any case, one thing is clear: Given the relatively infrequent use of the V-chip, the volume of teen television viewing, and the prevalence of sexual content on television—particularly on the programs targeted to them—American young people are hearing (and seeing) a lot of sex, every day, when they turn on the TV.

The Message Behind the Medium

So what, exactly, are girls learning when they watch television? Certainly there's very little that explicitly values chastity or sexual self-restraint. In fact, one study found that the three most frequently occurring sexual messages on television were that sexual relationships are recreationally oriented, men are sex-driven, and women are sexual objects.[48]

Indeed, a study of the television programs that children and adolescents view most revealed that the most common theme underscored a playful, permissive attitude toward sex.[49] Sex is, in large part, treated as a competition—with men and women strategizing, manipulating one another, and swapping strategies about the best way to appeal to the opposite sex. Another prominent theme is that sex is fun and natural, typically enjoyed without reference to relationships or commitment[50]—an attitude that seems to manifest itself to some degree in virtually every televised allusion to sex.

Given the emphasis on sex as recreation, it's not surprising that most sexual language and action on television takes place between characters who are not married (at least to each other).[51] Happy, hip, functioning married couples are few and far between in a television world where 35 percent of all sexual intercourse depicted takes place between unmarried characters with no strings attached whatsoever.[52]

Significantly, women are portrayed as the initiators of many of these casual encounters. Far from treating women as passive or indirect with regard to sexual matters, television includes almost twice as many messages that run counter to that stereotype[53]— a finding that surprised researchers. In other words, television portrays sexually aggressive women who are willing to pursue, engage in, and talk about sex with the same gusto as a stereotypical television male. Messages either depicting women as sexual limit setters or suggesting the existence of a link between sexuality and virtue likewise are surprisingly uncommon.[54]

All in all, girls are being exposed to a fairly one-sided image of female sexuality on television. Allusions to sexual patience (waiting to have sex) are rare. Indeed, although virgins occasionally show up on popular teen shows, for the most part their abstinence is treated as the characters' defining trait, which suggests to teens that sexual restraint is both noteworthy and unusual. Sexual activity is treated as the norm, and most of the most alluring and exciting girls in teen dramas are presented as liberated and uninhibited when it comes to sex.

One of the reasons that sexual activity may seem carefree and glamorous is that allusions to sexual precautions or depictions of risks or negative outcomes from irresponsible sexual behavior are infrequent.[55] A Kaiser Family Foundation study found that only 14 percent of all shows with sexual content included a scene referencing sexual risks or responsibility—and the figure falls to 10 percent among the twenty most highly rated shows for teens.[56] In fact, among the programs most popular with teens, only 5 percent of those with sexual content include a strong risk or responsibility theme.[57]

With sex playing such an important role in television content, it's hardly surprising that TV often sends girls the message that sexiness and appearance constitute the core of their appeal to boys—intelligence, kindness, and other truly important qualities are routinely minimized. In fact, the television programs heavily watched by teens and adolescents emphasize that men see women as sexual objects and value them by their physical appearance.[58] Even a cursory survey of prime-time television programs yields numerous examples of boys pursuing, talking about, or interacting with "hot" girls while shunning the "dogs," who most often appear in sitcoms for comic relief. And entire reality shows, such as *The Swan,* are predicated on the understanding that life simply isn't worth living if one isn't thin, beautiful, and sexy.

It's not difficult to calculate the effect of these messages on young girls as they learn how to relate to boys romantically and find their place in the world of adult women. It may help explain why the number one wish of girls aged eleven through seventeen is to lose weight.[59] It certainly suggests that girls are being taught that superficial qualities such as appearance and sex appeal are the paramount concern of their male counterparts. That's hardly a message designed to encourage personal strength, lasting self-esteem, or responsible sexual behavior.

Movies

Sixteen-year-old Cady learns that her "queen bee" classmate, Regina, is cheating on her boyfriend—a guy Cady herself

likes. Cady sends Regina's boyfriend to the projection room,
where she hopes he will catch Regina in the act. The ruse
is unsuccessful (Regina's actually off kissing another boy,
both in their underwear); but the boyfriend does discover
the school coach, passionately kissing a female student.

Partial plot summary of Mean Girls (2005)

The November 2005 Kaiser Family Foundation study on television found that movies broadcast on TV were the genre most likely to feature the most frequent discussion about sex, as well as sexual behavior itself.[60] Some of these movies are made for television, but many originally played on the big screen—and there, sex does indeed seem to rule the day, especially when it comes to movies aimed at teens.

Recent years have seen an "explosion of girl-power movies."[61] *Mean Girls* received good reviews when it was released. Film critic Roger Ebert called it "smart and funny,"[62] while the *San Francisco Chronicle*'s Mick LaSalle praised it for being "wild and real,"[63] and *The Washington Post*'s Anne Hornaday commended it as "smart, funny, well-acted and visually lively."[64]

They were right—*Mean Girls* was a very acute and entertaining movie. With teen queen Lindsay Lohan in the lead role and a PG-13 rating, it seemed to be aimed squarely at young teen girls. What's remarkable is that none of the critics thought to question any of the movie's bawdy content—possibly because, compared with so many others on the teen market, it was actually pretty innocent.

Even so, the movie includes an episode in which the clique of "cool" and desirable girls, the Plastics, shows up in revealing "Santa's helper" costumes for a skit where they sing "Jingle Bell Rock" complete with seductive dance moves. Earlier in the film, one of the Plastics dresses for Halloween as a *Playboy* bunny. And Regina, the movie's queen bee, not only is seen in her underwear and bra (with a boy in briefs) but also announces that she was "half a virgin" when she met one of her former boyfriends, and asks the movie's heroine bluntly whether she'd like to have sex with a particular boy at school. Safe-sex messages are mocked, albeit amusingly; the school coach (who's later found locked in a passionate embrace with a student) tells his students not to have sex standing up or they'll die (and then offers them condoms), and insists that if students succumb to the urge to remove their clothes, they'll catch chlamydia.

In other recent teen girl movies, the sexual content is just as vulgar, though less cleverly presented. The 2006 film *John Tucker Must Die* was likewise directed at the teen and preteen girl set. Featuring heartthrob Jesse Metcalfe, its plot centered on the decision of a group of teen girls to seek revenge on the popular boy who had broken their hearts by dating all of them simultaneously. Teen sex is taken for granted in the film; in one scene, one girl sensuously kisses another in preparation for an encounter with the high school heartbreaker. Vulgar language is plentiful; for example, one character, a vegan, tells John that she doesn't have to give up all meat (referring to his private parts). The title character is even paraded before his peers in a woman's thong.

The PG-13-rated *13 Going on 30* (2004), starring Jennifer Garner, is a mostly sweet film about Jenna, a thirteen-year-old magically transformed into her thirty-year-old self. As a grown-up, Jenna finds herself living (or at least sleeping) with her boyfriend, who drops the towel he's wearing in preparation for a shower (viewers see no nudity, although she does). The boyfriend, whose nickname for Jenna is "Sweet Bottom," later does a striptease on screen (down to his very small briefs), prompting thirteen-year-old Jenna (in her thirty-year-old body) to beg him to "put it away!" And article topics being discussed at the magazine where the thirty-year-old Jenna works include "57 Ways to Have an Orgasm" and "He Loves You . . . He Loves Your Butt."

What stands out about the sexual content in movies such as *Mean Girls* and *13 Going on 30* is its gratuitousness. The characters are likable (and relatable for young girls), and the plots, while imperfect, are engaging. Even films like *John Tucker Must Die* could have been clever and highly entertaining without all the sexual content. So it's worth wondering whether including the content was a conscious decision. If so, what was the point?

Using sexual humor to titillate or amuse, of course, has long been a staple of teen comedy—no surprise to those who grew up in the era of classics like *Animal House* and *Stripes*. But these films, along with 1970s comedic offerings like *Smokey and the Bandit*, are downright modest next to the sexual humor in comedies currently marketed to male and female teens alike.

In 2004's *The Girl Next Door*, a teen boy's life is changed when he falls for a seemingly wholesome new female neighbor who turns out to be a porn star. And one of the most popular teen movies in recent years, *American Pie*, is a comedy predicated on the efforts of four seniors to lose their virginity before prom night. The name of the film, of course, comes from the well-known scene showing the lead character having sex with an apple pie.

Some of the other innumerable examples of the film's sexual content include a scene in which a teen character watches a pornographic channel on his bedroom TV as he masturbates, before being surprised by his mother. Later, a girl tells her male partner that she doesn't want to have sex, but nonetheless unzips his pants and moves down his body. After more byplay between them, the audience then witnesses his reaction as he ejaculates, before seeing his semen floating in a cup of beer. Subsequently, the audience sees the boy performing oral sex on her. She later discusses sex with her friend, who tells her that intercourse hurts at first, but then "It starts to feel good . . . really good."

A different male character, having allowed a beautiful girl to change clothes in his room, races over to his friend's house so that they can watch her undress through a remote camera. The girl finds a pornographic magazine in the bedroom and begins to masturbate, prompting him to run home and try to have sex with her (he fails, the audience sees, because of two instances of premature ejaculation). Yet another character's mother seduces one of her son's friends.

American Pie was enough of a hit among the teen set to rate two sequels, which feature more of the same. Among other sexual content, *American Pie 2* incorporates phone sex, dildos, pornography, homosexual sex (treated as a joke)—and, in one excruciating scene, a youth accidentally masturbating with fast-drying glue, rather than lubricant. The mother–son's friend sex theme is repeated, too, with the mom asking her son's friend if he wants to "get it on." During a scene that features a car rocking rhythmically back and forth, the audience hears her instructing her young lover to call her "Stifler [her son]'s mom" during sex, rather than referring to her by her real name.

Likewise, the most memorable scene in the popular, innuendo-laced Farrelly brothers comedy *There's Something About Mary* is one in which the female protagonist smears semen in her hair by mistake; moments earlier, there's a scene in which the male protagonist masturbates audibly, as the camera shows his arm stroking. Other scenes imply that a man and woman are simultaneously performing oral sex on each other; elsewhere in the film, when his face is seen near another man's crotch, a male is misunderstood to be providing him with oral sex.

Graphic allusions to or depictions of sex aren't limited to comedies, however. Like *American Pie,* the plot of the popular teen drama *Cruel Intentions* centers on sex. In that film, two rich stepsiblings, Sebastian and Kathryn—their own relationship rife with sexual tension—bet on whether the brother can bed a virgin and help his stepsister get revenge on a former boyfriend. If Sebastian wins, Kathryn promises him, "I'll f**k your brains out," assuring him that "you can put it anywhere." Later in the film, the stepsiblings caress each other seductively, and Kathryn fondles Sebastian's crotch.

Sebastian seduces another girl in the film, Cecile, and the camera shows her reaction as he performs oral sex on her. Later, when Cecile confides in Kathryn about her experience (the two have French-kissed earlier in the film), the latter advises her to have sex with as many boys as possible, assuring her that everyone does it.

She's right—at least when it comes to teen movies.

The Facts

Teen films featuring explicit sexual content, such as *American Pie,* are rated R, which means that those younger than seventeen must attend with a parent or guardian, at least in theory. But it's worth noting that the ratings system is completely voluntary and carries no force of law. As *Hollywood Reporter* columnist Paul Hyman noted, "If a 16-year-old is intent on viewing [an R-rated film] . . . chances are he'll find a way to do it."[65] Although proposed federal legislation[66] has attempted to penalize the sale or rental of video games with either adult or pending ratings, movies are conspicuously exempt.

Whether it's because the guidelines aren't being strictly enforced at the theaters or because older caretakers are permitting it, teens are seeing plenty of R-rated movies. According to one study of 2,596 middle school students, 52 percent were permitted to see R movies all or most of the time, 29 percent could see them once in a while, and only 19 percent of the teens were forbidden ever to view the films.[67]

Even a PG rating may not mean what it used to. Online movie

critic, attorney, and activist Nell Minow has estimated that movies with a PG-13 rating are comparable to standard television fare.[68] To take one example, sexual content in the PG-13-rated *Anchorman,* starring teen favorite Will Ferrell, includes one character explaining that he's bestowed nicknames on his penis and testicles. Another tells the female protagonist, Veronica, that he'd like to put barbecue sauce on her behind, then makes dog noises as he simulates having sex with her from behind. In an additional scene, Veronica points out that Ron has a massive erection before the audience sees it (covered by his pants); Ron informs Veronica that *San Diego* means "whale vagina" in Spanish.

Given the coarse content of even PG-13 films, it's no surprise to learn that today's movies include "significantly more violence, sex, and profanity on average than movies of the same rating a decade ago," as one of the authors of a 2004 study from the Harvard School of Public Health concluded.[69] The report found that many of the current crop of PG-13 films would have received R ratings a decade ago[70]—which means that teens today can see movies on their own that would have once required being accompanied by a parent. It's hard to imagine a film like *When Harry Met Sally* (which received an R rating when it was released in 1989) receiving anything stricter than a PG-13 today.

This ratings creep may signal a dulling of Americans' collective sensitivity to sex, violence, and profanity. It also suggests that over the years, content once deemed acceptable only for adults has been increasingly finding its way to teens and children.

The Message Behind the Medium

Many of the more modern films are distinguished from their older counterparts not just in the explicitness of the sexual portrayals and language, but also in the fact that sex has become indispensable to many key plot points—or has even become the point of the film itself.

Older teen films, like the most celebrated and successful teen movies of the 1980s, managed to provide heartfelt and fairly accurate portrayals of relationships and adolescent life without constant sexual references. Although there is some sexual content in such films as *The Breakfast Club, Pretty in Pink, Some Kind of Wonderful, Say Anything,* and *Ferris Bueller's Day Off,* it is far less frequent and less graphic than that in modern teen fare. The older films certainly lack the gratuitous allusions to oral sex and the implied approval of casual sexual encounters; intimate activity on the part of protagonists (female protagonists, in particular) is undertaken only in the context of close and loving relationships.

What's more, in the 1980s movies humor derives, in many cases, from the outspoken, cartoonish sexual frustration of "nerds" (for example, geek Anthony Michael Hall's attempts to "bag a babe" in *Sixteen Candles*) rather than from the sexual humiliation or slapstick so prominent in movies such as *American Pie*. In other instances, even relatively intense sexual content is portrayed as part of an entertaining but ultimately fantastic scenario, as in *Risky Business,* when the character portrayed by Tom Cruise makes money and ultimately wins admission to Princeton by holding a party including prostitutes at his vacationing parents' house.

In the older films, promiscuous or overtly sexy girls tended to be peripheral characters, often antagonistic to the movies' heroines (like those preferred by bad-guy James Spader in

Pretty in Pink, for example, or Molly Ringwald's rival for her idol Jake's affections in *Sixteen Candles*). In 1985's *Teen Wolf*, starring Michael J. Fox, the blond, "sexy" girl makes a play for the hero once he's demonstrated his prowess on the basketball court; he rejects her, however, in favor of the brunette who has liked him for who he really is.

Today, in contrast, the sexy girls have become the protagonists of movies like *Cruel Intentions* and even *Mean Girls*. Even if they're not depicted altogether favorably (and the worst receive their comeuppance in the end), they are without doubt frequently presented as the exemplars of sophistication and cool, worthy of emulation.

The plot of *The 40-Year-Old Virgin*, released in the summer of 2005, focused on a man's efforts to have sex for the first time. Most of the movie's comedy derives from the measures that the virgin endures on the recommendation of his friends—such as chest waxing—so that he may reach the nirvana of commitment-free recreational sex. The entire point of *The 40-Year-Old Virgin* is to poke fun at a lovable loser who has reached early middle age without (gasp!) having slept around. Remarkably, a *Los Angeles Times* feature on the movie noted that film executives worried about the idea that the audience might associate the lead character with a serial killer.[71] In today's movie culture, apparently, virginity is just that *weird*.

In a revealing episode, a student in Lexington, Kentucky, actually thought the film was appropriate enough to bring to school, even though, as the *Times* described it, the content "resides at the outer limits of the R rating."[72] Despite its title (which one might suspect would raise a few red flags), a teacher saw no problem screening it for his high school class upon the student's recommendation that "it was very funny."[73]

Ironically, popular culture often portrays the era before the sexual revolution as a time of prurient and unyielding obsession with young women's sexual status, when nosy prudes just couldn't wait to destroy the reputation of free-spirited girls who refused to abide by society's sexual mores. But judging by today's teen movies, one's sexual status is *still* everyone's business—though this time the goal seems to be to ensure that no one remains a virgin until marriage.

Certainly, there's little in the movies—or on television—that would make married sex seem appealing. Of the top-rated prime-time television shows in spring 2006, only high-camp *Desperate Housewives* portrayed a happily married couple.[74] In films, one study found that sexual behavior among married characters was presented as boring and infrequent compared with sex out of wedlock.[75] Of all the sexual behavior in the top twenty-five movie rentals of 1998, just 15 percent took place among the married—and most of that action (63 percent) consisted of passionate kissing. In contrast, intercourse was portrayed as the most common sexual activity among unmarried partners.

Given what they're seeing, one can hardly blame young people for looking on premarital sex with a friendly eye. After all, who wants to abstain until marriage if married people rarely have sex—and when they do, it's no fun? Little on the screen suggests that married couples can and do have exciting relationships, and that sex can be even more meaningful and enjoyable in wedlock than out of it. Being exposed to these ideas might be healthy for young people, helping them to understand that committed sex is both worth waiting for and wonderful—not just the purview of the old and boring.

The Impact

It's difficult to prove that watching sex-laden content on the screen *causes* young people to have sex. Even when studies show correlations between watching sexy television or movies and particular sexual attitudes or behaviors, it's hard to determine whether the viewing causes them, or whether young people who exhibit certain attitudes or behaviors are drawn to sexually charged programs.

But the same problems of proof exist when it comes to the issue of violence and television—which has a much longer history as a subject of scholarly research. Over time, on the basis of countless studies, Americans have largely come to accept the existence of a causal connection between television and real-life violence.[76]

As the television violence studies indicate, other factors must come into play before watching violent television will actually alter a viewer's behavior. Even so, exposure to entertainment violence isn't discounted as an important part of the mix. If entertainment violence can lead to an increase in violent attitudes, values, and behavior, it follows that viewing entertainment sex could likewise promote the adoption of the sexual attitudes, expectations, and behavior portrayed.

Similarly, research on the impact of smoking in the movies certainly indicates that films exert a powerful influence on teen behavior. For example, one study found that an adolescent girl (aged twelve through fifteen) had *more than an 80 percent greater chance* of smoking if her favorite star smoked on screen, compared with girls whose favorite stars weren't onscreen smokers.[77]

If that's true when it comes to smoking, why would sex be any different? Like smoking, sexual activity is presented in the movies as largely undertaken by the young, hip, and beautiful. Information about the serious risks posed by cigarettes has long been widely disseminated—longer, in fact, than information about AIDS and the dangers of various STDs has been generally available. But it's a good bet that with sex, as with smoking (and with violence, for that matter), if a risky behavior is portrayed as sufficiently glamorous, at least some young people will ignore even obvious dangers in order to emulate it.

Many people intuitively understand that, to some degree, public behavior is shaped by what's seen on the big and small screens. That's why the shooting spree in the 1994 film *Natural Born Killers* elicited so much criticism—and why, in the wake of the Columbine shootings, filmmakers removed a scene from *The Basketball Diaries* in which a character dreams about storming his school and shooting his classmates. It's also why tobacco advertising is prohibited both on television and in the movies.

Ultimately, whether television and movies are primarily reflecting reality or helping to shape it, evidence suggests that the behavior, attitudes, and expectations associated with exposure to sex on the screen are hardly positive.

On Attitudes

A definite correlation exists between television viewing and adolescents' sexual attitudes. In two different studies, more frequent exposure to sex-oriented prime-time programming and talk shows was associated with stronger support for recreational sex among both teens aged fourteen through eighteen[78] and young women eighteen through twenty.[79] Young people in general tended to be more permissive about pre-, extra-, or non-marital sex when they had been exposed to such behavior on television.[80]

For girls, another important factor concerned the level of their identification with popular television characters—that is, the extent to which they admired, empathized with, or related to someone on TV. More involved television viewers, especially young women, were more likely to accept the most frequently occurring sex-related messages on television, including the idea that sexual relationships are recreationally oriented.[81]

Both teens[82] and older adolescents[83] who strongly identified with television characters in sexual situations reported greater experience with sexual activity.

And the reason a girl watches TV may also matter. Young women who watch for companionship (rather than for simple entertainment) were more likely to accept the most frequently recurring sex-related messages.[84] Perhaps the girls watching television for company, rather than simply for entertainment, are more likely to identify with the characters they see—even looking on them as surrogate friends.

In any case, chances are that they're lonelier. And it stands to reason that those who have fewer other sources of sexual norms (like parents or friends) will be more open to adopting the sexual standards shown on television as their own.

On Expectations

It also seems that watching television more frequently heightens young people's estimations of their peers' sexual experience. In essence, television viewing lends credence to the notion that "everyone is doing it."[85] In one study of male and female eighteen- through twenty-year-olds, researchers found that the more realistic the participants deemed television portrayals to be, the more sexually experienced they expected peers to be.[86] And among the young women in that group, those who identified most closely with female television characters had higher expectations of the sexual experience of both their male and female peers.[87]

It shouldn't be surprising to learn that exposure to particular behavior or attitudes increases teens' perceptions of how common they are in the real world. That may be why, for example, male and female students who watched television talk shows overestimated the frequency of the behaviors portrayed on them.[88] By affecting their perceptions about sexual behavior and attitudes, television is, obviously, shaping (and distorting) young people's view of reality.

On Behavior

Research suggests that exposure to movie sex may have a definite impact on girls' behavior. For example, one study found that watching X-rated movies was associated with higher numbers of sex partners, more frequent sex, and less frequent contraceptive use among a group of girls aged fourteen through eighteen.[89]

When it comes to television viewing, similar results were obtained. It's been reported that twelve- through seventeen-year-olds who watch more sexually oriented programming are more likely than others in their age group to become sexually active.[90] In fact, the more sex-related scenes they viewed, research has found, the greater the likelihood they'll initiate sexual activity.[91] As one scholarly study summarized it, "[A]dolescents who are exposed to more sexual content in their media diets, and who perceive greater support from the media for teen sexual behavior, report more sexual activity and greater intentions to engage in sexual intercourse in the near future."[92]

Anecdotal evidence supports these findings. In "The Lost Children of Rockdale County," a 1999 documentary about widespread sexual activity among middle-class teens in a largely white Georgia community, teens were imitating the behavior they saw on the Playboy Channel.[93] That's hardly a surprise—almost every adult can remember wanting to emulate someone on television, from the Lone Ranger to Donna Reed to Perry Mason. Today, however, most of television's visible role models for young people are sexually active, sophisticated teens and twenty-somethings.

In fact, one respected and influential study found that exposure to sexually oriented TV appears to have the effect of "aging" young viewers, at least in sexual terms. Teens who saw the most sex on television were found to be *twice* as likely to begin having sexual intercourse (or progressing to more advanced levels of sexual activity) within the next year as those who saw the least.[94] Twelve-year-olds with the most exposure to TV sex acted like fourteen- or fifteen-year-olds at the lowest levels of exposure.[95] That alone indicates that heavy television viewing is an important element in influencing sexual behavior. It's a concept that teens themselves understand—75 percent of fifteen- through seventeen-year-olds believe that sex on television influences the behavior of their peers.[96]

Ultimately, perhaps the greatest problem is that what's presented on the screen offers a skewed version of reality to many young people who lack the life experience to understand just how preposterous some of the content is. One unusually mature senior at a Midwestern high school observed: "The movies that we watch, the shows that we see on TV—it's not real. These people don't have values . . . They make life seem perfect, like every time you do something, it's with that special someone and it means something special. You don't ever [see] those bumps in between." If all young women were as insightful, there would be much less reason for concern about the impact of onscreen content on sexual decision making.

A Word About Celebrities

In stark contrast with films from Hollywood's Golden Age, smoking today is much less frequent than sex on the big screen; many more impressionable young women are likely to be watching their favorite stars engaging in sexual behavior than smoking. So to the extent that young girls are modeling their behavior on that of their screen idols, it seems much likelier that sex will become their (socially sanctioned) risk behavior of choice.

In fact, information about stars' sex lives seems ubiquitous.

In the spring of 2006, for example, the tabloids were full of stories about Katie Holmes and Angelina Jolie. Both were pregnant out of wedlock, the former by Tom Cruise, a man sixteen years her senior, and the latter by Brad Pitt, with whom she had allegedly begun an affair while he was still married to Jennifer Aniston. And the entertainment press, predictably, reported all this news as though it was just fine.

Girls in general are, understandably, attracted to what is portrayed as the glamorous lifestyles of Hollywood celebrities. In a 2005 study conducted by Teenage Research Unlimited, starlet Lindsay Lohan was the most envied person among girls—with Paris Hilton and Christina Aguilera also among the top five.[97]

If the views and behavior of teen girls are being influenced by Lindsay Lohan and Paris Hilton, parents have reason to worry. Lohan, often described as a "wild child," moved in with her then boyfriend at the age of seventeen. She confessed to dabbling in drug use and suffering from bulimia.[98] Papers spotted her with much older actors such as Bruce Willis[99] (both denied any improper relationship) and reported on her alleged messy breakup from thirty-seven-year-old director Brett Ratner, when she reportedly caught him in bed with another woman.[100] She allegedly completed a stint in rehab in early 2007, before reaching the age of 21, and has become a tabloid staple for alleged behavior of dubious legality.

If anything, Paris Hilton's lifestyle is even more flamboyant. She came to prominence in 2004 when she was featured on a graphic sex tape released by a former boyfriend without her consent; that year, Barbara Walters featured her as one of the "10 Most Fascinating People." On her television show, *The Simple Life*, Hilton has been shown making out with various boys, and tabloids have linked her with a seemingly endless parade of celebrity alleged lovers. *Playboy* magazine named her the "Sex Star of the Year" in March 2005; she appeared on the magazine's cover in a red bustier and fishnet stockings, although she denied having posed for the picture and claimed that *Playboy* had obtained it some other way.[101] She's likewise faced legal trouble for violating probation and for alcohol-related reckless driving. It's hard to imagine any responsible parent hoping a daughter will follow in Paris's footsteps.

Loveline's Dr. Drew Pinsky has observed, "It's mortifying that it's so hard to find a female role model . . . in the culture, there's just not much that you want your young female to hang on to." Even celebrities such as singer Pink have complained about the quality of female role models, insisting that only three celebrity women—Reese Witherspoon, Natalie Portman, and Angelina Jolie—were generally recognized as being intelligent.

As distressed as parents might be to learn that their daughters have put Lohan and Hilton on their "most envied" list, they can, at least, be grateful that aging sex symbol Sharon Stone didn't appear there. In March 2006, Stone reported that she always carries condoms with her as a way to promote safe sex. She likewise noted: "Young people talk to me about what to do if they're being pressed for sex. I tell them what I believe: 'Oral sex is a hundred times safer than vaginal or anal sex. If you're in a situation where you cannot get out of sex, offer a blow job.' I'm not embarrassed to tell them."[102]

Perhaps she should be.

What It Means

Responding to a study tracking how television viewing predicts sexual activity, an HBO spokesman asserted firmly, "[W]e do not believe that one show can alter a person's sexual behavior."[103] It's easy to understand his position—especially given that HBO was the television home of *Sex and the City*, one of the programs that the study followed.

Of course, he's right. And the same statement would be true if he had substituted *movie* for *show*. But he's sparring with a straw man. Seeing an occasional sex scene on television—or a movie with even a series of sex scenes—will hardly prompt young girls to immediately begin engaging in oral sex or intercourse. That's because if sexual content appears in just one show or one movie, it remains out of the mainstream. And that's true even if it's entertaining—or presented in conjunction with attractive, relatable female protagonists such as those on *Sex and the City* or *13 Going on 30*.

But here's the problem that the HBO spokesman ignores: Today there is significantly more than one sexually explicit program at issue. In a world that includes movies such as *American Pie* and television programs where nearly 50 percent of the interactions contain statements or behavior related to sexuality[104]—and 70 percent of all shows contain sexual content[105]—it's almost impossible for young people *not* to get a skewed impression of the extent to which sex is experienced, seen, or discussed in everyday life. On the screen, sex comes off as something of a constant human fixation.

Over time, the sheer repetition and volume of sexual messages may make recreational and uncommitted sex seem more common, more acceptable, and more integral to the lives of normal Americans than it actually is.[106] Young people become desensitized to sex on the screen. In fact, a 1977 Gallup poll found that 44 percent of young people aged thirteen through seventeen believed there was too much sex in the movies—but by 1999, only 28 percent thought that movies included too much sex.[107] They'd grown used to it.

And because programs help set expectations for those who haven't begun to date and provide young boys and girls with a template for how to behave in romantic relationships, the way sex is portrayed on the screen will, inevitably, affect the way those romantic relationships are understood and conducted. In fact, research has found that girls use the media more than boys do in order to learn about interpersonal relationships.[108] One study even suggested that female adolescents were more likely to enjoy sexual content than males.[109]

In any case, teens of all ages and both sexes are seeking role models to emulate, as well as guidance on how to define, confront, and overcome the challenges they face at home or school. As they watch the characters and situations presented on television or in movies, young people often do so with an eye to modeling themselves after the characters,[110] hoping that they may attain the same status and rewards as those they admire. When the most glamorous teen characters on television are portrayed as enjoying active sex lives, pursuing a similar course is likely to seem acceptable—even desirable—to the ordinary American teens watching at home.

Because they're defining and constructing their views of the world, the attitudes, values, and behavior of both girls and boys are malleable. In contrast with adults, who know (or should know) that there's an element of fantasy involved in the programs they're viewing, adolescents are more likely to take what they see seriously. They haven't yet developed the skills to evaluate television's images critically or the experience to determine if they're realistic—and whether the goals and lifestyles they promote are either attainable or worthy of emulation, especially when the images are being presented as though they represent real life.

Given their youth and lack of experience, it's profoundly unfair to expect teens to be able to watch television and movies and understand them from an adult's perspective. In fact, it's because of their relative lack of life experience that young people often look to the screen for guidance. Several studies have found that students rank the media among their top sources for sexual information, often before parents (although after their peers).[111]

Not surprisingly, the very teens who are looking to television for guidance are the ones most likely to believe what they see. Research indicates that the adolescents who use television as a way to learn about social relationships believe even more firmly than others that what they see is realistic.[112] The problem is that it may likewise be simultaneously shaping young girls' understandings of what's expected, acceptable—or even desirable—in male–female relationships.

CHAPTER 6

AURAL SEX

Like a virgin, touched for the very first time
Like a virgin, when your heart beats next to mine
"Like a Virgin," Madonna, 1984

Don't really wanna be a tease
But would you undo my zipper please
Uh uh, please don't talk
Listen
I'll let you touch me if you want
I see your body rise, rise
And when you come, don't get too hot
"Showdown," Britney Spears, 2003

hen Madonna burst onto the pop music scene in the early 1980s, she caused a sensation. As she writhed onstage in a wedding dress and bustier during the first MTV Music Awards in 1984, much of America was shocked—and incensed. Even a cursory viewing of MTV today, however, indicates that standards have loosened quite a bit since then.

For every generation of adults, the exploits of young pop singers frequently seem like little more than pathetic bids for attention. But given that girls aged thirteen through eighteen listen, on average, to three hours of pop music daily,[1] these musicians exert a very real influence on young women—as do the lyrics to the songs that the singers warble and the music videos that provide visual interpretations of them.

Girls are devoted consumers of music. One study found that they spend 15 percent more than boys do on music purchases and are bigger digital music users in general.[2] Over a three-month period, 78 percent of teen girls made a music purchase,[3] and nearly half of the girls who have access to the Internet spend more than a hundred dollars per year on music.[4]

Music has long played a central role in the lives of teens of both sexes. One study found that 24 percent of high school students studied ranked music as one of their top three sources for information on social interaction; 16 percent listed it as one of their top three sources of moral guidance.[5] It is important to teens for several reasons: Music has the capacity to intensify or alter their moods and emotions;[6] it's likewise a way to identify themselves as part of a peer group ("we're the ones who like Eminem!"), as well as a vehicle for channeling the rebellious impulses that are a normal part of the teen years.

Girls readily admit that music has a great impact on them. "It does influence the way you act, the way you talk," a high school freshman said as her friend nodded in agreement.[7] In fact, it provides a soundtrack for young people's lives; according to a 2002 *USA Weekend* poll, 79 percent said that they listen to music while they do chores, 73 percent when they're on the computer, and 72 percent when they're doing homework.[8] In fact, 18 percent reported that they listen to music even while they're in the classroom![9] Among seventh through twelfth graders, rap/hip-hop music is most popular (65 percent of teens who listen to recorded music in a given day list it as their choice), followed by alternative rock (at 32 percent) and hard rock/metal (at 27 percent).[10]

In almost every musical genre, much of what girls and boys alike are hearing is coming wrapped in an overwhelmingly vulgar package.

Madonna and Her Progeny

Ever since parents across America were scandalized by Elvis's pelvic gyrations, pop music has served as a symbol of teen rebellion, growing increasingly aggressive[11] and sexualized over time.[12] But no female singer has been as successful in exploiting the link between music and sex as Madonna, from her "boy toy" persona at the outset of her career, through her Jean Paul Gaultier–costumed dominatrix phase (complete with a conical bra), to *Sex,* her book of explicit photographs. As Dan DeLuca, music critic for *The Philadelphia Inquirer,* wrote, "She sexualized pop like never before."[13]

Today the sexual display that made Madonna's act so shocking has become par for the course in the music world—even for artists far younger than Madonna was when she made her debut. Madonna's significance lies not just in her longevity but also in her influence. Two of the most popular female stars of recent years among young girls—Britney Spears and Christina Aguilera—have cited her as an inspiration. It's perhaps symbolic that, at the twentieth MTV Music Awards in 2003, Madonna indulged in lingering openmouthed kisses with both of them.

Britney Spears, in particular, has provoked much of the controversy and attention that Madonna once courted. As she burst on the pop music scene in 1999, Spears attracted a legion of fans that most prominently included teen girls and their younger tween sisters. At first, Spears cultivated an image of sexual modesty, declaring even that she wanted to remain a virgin until marriage; the press wrote about the "Bible book" that contained her daily prayers.[14]

But it wasn't long until her public persona became more overtly sexy. By 2003, Spears confessed that she wasn't, in fact, a virgin,[15] posed semi-nude for the covers of *Rolling Stone*[16] and *Esquire*[17] magazines, wore increasingly revealing fashions, and simulated sex in her concert routines before audiences composed largely of young girls. During a 2004 concert, a reporter noted that Spears, clad in a body stocking, "bathed" in a transparent bathtub, simulating masturbation, while scantily clad male dancers writhed suggestively on mattresses. Audience members, some as young as eight, looked on.[18]

In November 2003, during a *Primetime* interview with Diane Sawyer,[19] Spears denied any responsibility for serving as a role model to her young fans. Even so, as Spears has morphed from wholesome teenybopper into full-fledged adult sex symbol, they have watched, admired, and imitated. When she sings that her "sex drive" is "outrageous," they've listened.

Britney Spears's songs, clothes, and attitude are so sex-saturated that they would have been too daring even for Madonna, circa 1984. But the sad fact is that Spears is hardly alone.

Though she has recently tried to moderate her image, Christina Aguilera—after Spears, the most popular female singer to emerge from the teen pop revival of the late 1990s[20]—likewise used to engage in outrageously provocative antics that influenced scores of young women. She has posed, both scantily clad and in dominatrix-style attire, for newspapers and magazines and released an album, *Dirrty,* that was full of graphic lyrics. The video Aguilera released to accompany the album's first single featured her dancing seductively in the shower; its over-the-top suggestiveness prompted mention on *Saturday Night Live,* where Tina Fey joked that it "gave [her] television genital warts."[21] Overall,

Aguilera's behavior prompted the gossip pages of the *New York Post* to initiate a "Christina Aguilera skank watch" to document her trips to local strip clubs.[22]

Like Aguilera, singer Nelly Furtado also altered her image—but in the opposite direction. After a relatively innocent initial album, along with a follow-up about inner beauty and ethnicity that wasn't a great success, Furtado remade herself into a sexier singer—in both appearance and subject matter. During the summer of 2006, she released an album titled *Loose*, featuring the hit single "Promiscuous," a duet with Timbaland about a man and woman deciding whether or not they will "hook up" in an implied one-night stand. Timbaland tries to win her heart by singing that he can "see her with nothing on," to which Furtado replies that she's "trying to get inside his brain" not to see what kind of man he is, but rather, to find out "if he can work" her "the way [he] say[s]." "Promiscuous" stayed at number one on the Billboard charts for six weeks and earned Furtado a 2006 Billboard Award. It seems that the ploy of adopting a new, racier persona succeeded.

Another singer popular with teen girls is Lil' Kim, who was sentenced to a year and a day in prison for conspiracy and perjury. Winner of a Source Award for Female Artist of the Year in 2003 and a nominee for Black Entertainment Television's 2006 Best Female Hip-Hop Award, Lil' Kim is known for what *Jet* magazine has called her "sexy, outrageous and revealing outfits."[23] In 2003, she was nominated for a Grammy for Best Rap Performance by a Duo or Group for her performance of the song "Magic Stick," which includes lyrics referring to the singer's "magic clit" and boasting that "I sex a nigga so good."

It's hard to imagine the kind of vulgarity being purveyed by the likes of Spears, Aguilera, Furtado, and Kim being condoned even as recently as the late 1980s. But now it's practically expected. An MTV documentary titled "When Sex Goes Pop:

Not That Innocent" (the latter part of the title playing off lyrics from Spears's hit "Oops! I Did It Again") summarized the trend: "Eager to keep pace with an increasingly sexualized culture, young female pop stars have amped up their raciness with bare skin and bold moves in live performances that delight some and shock others."[24]

What's troubling to many parents is that these pop music performers are role models for adolescents.[25] On MisterPoll.com, a survey targeted to girls between the ages of thirteen and nineteen asked who they considered a good role model—with Lil' Kim, Britney Spears, and Christina Aguilera listed as possible responses. (Others were Jessica Simpson, Mandy Moore, Jennifer Love Hewitt, Paris Hilton, and Alicia Keys.[26]) And the influence of these singers isn't limited to teens. Sesame Workshop research found that girls aged six through eleven usually chose Britney Spears or Christina Aguilera when asked what famous person they would like to be.[27]

With many girls looking to singers as role models, it's worth examining exactly what some of them are singing about.

Lyrics

In an arresting snapshot of the themes and ideas being purveyed to young girls through popular music, in June 2006, AOL Music ran a "face-off" between two sultry singers' hits: Nelly Furtado's "Promiscuous" and Rihanna's "Unfaithful."

Certainly, it would be inaccurate to assume that every song is about sex—or that every female singer tries to present herself as a sexpot. Performers like Joss Stone keep their clothes on and focus largely on topics other than sex. And adults have long objected to supposedly inappropriate rhythms, lyrics, or behavior on the part of rock stars.

Even so, over time, "The portrayal of sexuality in popular

music has become less subtle, more explicit."[28] In fact, there seems to be a growing expectation that music is one area where vulgarity can thrive unchallenged. In July 2006, a California radio station renamed itself Porn Radio, playing "all sex radio, all the time." With the suggestion that those under twenty-one not listen, the station proceeded to put together a play list made up of suggestive titles and songs with risqué lyrics—occasionally adding recorded moans and groans to more conservative fare.[29]

At present, a significant portion of the "hottest" songs and acts in America routinely purvey the tawdriest, most unwhole-some messages both about sex and about male–female rela-tionships. Emily Limbaugh, coordinator of the Best Choice sexual integrity program, who speaks with girls in schools, youth groups, and churches, notes: "The beat is fantastic. But the lyrics are absolutely disgraceful. I tell [young girls] 'These words are so demeaning. You're getting punked here—you're calling yourself a whore.'"

⌒∞⌒

Taken together, the volume of sexualized lyrics and pro-easy-sex messages heard by young girls daily is staggering. The *Seventeen* magazine Web site,[30] aimed primarily at teen girls, recommends the album *So Amazin'* by Christina Milian, on which she invites her lover to "Do what you want with me" and, in another selec-tion, begs him to "Lemme set your body on fire."

On Rihanna's first album, *Tears of the Sun,* she sings, "Boy let me fill your appetite / Won't you let me know what it is you like / And I'll do those sexy things for you."

One online merchant suggests that Rihanna fans might want to check out *PCD,* an album by the Pussycat Dolls (a group that, according to its "creation myth," began as a burlesque troupe[31]). It includes the hit single "Beep" (all the suggestive words are sup-posedly "beeped" out but are nonetheless plainly discernible). In the single, featured artist Will.I.Am sings about the fact that the Dolls may have a "big heart" and "big brains"—but he's looking at their bodies, as a "beep" sound covers his mention of the specific body parts to which he's referring.

The Pussycat Dolls respond, "[I]t don't mean a thang if you're looking at my . . . [beep] / I'm a do my thang while you're playing with your . . . [beep]," referring, presumably, to masturbation. That's apparently what passes for feminist empowerment, pop music style.

In 2005, the Black Eyed Peas released a hit titled "My Humps" extolling the virtues of female band member Fergie's breasts and buttocks. In one portion of the song, the male members of the band invite her to "mix your milk wit my cocoa puff" and ask, "What u gon' do with all that ass? / All that ass inside those jeans?"

She answers: "I'm a make, make, make, make you scream." Later, she announces: "They say I'm really sexy, / The boys they wanna sex me . . . / Tryin'a feel my hump, hump. Lookin' at my lump, lump."

Likewise Eminem, the critically acclaimed rapper, sings in "Ass Like That" from his hugely popular album *Encore:* "I ain't never seen an ass like that / The way you move it / You make my pee pee go / Da-doing doing doing." It's a far cry from the love songs of earlier eras.

In fact, there's an embarrassment of riches when it comes to quoting outrageously vulgar pop music lyrics. For every song and every artist cited above, there are many, many more that adopt the same attitudes and who sing the same kinds of songs, replete with the same kinds of messages. In indie band Saosin's "Rap Party," the singer announces that he "like[s] pussy" and that he's "going to lick it for an hour," adding that he "like[s] fat chicks / Cause they suck [him] for days." Similarly, the refrain of the Brazilian Girls hit "Pussy" includes the lyrics "Pussy pussy pussy marijuana."

One study of the top ten CDs as far back as February 1999 found that each contained at least one song with sexual content—and of the 159 songs studied, 42 percent contained sexual content consisting either of sexual innuendo/seductive lyrics (23 percent) or a direct description of sexual intercourse (19 percent).[32] Of the songs that did contain sexual content, 41 percent were deemed "pretty explicit" or "very explicit." In 68 percent of them, it was unclear whether the sexual encounters being described were within or outside an existing relationship; 14 percent alluded to an encounter outside or before a relationship.[33] And 18 percent of the songs with sexual content also featured sexual sound effects.[34]

Not surprisingly, few songs included messages about sexual planning or responsibilities (6 percent) or consequences or risks (8 percent). Only 6 percent of the songs alluded to sexual fidelity or monogamy, while 5 percent mentioned the benefits of sexual patience or abstinence.[35] There's no evidence that anything has changed for the better in the intervening years—if anything, the lyrics have grown more outrageous.

In fact, even though the words often seem difficult to discern, a significant percentage of young people have mentioned lyrics as a primary gratification in listening to music, and most mention them as a secondary gratification.[36] Even when the words are hard to understand, it's been found that those listening are able to recognize themes (such as aggression or sex) in the music itself.[37] And the more controversial the music is, the more likely its listeners are to pay close attention to its lyrics.[38]

Some girls are embarrassed to have to hear the words in public. A sophomore at a private high school observes, "A lot of people sing along [to raunchy songs]. We bring our iPod speakers to [free periods] every day at school. One day, this guy put something in about two people having sex, and it was the most disgusting thing ever." And many concede that a lot of lyrics are inappropriate. In a typical comment, a public high school fresh-man says, "I'll catch myself singing along to the music, and my mom will say, 'Do you know what you're saying?' But most of the time, you start to like the beat and you just hook on to the words, and half the time, I don't even realize what I'm saying until I listen to it and actually pull it out, singing it. And then it's like, 'Oooh.' "

Others have become completely desensitized. Another fresh-man at a public school says forthrightly, "[I]t's not shocking. I'm used to it already. Everybody says it."

Given the relentless vulgarity of many lyrics, it would seem nearly impossible to find a more effective delivery system for crass and unwholesome messages. But there is one: music videos.

Music Videos

With the advent of the music video, the power of popular music has extended beyond words and sound to the visual sphere. Music videos have become an extremely potent medium in the lives of teen boys and girls alike. As L. E. Greeson and R. A. Wil-liams, authors of an influential 1986 study on music videos, put it, "Music videos are designed to appeal to adolescent audiences, combining the impact of television with the sounds and mes-sages of youth transmitted through popular music."[39]

Music videos are readily available on a number of stations, ranging from Black Entertainment Television (BET) to Country Music Television (CMT), Music Television (MTV), and Video Hits One (VH1). The images and lyrics can vary depending on the music's genre;[40] when country music videos use sexual im-ages, they often appear in the context of dating and romantic love,[41] while rap music videos have been characterized as very graphic sexually, and often include images of violence as well.[42]

Of all the outlets for music videos, MTV—designed for those

between twelve and nineteen[43]—is by far the most prominent and the most widely viewed by young people in general. Its program *Total Request Live* is extremely popular across the country, and attracts a big crowd to Times Square each afternoon—all teens, of course, and largely girls. One relatively early study of ninth to twelfth graders estimated that adolescents spend more than two hours daily watching and listening to MTV, and found that 80 percent reported being exposed to it.[44] A different study found that 78 percent of girls watch MTV,[45] on average for 6.2 hours each week;[46] yet another study of students aged thirteen through eighteen found that 10 percent of the girls watched four to five or more hours *daily*.[47] According to Nielsen Media Research, girls eleven through nineteen watch MTV more than any other network.[48]

In any case, a study of ninth through twelfth graders found that they perceived MTV as "more visually profound and relevant" than other programming on television.[49] And teen girls, in particular, express deep interest in and forge personal connections with music videos.[50]

So it's worth taking a look at what they're hearing and seeing there—and why it matters so much.

The Unique Impact of Music Videos

Research suggests that music videos have an even more potent effect on young people than music and lyrics alone.[51] Experts have theorized that when visual images are added to the power of music and lyrics, the impact of the latter are magnified,[52] and that, by affecting the emotions, music can increase a listener's receptiveness to the accompanying lyrics and visual images.[53] One study noted that music videos are potentially much more influential than music alone for three reasons: First, they rely less on imagination and add new information about the music. Second, because teens are watching and not merely listening, music video viewing is more likely to be a foreground, rather than a background, activity. Third, less interpretation is needed to process the meaning of images than to understand lyrics.[54]

In fact, the American Academy of Pediatrics noted in 1996 that "Teenagers who may not 'hear' or understand rock lyrics cannot avoid the often disturbing images that characterize a growing number of videos" and that viewers who hear a song after having seen its music video may "flash back" to the video's imagery.[55] This is, of course, consistent with the theory that adolescents watch music videos in large part because they serve as visual aids that help to decipher the meaning of popular songs.[56]

These facts have particular relevance to girls, because research has indicated that they are more attentive to and involved in music imagery, and are, in fact, more likely than boys to recall a video's images when hearing the corresponding song played on the radio.[57] Much of what they're seeing is hardly wholesome.

The Content of Music Videos

The world portrayed in music videos is a distorted one, filled with plenty of scantily clad women and sexually aggressive men (not to mention bad language: One study found that MTV's music videos averaged thirty-two instances of foul language per hour[58]). Researchers have found that, on average, music videos portray ninety-three sexual situations per hour, including eleven "hard core" scenes that show behavior such as intercourse or oral sex.[59]

In 1997, it was reported that between 19 and 55 percent of music videos depicted sexuality or eroticism, depending on the genre of music;[60] other, earlier studies have pegged the percentage at 47 percent[61] or as high as 60 percent.[62] And as early as 1986, one study (which found that four sexual activities per music video was the norm) noted that adolescent sex on music television is "long on titillation and physical activity but devoid of emotional involvement"[63]—and it seems that little has changed.

Britney Spears's "Toxic" provides an example of a typical sexually charged music video. In it, viewers variously see Britney rub her rear end against the front of a man's pants, sport a black leather bodysuit as she rides on a motorcycle with a shirtless man, and then straddle a different man on a bed, whom she apparently poisons. Other images include two girls wearing fishnet stockings and lingerie with their legs intertwined—and the entire video is interspersed with scenes of Spears writhing on the floor in a nude bodysuit, wearing a thong. With the over-the-top sexual imagery of the "Toxic" video, perhaps it's not surprising to learn that its director has a background in directing pornographic movies.[64]

Given what they're seeing, it's troubling that the portrayals in music videos shape girls' perceptions of how women should behave and look more than any other kind of television programming.[65] One study, having analyzed sixty hours of music videos, found that a third of all the women portrayed wore lingerie or other revealing outfits, and were forty times more likely than men to be depicted as emotional, passive, and dependent—even as, in some cases, the women were portrayed as significantly more sexually aggressive than the men.[66] Another found that nearly half the victims of violence or other humiliating behavior were women.[67]

The images in these videos have a definite effect on young girls. Attending a middle school talent show, a *New York Times* essayist deplored the girls' performances, described as "elaborately choreographed re-creations of music videos." He noted, "They writhe and strut, shake their bottoms, splay their legs, thrust their chests out and in" and "straddle empty chairs, like lap dancers without laps."[68]

Accepting a trophy for a striptease performance in the movie

Sin City at the 2006 MTV Music Awards, where, as one account noted, "a teen-is-king attitude reigns,"[69] actress Jessica Alba offered these words of wisdom to her young fans: "Practice safe sex and drive hybrids if you can." Thanks, Ms. Alba—and MTV.

The Effects

An influential study reported that after viewing less than an hour of MTV, seventh and tenth graders were more likely to approve of premarital sex than were adolescents who had not been exposed to the channel.[70] A similar study of college students came to the same conclusion.[71] In short, both these experimental studies found that watching music videos may, in fact, influence attitudes toward early or risky sexual activity.

Relatively few studies have concentrated on the emotional and behavioral effects of music lyrics and videos specifically on teen girls. A study of thirteen- to eighteen-year-old adolescents, however, did find an even stronger relationship between music video exposure and sexual permissiveness and experience for girls than for boys.[72] Likewise, watching music videos frequently has been associated with a greater number of sexual partners among young college women,[73] and a positive relationship has been found between music video viewing and sexual permissiveness[74] and liberal sexual attitudes[75] in adolescent females.

Overall, the results of a significant number of surveys suggest an association between exposure to music videos and sexually permissive attitudes.[76] And these conclusions are buttressed by the opinions of teens themselves. When asked what accounted for the pervasiveness of sex in teen girl culture, an attractive blond seventeen-year-old from the Midwest answered immediately, "It's definitely MTV, because that's all people watch."

In fact, a 2003 study of young African American women aged fourteen to eighteen found that girls who watched the most rap videos were nearly twice as likely to have had sex with numerous partners; likewise, they were two and a half times as likely to have been arrested and three times as likely as other girls to have hit a teacher.[77]

Another study of African American high school students found that more frequent viewing of music videos and listening to pop music were associated with imputing greater importance to "showy" qualities such as sexiness.[78] Other research has shown that female students who saw sexy music videos were more likely to be accepting of teen dating violence,[79] and students of both genders were more likely to agree with the notion that sexual relationships are adversarial, rather than cooperative.[80]

The effects aren't simply academic. Critics have attributed a 2000 episode in which a mob groped and harassed almost fifty women near Central Park to the desensitizing effects of music videos.[81] And hip-hop music's suggestive beat and lyrics, favored by boys and girls alike,[82] have given rise to "freak dancing" (otherwise known as "grinding" or "the nasty")—itself popularized by MTV.[83] Because of its graphic nature, freak dancing has been banned from numerous school dances; as one principal explained to The Washington Post, "If they didn't have their clothes on, you would swear they were having sex."[84]

Perhaps the parents so concerned about Elvis's pelvis half a century ago didn't realize how good they had it.

What It Means

As always, it's almost impossible to come up with a hard-and-fast conclusion about the effect of listening to vulgar pop music lyrics or watching music videos on *all* young girls' sexual activity. In fact, music or videos doubtless impact some young people more than others; as one study noted, music videos have a greater influence on at-risk youth.[85] Each viewer or listener will respond based on her own unique psyche and life conditions—which affect how she uses or interprets music, and whether she has the time, means, and inclination to act on what she's learned.[86]

Likewise, some of the evidence about the effects of lyrics and videos is correlational. A study of 326 Cleveland teens, for example, found that those who preferred music television had increased amounts of sexual experience in their midteen years.[87] The studies don't indicate whether watching the videos helped shape attitudes—or the sexually permissive were drawn to the sexual content of the videos from the beginning.

Studies that are experimental—for example, that measure attitudes toward premarital sex among the same subjects before and after viewing music videos—likewise are subject to some caveats. Even when they find that girls are influenced by music videos, they can't always specify whether the influence will last for a short period or a lifetime.

Nevertheless, these caveats don't ultimately undermine the commonsense conclusion that the vulgar song lyrics and graphic images of music videos are pernicious for young girls (and boys, too). Some research has indicated that music has an "amplification effect" on teens' moods—in other words, it heightens whatever emotion the listener is already feeling.[88] That phenomenon raises the possibility, at least in theory, that music can lead a hard-partying or romantic girl to push the limits farther than she otherwise would in a moment of youthful exuberance. Even if the effects of lyrics or videos are temporary—well, life-changing choices (such as the decision to engage in unprotected sex) can be made during the course of an afternoon or a wild night out.

And the lessons about sex that the lyrics and videos are teaching are profoundly damaging. In a study of forty MTV music videos, researchers found that women in them participated in more subservient sexual behavior, and were often the recipients of graphic and aggressive sexual advances.[89] The researchers concluded, "[T]he concept of the whole person involved in a complex relationship with another whole person is clearly absent from the video's message."[90]

In other words, relationships are portrayed as little more than sexual pit stops along life's highway, with scant reference to the deeper emotions, obligations, responsibilities, and opportunities that they may likewise occasion. Discussing rap music, Dr. Michael Rich, the spokesman for the American Academy of Pediatrics' Media Matters campaign, put it this way: "I see an acceptance among teenagers—both girls and boys, of the kind of sexual objectification celebrated in this kind of music. There is this notion that it's okay to be used for sex and that there is not any emotional commitment necessary."[91]

When admired pop or rap stars model over-the-top sexual availability and sexual aggression, and when sexuality is portrayed as the everyday (and virtually exclusive) currency of male–female interaction, that behavior normalizes and romanticizes the vulgarity and makes it acceptable. The repetition of the message ingrains unwholesome concepts and builds on them.

The influence of sexualized pop singers like Britney Spears can be harmful to girls as young as six. Even as the "pop tarts" project a youthful image that encourages young girls to identify with them, they show young girls, who are still in the process of developing their own sense of self, that sex appeal is the only quality that matters. In the MTV documentary "When Sex Goes Pop: Not That Innocent," a fourteen-year-old girl comments, "You men are seeing Britney Spears pretty much naked except for her bra and a thong and sparkles, you know, and they are gonna want every girl to dress like that also."[92] That's a lot of pressure and big shoes (or bra cups) for a teen girl to fill.

Perhaps that's why one Chicago radio station ran a "Boobies Like Britney" contest for its young female listeners. The contest's tagline ran, "Wanna be like Britney? . . . You've watched her grow into every guy's fantasy slave. Now you want what she's got!"[93]

The contest offered a five-thousand-dollar grand prize (enough, presumably, to cover breast augmentation surgery).

How are girls who have been exposed to crass come-ons like this supposed to learn how to form healthy relationships with boys who have come to admire performers and lifestyles that demean women? They're all living in a world where celebrities like Britney Spears and Kevin Federline provided their bridal party with hoody sweatshirts reading PIMP for the boys and HO for the girls—and then donned them themselves. As one boy told Katie Couric in a 2005 interview on *Today*, "I personally think if you're going to call someone a 'ho' then, that your respect for them drops down to nil. You know, young men who are going to look up to these rappers as role models are going to start, in my opinion, treating their girlfriends this way."[94]

In fact, girls attribute a lot of undesirable male behavior to the influence of their music. One high school freshman said that boys' ideas about sex come from the lyrics. "A lot of music that they listen to, that's all it talks about," she said. "In the music, they give you, like, detail by detail."

Vulgarity has become normal, even mainstream, thanks to the vocabularies and behaviors of music stars. When Grammy Award–winning rapper Nelly builds on the success of his hit song "Pimp Juice" with an energy drink called Nelly's Pimp Juice—which then totals over a million sales in just three months[95]—the term *pimp* starts to take on a luster, and young boys begin to believe that being a pimp (presumably with "ho's") is something admirable, to be emulated.

In fact, the 2006 Oscar for Best Song went to "It's Hard Out Here for a Pimp." In order for the song to be broadcast, three words (*f**k, s**t,* and *ni**az*) repeated a total of ten times had to be omitted; even so, producer Gil Cates approved the use of *bitch* and *ho's,* because they are already heard on network news.[96] When terms that were once coarse epithets for men and women alike are celebrated by the hip and famous, it's unfair to expect boys and girls alike *not* to take notice.

Britney Spears has insisted she's not a role model,[97] and Nelly has said that he hates the idea of being one.[98] But ultimately, whether pop singers consciously *intend* to motivate young people to imitate them is irrelevant. Most human learning is, after all, incidental[99]—and the most harmful messages that teens receive from music lyrics and videos aren't necessarily those that are intentionally transmitted.

Of course, there's no doubt that some pop stars are more wholesome than others. At least for now, Mandy Moore and Hilary Duff are far more restrained than Britney Spears and Nelly Furtado in the way they present themselves and the music they sing. But their approach will be emulated by others only if they're successful—and that's defined by how well their albums and movies perform.

The importance of encouraging pop stars who are trying to disseminate worthwhile messages has been recognized by Oprah, a cultural arbiter in her own right. One of her guests has been the singer Pink, who—despite her rough persona and sometimes outrageous fashions—has spoken out against a celebrity culture that glorifies "stupid girls," who are content to be nothing more than sexual objects.[100] And despite some criticism from the artists themselves, Winfrey has refused to host prominent African American rappers who purvey music that could be construed as crudely misogynistic.

Girls deserve better than the ugly, aggressively graphic sexual messages they're receiving. So do their parents. So do we all.

CHAPTER 7

BARELY THERE

Want to know what gets between me and my Calvins?
Nothing.
Brooke Shields in an ad for Calvin Klein jeans, 1980

Who needs brains when you have these?
Abercrombie & Fitch girls' T-shirt, 2005

n 1980, when Brooke Shields declared that "nothing" came between her and her Calvins, her declaration elicited a public outcry[1]—even though a close reading of the statement suggests that it was, in fact, the opposite of a sexual come-on. Today, of course, the controversy that the ad provoked seems almost as quaint as, well, the high-waisted, relatively modest jeans Shields was touting.

In one sign of how the times have changed, a back-to-school ad for JCPenney (later withdrawn) featured a little girl, clad in a cropped top and low-rise jeans, whose mother insists that she can't go to school the way she is dressed.[2] Only after lowering the girl's pants another inch or two does the mother proclaim with satisfaction, "That's better." Apparently, the little girl's pants had struck her as unacceptably demure.

There's been an element of sexiness in numerous fashion trends over the years—the miniskirts and hot pants of the late 1960s spring immediately to mind. Likewise, there have always been clothes for teens and tweens. But today the two categories overlap to an unprecedented degree. The world of fashion has become sexualized, even infiltrated, by elements of pornography as never before.

The explicitly sexy styles are being created for and marketed even to the littlest girls—almost as if the goal were to make them sexually attractive to adults. In spring 2002, Abercrombie & Fitch stocked thongs in its stores sized to fit those in the ten- to sixteen-year-old age group.[3] On the tiny thongs were catchphrases like EYE CANDY, KISS ME, and WINK WINK.[4] In response to complaints, the company's spokesman insisted that the thongs were "cute and fun and sweet."[5]

At the extreme is the almost unthinkable: companies selling "Child Pimp & Ho Costumes" for Halloween[6] so that thirteen-year-olds can dress up as prostitutes, complete with fishnet stockings, tube tops, and miniskirts.[7] Other costumes marketed to children and teens on recent Halloweens have included "Transylvania Temptress," "Handy Candy," "Major Flirt," and "Red Velvet Devil Bride," typically featuring fishnet stockings, knee-high boots, miniskirts, and low-cut necklines.[8]

Revealing clothes are marketed to children so young that the term *prostitots*[9] has entered parents' lexicon. Even the littlest girls can "design [their] own sexy skirt" with the Bratz Superstyling Funkitivity Book[10] or own their own Bling Bling Barbie doll, dressed in a micro-miniskirt and a plunging, navel-baring silver tank top.[11] Shoppers at FAO Schwarz last December could find dolls tricked out in high heels, fishnet stockings, garter belts, and bustiers.[12]

Even babies aren't off limits—witness the 2006 debut of Pimpfants.[13] The line includes a mini basketball uniform with JR. PIMP SQUAD emblazoned across the front and a T-shirt that proclaims that MY MOM IS A MILF (that is, a "mother I'd like to f**k").

What's Happening

A more detailed examination of teen girl style and its inspirations demonstrates just how central the concept of sexiness has become, even in fashions for the youngest girls.

The Styles

In recent years, fashion for teen girls—and their younger sisters—has consisted largely of remarkably body-baring styles, courtesy of such stores as Abercrombie & Fitch, Hot Topic, and Wet Seal, with Hollister, Abercrombie Kids, and Limited Too for the younger set (the latter, with a seven- to fourteen-year-old clientele, was marketing strapless tops in 2005[14]). A trip to the mall reveals young girls decked out in tight low-rise jeans; backless, strapless, tank, and halter tops; belly shirts (bare midriffs); miniskirts; "bondage pants" (for those affecting a punk style); and short shorts (inseams under three inches).

Tightly stretched terry cloth and clingy, gauzy fabrics likewise have been in vogue. As one high school writer noted, upon arriving at school, she's "accosted by un-tanned butt cheeks, breasts that spill out of barely there clothes . . . and ensembles that attempt to pass off bras as T-shirts."[15]

Indeed, as the president and fashion director of Robinsons-May (now part of Macy's) assured the *Los Angeles Times,* lingerie "goes from the sheets to the streets."[16] Like the other sexy fashion trends, it's been made available to teens and tweens. Along with fashions that include elements like visible bra straps and lacy camisoles, retailers are establishing lingerie shops targeted to the junior high set.[17] Victoria's Secret has reached out to teens with its Design Your Own Bra line, which allows them to add a bevy of charms and other decorative touches to their underwear.[18]

But few lingerie items have ascended to widespread popularity as quickly as the thong. It's hard to forget the trend that called for the coupling of low-rise jeans with a peekaboo thong.[19] Between August 2002 and July 2003, perhaps the height of the craze, thong sales in the United States climbed to $610 million from $570 million;[20] girls aged thirteen through seventeen spent more than $157 million on thong underwear in 2003 alone.[21]

Certainly, sexy fashions have created plenty of difficulties for parents and schools attempting to fight what writer Betsy Hart has nicknamed the "whore wars."[22] Even the CEO of Xcite, a company that released a line of skimpy prom gowns in 2005, candidly admitted that he would never permit his own daughter to wear one of the dresses he was selling to others.[23]

Parents might have breathed a sigh of relief, first in 2004,[24] and then again in 2005,[25] when fashion experts assured the public that the sexy look was no longer fashionable. (In the colorful parlance of *Fashion Wire Daily*, "The slut is out now. She's dead."[26]). But even a cursory examination of popular teen magazines and clothing Web sites indicates either that the fashion experts were wrong—or that their idea of sexy clothes differs radically from that of the average mom and dad.

In June 2006, on the front page of its Web site, Wet Seal, a retailer targeting the fifteen- through twenty-three-year-old age group, was featuring a "rhinestone ring halter top"—bare to the top of the breasts, aside from a thin line of stones running up the top of the chest and around the neck. The two teenish models were sporting clingy, cleavage-displaying halter dresses. Even at the Gap, which generally sells less revealing items, tiny denim miniskirts and plenty of tank tops and short shorts were available.

On the site for the Limited Too (aimed at tweens), items denominated as "Top Sellers" included a "sparkle tube top," a "studded halter cami," and a "sequin band cami." Similar tanks and camisoles were likewise featured as options for juniors on the Target site. Abercrombie & Fitch was still selling low-rise jeans to girls, while their younger sisters could buy black-lace-trimmed camisoles with spaghetti straps at Abercrombie Kids. And at Abercrombie's surf-and-skate-oriented Hollister site, along with the predictable micro-miniskirts, girls could buy T-shirts with sassy little slogans like LAYING OUT MAKES ME HOT and SAVE A WAVE, RIDE A SURFER.

In fact, message T-shirts and accessories with lewd slogans or logos are widely available. The T-shirts, known as "attitude clothing," have become increasingly popular in recent years; 2005 sales at Wal-Mart surpassed by 50 percent the twenty million shirts sold in 2004.[27] On the Internet, options range from THERE'S ENOUGH OF ME TO GO AROUND to the straightforward SLUT (either in regular or babydoll[28] styles) and SKANKY WHITE TRAILER TRASH.[29] Merchandise bearing the *Playboy* Bunny logo—once deemed a symbol of male oppression and female subjugation—has enjoyed a surprising resurgence as a fashion accessory, appearing on everything from flip-flops to pencil cases.[30] Even the harder-core porn magazine *Hustler* has attempted to market a line of accessories such as makeup bags targeted at teen girls.[31]

Whatever the fashion mavens say, it's hardly likely that sexualized fashions will disappear altogether anytime soon. As *Women's Wear Daily* pointed out, "Millennials [born between 1978 and 1995] can't remember a time when strong sexual imagery and messages weren't widely available, or were considered controversial."[32] This may explain why many middle school girls don't believe that even skimpy tank tops, belly shirts, and low-rise jeans are provocative.[33] Body-baring styles seem normal to them; that's all they've ever known.

The Celebrity Influence

From the days of the flappers through the black leather jacket era to tie-dye mania to punk, fashion has always offered teens a way to rebel and to express themselves by choosing more daring styles than their parents would likely prefer. Understandably, being fashionable is important to teens generally; 39 percent describe themselves as trendsetters.[34] Like her choice of music or hairstyle, a girl's fashion choice is also a social identifier—a way of showing where, how, and with whom she fits in the great teen social hierarchy.

Not surprisingly, being "hot and trendy" when it comes to fashion is more important to girls than to boys; 44 percent of girls will even go over budget to achieve that goal, versus 35 percent of the boys.[35] And for many girls, "hot and trendy" is defined by their idols. As trend expert Irma Zandl noted, "The entertainment world is the single most important influence on shaping fashion and beauty trends among teen girls."[36]

In fact, the bare fashion trend actually began with pop idols like Britney Spears, Christina Aguilera, and Beyoncé Knowles.[37] Popular songs often reference high-fashion labels; in their hit "My Humps," the Black Eyed Peas sang about Dolce & Gabbana, Fendi, and Donna Karan, as well as Seven and True Religion jeans, just as rapper Nelly referenced Prada, Gucci, and Dolce & Gabbana in his hit "Pimp Juice."

The association between music and fashion is evidenced by the number of singers with their own clothing lines, including Beyoncé Knowles,[38] Jennifer Lopez,[39] and Gwen Stefani—and all have made efforts to reach out to the teen fashion market. Even Britney Spears told Matt Lauer in a June 2006 interview that she had plans to introduce a children's clothing line called Baby Soul Rock 'n Roll.[40]

In fact, the retail chain Hot Topic has achieved solid success by explicitly focusing on the nexus between music and fashion, selling rock-, punk-, and goth-inspired clothes along with music discs and accessories. Its Web site, designed to target young people between twelve and twenty-two, offers merchandise such as "black garter thigh-highs," a "black and pink mesh ruffle bustier and pantie [sic] set," and "black mesh lace hot pants," among other provocative items.[41] Touting "hot costumes for cool chicks" in the run-up to Halloween 2006, the site featured a picture of two teen girls, one wearing hot pants with fishnet stockings, the other clad in a short skirt and bustier, wielding a billy club.

Clearly, there's been no sign that the artists most popular with young girls—like Britney or Beyoncé—have received the memo about the new modesty that was supposed to have emerged. For a television interview in June 2006, Spears chose a denim miniskirt and low-cut, gauzy top; Robin Givhan, the merciless *Washington Post* style critic, noted that Spears's skirt was so short, "when seated it practically disappears beneath the protuberance of [Spears's] pregnant belly"; her top gave the appearance of "serving up one's bosom like melons at a picnic."[42] Likewise, singer Lil' Kim once showed up for the MTV Music Awards garbed in little more than pasties.

And many of those who should know better simply defend the trend. When Robin Antin, the creator of the Pussycat Dolls, was asked to defend the sexualized depiction of young women in the group's new reality show, she replied, "It is empowering to get up there and dress like a doll . . . There's nothing skanky about it. Their clothing is cute. It's fun. Yes, of course, it's sexy."[43]

As retailer Nanci Frisby noted in the pages of the *Los Angeles Times*, "If you think these celebrities are your style icons, then the way they dress . . . is going to resonate with you as well. If a celebrity has everything in the world to choose from and they choose item A, then item A must be pretty cool. We look to them because they can choose whatever they want."[44] Frisby was talking about the parents who outfit their babies in the same garb as celebrity newborns, but the concept holds true for teen girls as well. That's why a snapshot in *Teen People* of a celebrity wearing even the most outrageous style is pure gold for the retailer selling the item.

Ads

Teen girls have unprecedented freedom to spend, thanks both to the widespread availability of credit cards (22 percent of current college students had them in high school)[45] and the Internet, which allows them to shop at home. Of all consumer categories, clothes are the most popular item that teens plan to buy—and actually buy—with their own money.[46] Those between the ages of fourteen and seventeen visit malls more frequently than any other age group, at a rate averaging once a week.[47] Of course retailers make extraordinary efforts to solicit teens by seeking models popular with them.

Not surprisingly, these ads often play on sexual themes. In recent years, Britney Spears sang that she "can't wait another minute" because she's "got the urge" for Herbal Essence Shampoo—a product so superior that, according to its ads, it renders women virtually orgasmic. In a Pepsi commercial, Britney pranced through a warehouse in a white bustier sucking down a soda, thereby stimulating Bob Dole, shown watching on a TV in a diner (the ad concludes with Viagra pitchman Dole exclaiming, "Easy, boy!"—presumably to his dog).

In another Pepsi ad, singers Beyoncé Knowles, Pink, and Britney Spears vamped it up in sexy gladiator costumes. And Paris Hilton, one of Barbara Walters's 10 Most Fascinating People of

2004, lathered herself and writhed on a car while devouring a Carl's Jr. burger in an ad so explicitly sexual that it triggered strong objections from at least one watchdog group.[48]

But most remarkable is the ubiquity and the explicitness of the sexual images used to sell teen fashions. As the face of bebe, a fashion house popular with teen girls, teen favorite Mischa Barton participated in a dominatrix ad campaign launched in May 2006. In one photo, she's shown in a strapless minidress with a man—naked but for a pair of bikini briefs—kneeling submissively beside her. In another image, she digs her stiletto shoes into a male model's back.

Skechers, a favorite footwear company for teens and pre-teens, hired Christina Aguilera for an ad campaign in August 2004. In one photo, she's wearing a "naughty nurse" uniform, complete with exposed bra, tiny skirt, garter belt, and white leather boots, as she wields an enormous needle; another image of Christina looks on helplessly from a hospital bed. In a separate ad, Aguilera portrays both a police officer tarted up in dominatrix style—thigh-high leather black boots, fishnet stockings, hot pants, exposed cleavage, and dangling handcuffs—as well as the detainee spread and bent over the car's hood, wearing the requisite tiny tank top. Yet another image shows the singer in provocative schoolgirl attire, pencil to her lips, with a short plaid jumper and white shirt unbuttoned to display her bosom; at the same time, she appears as the "hot teacher," in full cleavage-display mode as she brandishes something oddly resembling a pool cue.

Even tween favorite Ashlee Simpson turned up sporting hot pink high heels in an ad for Candie's shoes. Scantily clad to display maximum cleavage, wearing little that's visible below the waist besides some crocheted white socks, she's perched seductively on a bed with a teddy bear in the corner. Perhaps to defend against the objections that such ads are likely to elicit, Candie's also markets a shirt that reads BE SEXY: IT DOESN'T MEAN YOU HAVE TO HAVE SEX, a motto Simpson parrots in appearances for the company.[49] Of course, the point is somewhat muted by the fact that SEXY is printed in big print across the bust, and the tagline appears in tiny letters below; even so, it's about as close as any company comes to a pro-abstinence message. Yet the question remains: Why would young girls be encouraged to "be sexy" in the first place?

Taken as a whole, the influence of such ads is substantial. In fact, 30 percent of teens aged thirteen through eighteen have bought clothes because of seeing a magazine ad about them.[50] And even ads that don't feature celebrity models rely on graphic sexual imagery.

Abercrombie & Fitch, often described as "the runaway leader in teen fashion,"[51] has been one of the most provocative retailers in marketing its goods—in fact, it's sometimes seemed that for the retailer, selling clothes is incidental to selling sex. Until it ceased publication in 2003, the company's magalog (magazine/catalog) engendered ongoing controversy with explicit photos of naked young people. The Christmas 2003 issue—withdrawn under threat of a boycott—included a "sexpert's" column advising readers to engage in oral sex in movie theaters,[52] along with information on threesomes and masturbation.[53] Earlier editions had included tips on seducing nuns and teachers and even pictures of Santa Claus with his elves, arranged in sadomasochistic poses.[54]

Abercrombie has continued to push the envelope. Its summer 2006 Web site gallery included a picture of a naked young woman in the arms of a naked young man,[55] and the shots advertising low-rise jeans for men show pants positioned so far down the models' torsos that they leave little to the imagination.[56]

Other companies have followed Abercrombie's lead. In an ad campaign appearing in *Cosmo GIRL!,* a Buffalo jeans shot displayed a very young model, thumb pulling down her jeans to the crotch, her hand covering her pubic area so that her fingers reach (over the jeans) between her legs, as her thong, likewise, is clearly exposed. Another ad in the same series showed a young woman lying on her back with her hand down her open jeans.

Diesel jeans, another brand popular with teen girls, created a similarly risqué campaign in spring 2006. Perhaps the tamest shot ("Apartments") featured a young jeans-clad man looking seductively at the camera as he pulled apart his raincoat in the manner of a flasher. Another ("Office") showed a woman straddling a man on a daybed while others watched (with binoculars) from surrounding windows. Yet another ("Whip") displayed three topless jeans-clad women from the back, two of them wielding whips while one's hands were tied and secured above her head (two of the women had welts in the shape of tic-tac-toe boards emblazoned on their backs). Finally, one image ("Statue") was of two women on the ground beneath a statue with its pants around its ankles; one of the women, on her back, arches her hips as if to pull her jeans up, while the other, on her knees, smiles suggestively at the camera.

For some teen products, a titillating marketing campaign begins even with the name of the product. Teen fragrances "FCUK Him" and "FCUK Her," created for FCUK (French Connection UK) capitalized on a provocative name with message T-shirts reading SCENT TO BED; invitations for the product's New York launch party came shaped like a hotel door hanger that read FCUK IN PROGRESS.[57] On FCUK's Web site, advertising images have included a young girl in her underwear, with a shirtless boy on a rumpled bed. The product has been marketed in *Teen People* and *Maxim*.[58]

And there are other, novel ways that retailers purvey sexy fashions and accessories to teens. Innovative marketing strategies include *Playboy*'s reality show, *The Girls Next Door,* filmed at the Playboy Mansion and broadcast on E!, as well as product placement on outlets popular with teens such as MTV.[59] The teen novel *How Opal Mehta Got Kissed, Got Wild, and Got a Life* (subsequently withdrawn after allegations of plagiarism), presented by Alloy Entertainment, included mentions of La Perla bras—and was to have been developed for the big screen by DreamWorks, where an image or mention of the referenced product would have been infinitely more valuable.[60]

Certainly, sexy products are nothing new, and they've long been marketed to consumers who have expressed an interest in them (or sought them out) in ways that are correspondingly risqué. But today explicit sex in marketing has become so widespread that it's virtually unavoidable by the public as a whole.

A prime example is the controversial displays set up by Victoria's Secret in late 2005 in its suburban Virginia and Milwaukee-area stores. Titled Backstage Sexy, an in-store display featured two female mannequins lying on a bed, with "one scantily clad female mannequin crawling toward another who reclined on a left hip and leaned back on both hands," as *The Washington Post* described it.[61] Other mannequins in the store windows were decked out in fishnet stockings, thongs, and accessories with a bondage theme.

Surely Victoria's Secret would insist that such displays were not specifically intended for young girls. Even so, the images they employ influence not only the way that less expensive brands— or those specifically targeted to teens—will be advertised, but also popular conceptions both of what's acceptable and of what it means to be beautiful, desirable, and hip. Such images offer young girls and boys alike an inappropriately provocative (and often undesirable or unattainable) definition of female sexiness.

Some lines have even made explicit links to the pornography industry. Pony, an athletic footwear and apparel company targeting teen boys and young men, hired porn stars including Jenna

Jameson for an ad campaign in 2003.[62] There's a whole line of T-shirts emblazoned with the phrase PORN STAR on the front; not surprisingly, the babydoll T-shirts are available in junior sizes.

These ad campaigns—and others like them, some going so far as to flirt with bestiality[63]—represent what critics have called "the increasing coarseness of commercial discourse,"[64] and their effects on American culture as a whole are unfortunate. Over time, confronted with ever-more-outrageous sexual images, consumers' collective tastes become degraded and their sensibilities are dulled, all as part of a marketing race to the bottom. Eventually, smutty advertising loses its shock value—the over-the-top sexiness celebrated in the ads begins to seem normal. And our common culture is vulgarized as a result.

The effects of sexy advertising are profound. Retailers' efforts to create a market among young people for even mature products have resulted in age compression,[65] in which tweens and younger teens are encouraged to want products once exclusively reserved for adults. The ads designed to drive demand for these products (and public acceptance of them) teach inexperienced teen (and younger) boys and girls that exaggerated, sexualized attitudes, fashions, and behaviors are a standard part of mainstream culture. Over time, teens and their younger siblings receive the message that it's expected—even desirable—for them to present themselves as flagrantly sexual beings, long before they're old enough to handle (or even understand) the accompanying responsibilities.

Ironically, what many young people don't realize is that, despite the critical and elite approval that frequently greets cutting-edge ads with risqué sexual images, they actually represent a lack of creativity. After all, it's not nearly as difficult to find some gross or outlandish sexual image that will shock and titillate viewers as it is to come up with tasteful ads that are nonetheless effectively creative or heartfelt or funny.

Certainly it's impossible to know whether the very bright and talented people behind the ad campaigns realize how they're influencing young girls—or if they just don't care. But one thing is certain: With the ads (and the products they popularize) come implicit messages about what constitutes being cool and desirable and admired. And ultimately, it's difficult to expect young girls besieged by images of rail-slim, highly sexualized peers to develop healthy attitudes either toward sex itself—or toward their own imperfect but beautiful bodies, stuffed like "sausage casings" (as one *Los Angeles Times* article put it) into the tight, skimpy clothing that, too often, is all that's available to them.[66]

What It Means

In the past, young girls might have chosen audacious clothing styles as a way to showcase their individuality and send a message that they were daring nonconformists. But the bare look has become so available and so widely accepted for women of all ages that, in truth, little remains to rebel *against*—unless it is the salacious fashion status quo. As Alison Pollet and Page Hurwitz pointed out in *The Nation*, "It's a strange day when Hot Topic's 'Pay up, sucker!' thong (the words, in bubble letters, encircle a dollar sign) seems a better option for girls than the padlock one, because it smacks less of sexual Puritanism."[67]

Indeed, in the elite media, sexualized dress isn't just accepted—it's celebrated. In early 2006, the *Los Angeles Times* splashed a feature story across the front of its calendar section about "fashion's 'it' girl."[68] The subject of the piece—"who the fashion world is buzzing about"—was "burlesque queen and fetishist" Dita Von Teese, "known for stripping down to her pasties while frolicking in an overgrown martini glass."

Of course, not every girl is going to share the *Times*'s fawning admiration for Dita Von Teese. But the sensibility that glorifies her trickles into the mainstream, perhaps explaining why, as radio talk-show host and writer Dennis Prager put it, "A young woman who wore a dress or even a skirt and blouse to a college, let alone high school, class would probably be considered stranger by her peers than one who wore a see-through top."[69]

Despite its outrageousness (or perhaps because of it), the bare trend has had a lot of staying power. It's popular with many teen girls, perhaps because revealing clothes garner attention from the opposite sex at an age when attracting male attention is a key element of being deemed successful and popular. The sexy clothes and accessories offer girls who are learning about their own sexual power a way to develop a "coy yet brazen, look-but-don't-touch sexual persona,"[70] as Pollet and Hurwitz theorized in *The Nation*.

Widespread social acceptance of young girls wearing sexy styles puts those who refuse to do so (or whose parents forbid it) at a significant disadvantage in the world of teen romance; not only are they often deemed unfashionable for choosing modest styles, but they also must compete for male attention with girls who wholeheartedly embrace the sexy look. A sophomore in a private school in California observed, "It really bothers me—I have this friend who always wears low-cut shirts and high skirts. She's really pretty, and you don't need your boobs hanging out all the time in order to get by, but it seems like she's just doing this all for [guys]."

But there are good reasons for girls and parents to resist simply following the crowd. As adults have long understood, provocative fashions make a girl look older and more sophisticated. By wearing short shorts, micro-minis, tank tops, and other revealing styles, young girls send the message, consciously or not, that they're sexually aware and active. Seeing sexy clothes on young girls suggests that it's acceptable to view them as sexual objects, and provides a rationalization for those who already have an unhealthy tendency to do so.

What's more, as clinical psychologist Patricia Dalton notes, "When a [teen] moves straight from girl to woman, she's playing a role rather than gradually learning to live her own life. These girls may seem whole, but they aren't. There is often a lost girl inside."[71] Perhaps that's because they've developed an identity that is almost exclusively bound up with their appearance and their sexuality.

When a girl's attention is directed primarily to her appearance, there's less time for her to pursue other interests and develop other skills that can serve as sources of self-esteem. When she's learned to garner male attention simply by displaying her body, it's less likely that she'll develop the other, inner qualities that are conducive to strong relationships and lasting happiness; indeed, a lifetime of focusing primarily on her own appearance and body—and automatically expecting men to do so as well—can make it difficult to form deep, lasting bonds with any man. How, exactly, is all the superficial, ersatz sexiness supposed to translate into a joyous and mature sexuality when the right time comes?

The damage to girls who grow up using their sexuality as their calling card isn't necessarily limited just to the realm of the personal—it can follow them into the workplace as well. As a result of workers frequently sporting inappropriately revealing fashions on the job, employers have resorted to printing illustrated booklets with dressing dos and don'ts.[72] The Web site CareerBuilder.com has actually begun dispensing advice on what constitutes appropriate professional attire—advice that would have been laughably unnecessary even fifteen years ago.[73]

Failure either to understand or to follow these rules hurts women's chances of being taken seriously at work and can have real consequences for their careers. A 2005 study found both that women in "high status" (managerial) jobs who dress provocatively were perceived as being less intelligent and capable than those who dressed more modestly—and that women who wear racy clothing were seen to be using their sexuality to aid their professional advancement.[74]

More than anything, watching teen girls wear inappropriately sexy clothes is profoundly sad. Certainly the clothes send a message to boys. As one unusually perceptive high school sophomore noted, "Dressing in certain ways makes guys look at you in a different way. Yeah, they're going to like you, but they're not going to respect you as much."

The risqué clothes send a disheartening message to older women as well: Too many young girls wearing too-sexy styles haven't yet learned to distinguish transient sexual power from true, lasting personal power. After all, the kind of "liberation" that "empowers" young girls to become "eye candy" for older men isn't real freedom at all.

CHAPTER

PAYING THE PIPER:
THE TOLL ON YOUNG GIRLS AND
THE COST TO AMERICA

If it makes you happy
It can't be that bad
If it makes you happy
Then why the hell are you so sad?
"If It Makes You Happy," *Sheryl Crow*

In an era of omnipresent sexual messages, it's hard to
know: Would those who glamorize unmarried teen sex
through books and magazines, television and movies,
fashions, music, and the Internet continue to do so if they knew
what a heavy toll this easy-come, easy-go approach to sex can
take on young girls?

Certainly, sex can have serious physical consequences for
women generally. In fact, if HIV-related mortality is excluded,
more than 80 percent of deaths related to sexual behavior
are among women.[1] Teen girls are hardly immune from these

151

threats; in some ways, they are at particular risk. And along with the potential for physical harm, teen sex often condemns young women to a life of poverty and deprivation. Finally, there's another, rarely discussed result of sexual promiscuity: Girls can (and often do) suffer profound and even lifelong emotional damage as a result of having given too much, too soon.

As staggering as these costs are, they're not restricted to the young women who make the choice to have sex as teenagers. They extend to the children those girls bear—and American society as a whole.

The Physical Toll

One of the most obvious costs of teen sex is the impact it can have on the physical health of girls.

Sexually Transmitted Diseases

Several decades after the dawn of the sexual revolution, almost sixty-five million Americans have contracted an incurable STD.[2] Many of them become infected early; as of 2004, almost half of the nineteen million new cases each year were erupting among adolescents and young adults aged fifteen through twenty-four.[3]

This means that, even though fifteen- through twenty-four-year-olds represent about one-quarter of those who have ever been sexually active, they nonetheless acquire almost half of all new STDs.[4] Not surprisingly, the younger adolescents are when they first engage in sexual activity, the more likely they are to become infected; girls who begin having sex at thirteen are twice as likely to contract an STD as those who initiated sex at twenty-one.[5] That may be because teens and young adults are more likely than older people to have unprotected sex and multiple sex partners; for young women in particular, the risk is enhanced by choosing older sex partners.[6]

What's more, the risks posed by STDs are even greater for girls than for women generally. Young women are biologically more susceptible to certain kinds of STDs than their older counterparts:[7] Young women's bodies have fewer protective antibodies, and their cervical cells are immature, which can predispose their genital tracts to infection.[8]

The most common STDs today are:

Chlamydia. Between 1986 and 2005, the rates of reported chlamydia infection increased from 35.2 to 332.5 cases per 100,000 population.[9] In fact, because many of those who have chlamydia aren't aware of it, infection levels are likely to be even higher.[10]

As of 2005, girls between fifteen and nineteen had the highest age-specific rates of reported chlamydia.[11] According to the Centers for Disease Control, 5 to 10 percent of young girls have acquired this bacterial infection.[12] And because it can be transmitted through secretions during sex that moisten areas outside those covered by a condom, there's little meaningful protection against infection.

If left untreated, the consequences of chlamydia are serious. It increases the risk of becoming infected with other STDs, including the HIV virus, and the infection can lead to pelvic inflammatory disease, which itself can cause ectopic pregnancy[13] and lead to the heartbreak of infertility. What's more, pregnant women with chlamydia can pass the infection to their infants during delivery, which elevates the risk of their babies contracting pneumonia and conjunctivitis.[14] It likewise can lead to arthritis and bladder infections.

Genital Herpes. Herpes is an incurable malady that, in recent years, has been spreading fastest among teens—who, as of 2000, were nearly five times more likely to have the disease than they were in the 1970s.[15] Type 2 herpes is transmissible both through intercourse and from mother to child; what's more, it makes those infected with it more vulnerable to HIV, and renders HIV-infected individuals more infectious themselves. Because the virus lives in the infected person's nerve roots, sores, rashes, and blisters on the genitals can recur unpredictably and intermittently.[16] Overall, herpes is slightly more prevalent in women (about 25 percent) than men (almost 20 percent).[17]

Herpes can be spread by skin-on-skin contact anywhere in the genital region during sex. For that reason, the efficacy of condoms in preventing transmission is limited, as they cover only a relatively small part of the relevant area.

Human Papillomavirus (HPV). The most commonly sexually transmitted infection in the United States, HPV is most common in those in their teens or early twenties.[18] More than 20 million Americans are already infected, and the CDC estimates that there are 6.2 million new cases each year.[19]

For females, the most significant risk factor for contracting cervical cancer—of which there are 9,710 new cases annually— is being infected with certain strains of the virus.[20] In 2006, a CDC advisory committee recommended that a newly licensed vaccine for HPV be given to girls before they had engaged in sex. In a sad sign of the times, the committee suggested that vaccinations be routinely administered to girls as young as eleven and twelve—or even nine at the discretion of their doctor.[21]

As with herpes, HPV can be contracted from skin-on-skin contact in the genital area. Again, condoms are no guarantee against infection.

⌘

Other serious STDs include:

HIV/AIDS. In recent years, approximately 25 percent of all new HIV infections have taken place in those younger than twenty-one,[22] and a growing proportion of these new cases result from heterosexual transmission through sexual intercourse. In

2003, teen girls made up half of the HIV cases reported among those between thirteen and nineteen.[23]

The life-threatening consequences of HIV are well known. The virus limits the ability to fight disease, thus rendering its victims more susceptible to diseases such as cancer and infections ranging from pneumonia to other STDs.

It's worth noting that African American girls are at a disproportionately high risk of HIV infection. One study found that 4.9 per 1,000 black teenage girls were infected, compared with 0.7 per 1,000 for Hispanic girls and 0.6 per 1,000 among whites.[24]

Nor is condom use a guarantee against contracting AIDS. A 2001 report from the National Institutes of Health found that condom use can reduce the sexually transmitted spread of AIDS by 85 percent—but only if they were used 100 percent of the time.[25]

Gonorrhea. Rates of reported gonorrhea have fallen over the last decade, but compared with women in all other age categories, girls aged fifteen through nineteen have the highest rates of gonorrhea; in 2005, the infection rate in this age group was 624.7 cases per 100,000.[26] Like those with chlamydia, girls with gonorrhea often experience no symptoms—and like chlamydia, the infection increases the risk of infection with other STDs. In females, if left untreated, gonorrhea can spread to the uterus and fallopian tubes, causing pelvic inflammatory disease, which can cause infertility and tubal pregnancy.[27] What's more, it can lead to nervous disorder, stillbirth, premature labor, heart problems, and arthritis.

Trichomoniasis. This is the most common curable STD in sexually active young women; there are about 7.4 million new cases of this parasitic infection annually in women and men.[28]

Because trichomoniasis causes inflammation of the genitals, it can increase a girl's susceptibility to HIV infection as well as increasing the risk that girls also infected with the HIV virus will pass it to their sexual partners.[29] Trichomoniasis can also cause complications during pregnancy, increasing the risk of premature delivery or low birth weight.[30]

Syphilis. Syphilis elevates the risk of infection with other STDs, and if it remains untreated, the disease can eventually damage the brain, heart, and nervous system, in some cases causing death.[31] About seventy thousand new cases are reported each year,[32] but the rates among girls aged fifteen through nineteen remain low.[33] In women generally, syphilis rates are highest for those between twenty and twenty-four;[34] for pregnant women, the infection can significantly harm an unborn child.

✸

Overall, sexually transmitted diseases may account for as much as 15 percent of infertility cases in the United States—but only about half of those affected knew that they had contracted an STD.[35] In fact, one in five newlywed American couples are unable to conceive a child.[36] Given that an overwhelming majority of girls have reported that having children someday was somewhat or very important to them,[37] it's important that they learn that poor sexual decision making can result in heartbreak and regret—not just here and now but even, potentially, over the course of a lifetime.

Pregnancy

As noted above, condoms do not guarantee complete protection against any sexually transmitted disease.[38] Even so, they are generally considered to be the most effective device other than abstinence for preventing the spread of STDs. They also serve as a form of birth control. As of 2002, 54 percent of sexually active girls between fifteen and nineteen reported using condoms, with 43 percent using hormonal methods (such as pills, injectables, implants, patches, or emergency contraception), 20 percent using some combination of condoms and hormonal birth control, and 17 percent using no kind of contraception at all.[39]

Given that nearly a fifth of teen girls aren't using any contraception—and the fact that no form of contraception is guaranteed to be entirely effective—perhaps it's no surprise that almost one-third (31 percent) of girls aged fifteen through nineteen who have had sex have, at some point, been pregnant.[40] In 2003, the teen birth rate for unmarried women was 34.8 per 1,000 for girls fifteen through nineteen and 20.3 per 1,000 for girls between fifteen and seventeen.[41] Of the approximately one million teen girls who become pregnant in the United States each year, more than 80 percent do so unintentionally;[42] for girls seventeen and under, only 12 percent of the births are planned.[43]

In assessing the toll that teenage sex can take on girls, it's worth noting that pregnancy and childbirth can have serious complications, especially for teen mothers. Adolescent pregnancy is associated with higher rates of illness and death for babies and mothers alike.[44] Teen girls have an elevated risk of death or serious complications from conditions such as pre-eclampsia (pregnancy-induced hypertension), anemia, placenta previa, and premature delivery.[45]

The physical and developmental ramifications of teen pregnancy aren't restricted to the mother—babies can be affected, too. The offspring of teen mothers are two to six times more likely to have low birth weight than infants born to mothers aged twenty or older.[46] Even after adjusting for socioeconomic and other risk factors, post-neonatal death rates are higher for babies of mothers between twelve and seventeen than for older mothers.[47] What's more, even after a variety of risk factors are taken into account, the babies of girls seventeen or younger likewise are more likely to be of low birth weight—which, in turn, elevates their risk for conditions including blindness, cerebral palsy, mental retardation, deafness, chronic respiratory problems, and mental illness.[48]

Children born to mothers aged seventeen and younger have also been found to begin kindergarten with lower levels of school readiness than children born to older mothers, particularly those aged twenty-two through twenty-nine, even after controlling for factors such as mothers' marital status, family structure, and socioeconomic status.[49]

Would it make a difference if girls knew that the physical risks of teen pregnancy aren't being borne by them alone?

Abortion

Since abortion became legal in 1973, many young girls have simply terminated unwanted pregnancies. In 2000, 29 percent of all teen pregnancies ended in abortion.[50] In 2002, the most recent year for which the information is available, 17.5 percent of all abortions were performed on girls under nineteen, and 51 percent were performed on women under twenty-five.[51] Of all age groups, girls under fifteen showed the highest percentage of late-term abortions (approximately 15 percent), and the lowest percentage of early ones (about 40 percent).[52]

Overall, 80 percent of abortions were to unmarried women,[53] indicating that abortion tends to be a method of birth control favored predominantly by the unmarried. In fact, an analysis of the 1995 National Survey of Family Growth found that only 7.6 percent of women who'd had sex only with their husbands had had an abortion, while more than half the women with more than twenty nonmarital sex partners had undergone an abortion.[54] What's more, women who've had sex with nonmarital partners are fully four times as likely to have had abortions than those who've had sex only with a spouse.[55]

In recent years, claims about the existence and severity of the physical and emotional effects of abortion have been the subject of heated controversy. Given the profound political and ethical disagreement that the topic of abortion engenders, it's difficult to find authoritative conclusions about the risks of abortion from completely impartial sources. Nonetheless, this information still helps assess the threats to girls resulting from teen sex.

Physical Risks of Abortion. Like any other surgical procedure, abortion entails certain physical risks, including perforation as a result of a surgical instrument puncturing the uterus and possibly injuring an abdominal organ; excessive bleeding; failure to terminate the pregnancy (with the potential deformation or crippling of the surviving baby); infection; and infertility because of scarring from previous abortion(s). However, most agree that the risks to the mother are relatively small when the procedure is performed by a competent physician.

In recent years, the issue of whether a link exists between abortion and breast cancer has been hotly disputed. Some have asserted that available evidence doesn't establish any connection,[56] although others have asserted the existence of a link and characterized the studies to the contrary as flawed.[57] It is, in any case, a potential risk for young girls (and their parents) to keep in mind.

Emotional Risks of Abortion. Like the debate over abortion and breast cancer, the issue of whether abortion can cause mental health problems is passionately debated. Some studies have found that those who have had abortions experience higher rates of depression, anxiety, and suicidal behaviors.[58] Certainly, the creation of groups like WEBA (Women Exploited By Abortion) and the experiences of ministers and counselors who work with women mourning their abortions even years later suggest that for some, at least, the emotional aftermath is both profound and lasting.

Even so, the same kind of controversy that characterizes almost every aspect of the abortion debate surrounds this issue.

Some have found the evidence of emotional harm inconclusive.[59] Others have asserted that the psychological risks are minimal, if they exist at all.[60]

Whatever the ethical dilemmas that divide Americans when it comes to abortion, however, certainly everyone can agree that it's best for a young girl *never* to be in a position where she runs the risk of having to learn firsthand whether the emotional and physical risks of abortion are, in fact, real. Just as young girls need to understand that condoms do not completely guarantee protection from unwanted pregnancy or STDs, it's important for them to realize that although an abortion may eliminate the immediate problem of an unwanted child, it's not a risk-free cure-all to the problems caused by poor sexual decision making.

It's worth noting that delaying sexual activity reduces the risk of abortions. Based on the 1995 National Survey of Family Growth, almost 30 percent of girls who began having sex at thirteen or fourteen have had an abortion, compared with 12 percent of those who started having sex in their early twenties.[61]

Perhaps it's significant that more teenage boys than girls believe in abortion rights. According to a 2003 Gallup Youth Survey, 35 percent of girl respondents said abortion should be illegal, compared with 32 percent of boys; conversely, 23 percent of boys and 19 percent of girls who responded to the poll thought abortion should be legal under any circumstances.[62] The results make sense—for boys, abortion can seem like little more than a convenient way to avoid having an unwanted child. For girls, the hazards—and the emotional fallout—are much greater.

The Economic Toll

The risks of poor sexual decision making to a young girl aren't just physical. Setting aside the adverse impact that concern over an STD or emotional fallout from an abortion can have on girls' grades and other opportunities, there's an economic price for girls when they reproduce as teenagers.

For starters, most of the time their education is cut short. Teenage childbearing is associated with lower levels of completed schooling compared with those who delay childbearing. In fact, the gap in educational attainment between teenage mothers and others is as wide as ever.[63] Only 41 percent of teenagers who have children before age eighteen ultimately obtain a high school diploma, compared with 61 percent of teens from similar social and economic backgrounds who did not give birth until age twenty or twenty-one.[64]

What's more, only 30 percent of girls who have children at seventeen or younger receive a diploma by age thirty.[65] And that's if they graduate at all. After controlling for background and similar factors, having a child at seventeen or younger means a young mother is half as likely to finish high school.[66]

With an education that's been short-circuited, it's hardly surprising that teen mothers face a higher likelihood of economic dependency. Teens who give birth are more likely to come from economically disadvantaged backgrounds in the first place; even so, unmarried teen mothers are at greater risk for ending up on Welfare than women of similar socioeconomic status who have delayed childbearing.[67] Up to 80 percent of all teen mothers receive Welfare,[68] and more than 75 percent of all unmarried teen mothers go on Welfare within five years of the birth of their first child.[69]

A whopping majority of teen births today takes place out of wedlock. In 2001, 79 percent of teen births were to unwed mothers[70]—a sixfold increase over the preceding fifty years.[71] Teen girls who give birth at seventeen or earlier will spend 57 percent more time as a single parent during their first thirteen years of parenthood as well.[72] Indeed, any examination of the link between unwed teen pregnancy and poverty must take into account the fact that most teen mothers are bereft of the financial stability that marriage provides, even as their children are deprived of the innumerable emotional benefits of having a father in the home.

The economic deprivations are real, and they can be severe. Even so, of course, dollars and cents are a completely inadequate measure for counting the opportunity costs of missing the milestones of normal teen experience—proms, graduations, and the like. A strictly economic analysis can never fully account for the sacrifice of innumerable other professional, social, or academic opportunities that result from teen motherhood. And any economic calculation completely fails to consider how many more benefits would have been available to the children of these teen mothers had they been born just a few years later, after their moms had had an opportunity to get their own lives on track.

The Emotional Toll

Many girls learn both about the physical toll that early sex can take upon them, and the fact that unplanned pregnancy often results in economic disadvantage and thwarted ambition. But they hear much less about the high emotional price of giving too much, too soon. Even as girls are reminded that they could end up with an STD, or an abortion, or an unwanted child, or on Welfare as a result of poor sexual decision making, they're rarely told they could also end up with a broken heart. As developmental psychologist and professor of education Dr. Thomas Lickona has pointed out, "This relative silence about the emotional side of sex is ironic, because the emotional dimension of sex is what makes it distinctively human."[73]

Though it's seldom discussed, the danger is real, especially for girls. Part of this phenomenon is biological. Sexual activity typically elicits deeper feelings for girls than boys, at least initially.[74] As sex therapist Ian Kerner has noted, "[S]ex and emotions are more inextricably linked in women than in men . . ."[75] In fact, the female orgasm releases a burst of the hormone oxytocin, which engenders a sense of attachment toward one's sexual partner, helping women feel bonded to the men with whom they've had sex. The quick and uncommitted sex characteristic of the hookup culture therefore presents a double drawback for the females: Even as they're more likely to bond with their sexual partners, there's a smaller window of opportunity to forge a meaningful relationship with them.

The emotional wounds that can result from poor sexual decision making are varied and potentially profound. They include:

Regret. Many young women who decide to engage in intercourse come to regret having done so. An ABC News poll of thirteen- through seventeen-year-olds concluded, "Many [teens], in retrospect, acted too soon: Among those who've had sex, half (especially girls) say they wish they'd waited longer."[76] And those results are hardly unique. A survey from the National Campaign to Prevent Teen Pregnancy likewise found that fully 63 percent of teen boys and 69 percent of teen girls reported that they wished they had waited longer to have sex.[77]

Any sense of private regret is, of course, only intensified if negative social consequences result from sexual experimentation. School gossip or a loss of reputation (in more traditional social circles, or if one is avoided or rejected by a former sex partner) can also be sources of real, deep, and lasting anguish.

And, of course, there's the possibility of a life-changing unwanted pregnancy. Discussing an acquaintance who became pregnant during high school and dropped out, a high school freshman said, "She tells me, 'It's really hard now' . . . She thought he [the father of her child] would be the only man she'd ever love. But she found he didn't love her, and he left her. Before doing it again, she said she'd get to know him."

Apathy and Shame. One high school freshman in Southern California tried to describe the reaction of her acquaintances after they had engaged in sexual activity. "I don't know if they're exactly ashamed of it," she said, "but they're certainly not proud. I guess it's like 'oh, whatever' to them."

Dr. Adria O'Donnell, clinical and consulting psychologist whose primary focus is on adolescent girls, says, "It's so sad. The most common reaction [of girls who have had sex for the first time] is apathy. [They say] 'It wasn't a big deal. It was uncomfortable, I hated it. Whatever.'" She adds, "But there is shame. Most of the girls lie and say they didn't do it."

There's something quite poignant about these accounts. Led astray by a culture that too often celebrates girls freely expressing their sexuality, many young women find what should be a wonderful experience—at the right time and with the right person—transformed into an occasion for shame. And the "oh, whatever" attitude many girls adopt as a response hardly bodes well for more prudent sexual decision making, resulting in a more meaningful experience, in the future.

Disappointment and Betrayal. Many girls expect their sexual encounters to be beautiful and romantic—and to cement or strengthen their relationships with their sex partners. But what's portrayed in popular culture as a tender and life-changing experience often turns out instead to involve rushed sex acts with an inexperienced or inept boy—who may not even express romantic feelings for his sex partner. Disappointment—coupled with a sense of "Is that all there is?"—is a natural, even inevitable, result.

What's more, because young girls are more likely to infuse sexual acts with an emotional meaning, it's especially difficult for them when sex becomes divorced from love, relationships, and formal commitments. If a girl finds out that a boy she loves (and who, she thought, loved her) was only in it for the sex, it's almost impossible for her not to feel betrayed, used, and even degraded.

Discussing an acquaintance who had recently performed oral sex for the first time, one high school freshman reported, "She did it because the guy said, 'It's for me.'" Later, however, the boy made it clear that the liaison had meant nothing to him, and even ignored the girl at school.

Lack of Trust/Honesty. Over time, after experiencing sexual hookups that are supposed to involve no emotions whatsoever, girls are likely to suspect that sex is the only real reason boys are interested in them. Even in a relationship—at least when it's focused on sex—a girl will understandably come to believe that her boyfriend's primary interest is in her body, whatever he says.

And when girls don't trust boys, it's difficult to be honest with them about what they want. In a 2006 poll of ten thousand of its readers, *Seventeen* magazine reported that fully 40 percent of respondents had assured a potential love interest that they were okay with just a hookup when they really wanted a relationship.[78] In fact, girls rank intimacy as their primary goal in romantic relationships;[79] apparently, however, many of them don't trust boys enough to admit it. This dynamic is replayed over and over again in MTV's hit reality show *Laguna Beach,* which continuously lands in Nielsen's top twenty programs for viewers between twelve and seventeen. For example, in the 2006–07 season, Tessa, a sweet girl who is the show's lead character, constantly hooks up with the wrong kind of guy. By season's end, she confides to her ex-boyfriend Chase that she simply "doesn't trust guys anymore."

Guilt. Many of those who favor more liberal attitudes toward teen sex decry the notion that any teen would experience guilt after having sex.[80] But a 2001 Gallup poll of teenagers between thirteen and seventeen found that engaging in premarital sex would make fully 59 percent of teens feel guilty.[81] And rather than being the by-product of unduly repressive social attitudes toward sex, guilt can be an entirely normal reaction when girls realize they have made a choice that would deeply distress their parents, or that they themselves consider religiously or morally wrong.

Worry. Along with sexual activity comes a lot of anxiety. An ABC poll found that 57 percent of girls between thirteen and seventeen were "very" or "somewhat" concerned about becoming pregnant, and 66 percent of them were "very" or "somewhat" concerned about contracting a sexually transmitted disease.[82] Other worries can include ignorance about adequate or appealing sexual technique, and, for girls, concerns that sex will be physically painful.

Heartache. Even without the complicating factor of sex, romance tends to be fraught with more emotional danger for girls than for boys, because girls are likely to be more preoccupied with emotions and invested in relationships than their male counterparts. The breakup of a romantic relationship is difficult for any girl, especially when she's not the one who initiated it. It's natural for anyone who's been "dumped" to feel undesirable, or even to become convinced that her experience in one relationship is predictive of her future love life.

The sense of loss and grief that accompanies any breakup is exponentially increased when a young girl has given her body— as well as her heart—to a boy who rejects her (or worse yet, refuses even to initiate a relationship after acting like sex was a prerequisite for doing so). Having sex only intensifies the feeling that a relationship is serious and meaningful, and exacerbates the emotional wounds inflicted by a breakup.

Depression. Given the constellation of negative emotions that often result from or accompany girls' sexual activity, it's hardly surprising that a number of studies have found that sexually active adolescent girls (but not boys) are significantly more depressed than those without sexual experience.[83] One analysis found that of teenagers between fourteen and seventeen, 25.3 percent of sexually active girls reported feeling depressed either a lot, most, or all of the time, compared with only 7.7 percent of girls who weren't sexually active.[84]

In fact, academic research has recently confirmed that for girls (though not for boys), even modest sexual experimentation increases the risk of depression, while finding no support for the theory that girls' sexual behavior is a form of self-medication for preexisting depression.[85] In other words, depressed girls aren't having sex to make themselves feel better; rather, it seems that having sex (and/or engaging in other risky behavior) can actually cause depression.[86]

Early sexual experience among adolescent girls is likewise associated with other negative feelings. Most notably, a study published in the journal of the American Academy of Pediatrics found that nonvirginal girls (but not boys) were 6.3 times more likely to report having attempted suicide, were slightly more likely to report feeling lonely and upset, and were having difficulty sleeping.[87] Similarly, a Heritage Foundation analysis reported that 14.3 percent of sexually active girls between fourteen and seventeen had attempted suicide, compared with 5.1 percent of those not engaging in sexual activity.[88]

Damaged Self-Esteem. A 2006 study of girls between fourteen and nineteen reported that girls with lower self-esteem were more likely to engage in early sexual activity.[89] What's more, for all groups of adolescents except black males, girls and boys alike suffer a loss of self-esteem after their first act of sexual intercourse, compared with those who remain virgins.[90] Two female high school freshmen confided, "Before the first time they do it, [some girls] are pumped up about it. After that," they added, "they feel degraded."

When it comes to teen girls and sex, low self-esteem may well have a chicken-and-egg aspect. Those with low self-esteem initially are more likely to experiment with sex; as a result, their self-esteem is further eroded. What's more, the problems that low self-esteem creates when it comes to girls' sexual decision making may continue to impact their sexual experiences. According to an ABC poll of teens aged thirteen through seventeen, girls with low self-esteem are three times more likely to do something sexual that they didn't want to do.[91] Certainly *that* doesn't result in an enhanced sense of self-worth, and so the vicious cycle continues.

Impairment of Future Relationships. Having sex as part of a teen relationship can result in a kind of ersatz intimacy. Young girls begin to believe that they're close to their male partners (and may even become emotionally dependent upon them)—although, in reality, they know very little about the things that matter most. That's a poor pattern for future relationships.

Indeed, becoming sexually active as part of an adolescent relationship (or no relationship at all) can make it difficult for young girls to form healthy relationships in later years. When sex is everywhere and boy–girl relationships are primarily or frequently sexual, girls have fewer opportunities to learn how to relate to boys outside the context of sex.

A history of loveless sex, relationships focused primarily on sex, or painful breakups after having sex inhibits young women from forming intimate relationships later on. They don't know how to trust males as romantic partners, how to communicate with them, and how to develop the emotional and mental resources that are the bulwark for healthy, lasting love matches—all valuable lessons more easily learned in teen dating relationships unburdened by the complications of sex.

The negative impact promiscuous teen sex has on the development of relationship skills may explain why nonvirgins with multiple sex partners hold less favorable attitudes toward marriage than virgins do.[92] Certainly animus toward marriage could drive the sexual activity among nonvirgins—but it's just as likely that those who have been involved in multiple sexual relationships have simply learned to fear or distrust the prospect of the long-term intimate relationship that marriage implies.

❧

Given the massive emotional costs of giving too much, too soon, it's no wonder that the ring of sexually active young girls in Rockdale County, Georgia, rarely spoke about sex in terms of being pleasurable. Rather, the adults who had interviewed them noted, the recollections were so painful that some girls couldn't even remember what they had done.[93]

It's important to help young women understand that they may be able to emerge from a host of early sexual relationships without an STD or unwanted pregnancy—but that's no guarantee they won't be emotionally scarred. Girls have an entire adult lifetime to have sex. Given all the emotional damage that can result, isn't it crazy not to wait until the time is right?

The Cost to America

Certainly, the physical, economic, and emotional toll that teen sex can take falls overwhelmingly on the young girls who engage in it. But as a country, America also pays a heavy price for tolerating a culture that not only condones, but often seems to celebrate, early sexual activity.

Sexually Transmitted Disease

One study estimated that the economic burden of the lifetime direct medical costs of eight sexually transmitted diseases acquired in 2000 by young people between fifteen and twenty-four would total a hefty $6.5 billion.[94] Among teens alone, a member of the General Accounting Office in 1997 estimated the cost of STDs to be $4.25 billion each year.[95] That's a hefty price to pay—in more ways than one.

Teen Childbearing

The public costs of teen childbearing are even greater.

A recent study concluded that adolescent childbearing—defined as births to teens seventeen or younger—cost taxpayers at least $8.6 billion in 2004 in additional public services and reduced tax revenues.[96] What's more, the estimated cumulative public costs of teen childbearing (including eighteen- and nineteen-year-olds) between 1991 and 2004 top out at a whopping $161 billion.[97] Those hefty figures represent the effects of early childbearing alone; the study accounted for other factors, including race, ethnicity, and socioeconomic class.[98]

Adolescent mothers are significantly more likely to have both children placed in foster care and reported cases of abuse or neglect than women who first give birth in their early twenties.[99] In fact, if mothers seventeen and under waited until their early twenties to give birth, yearly total costs for foster care, adoption, and other child welfare programs would decrease by $1.8 billion each year.[100] And because the teen sons of adolescent mothers are 2.2 times more likely to go to prison than sons of girls who delayed childbearing until their early twenties, adolescent motherhood likewise costs the taxpayers a minimum of $1.9 billion each year in added incarceration expenses.[101]

Welfare costs for adolescent mothers are likewise significant: Compared with women who have children in their early twenties, teen mothers receive more than $2 billion in extra cash assistance, $680 million in additional food stamp payments, and $800 million in additional housing help.[102] Researchers also noted that the United States incurs a significant loss of tax revenue because of the effect of adolescent childbearing on the work patterns of those who are fathering the children with the young mothers, estimating that lost revenue at $1.7 billion.[103] The lost tax revenue resulting from young mothers' lower educational attainment and earnings totals $2.3 billion.[104]

It's worth noting that the problems caused by adolescent childbearing also create a loss in national productivity, absorbing time, energy, and funds that might otherwise be directed elsewhere. Altogether, researchers had earlier calculated these indirect social costs of adolescent motherhood to total a minimum of nine billion dollars yearly with strictest statistical control for factors such as race, ethnicity, and socioeconomic class—but perhaps as much as twenty-one billion with a somewhat looser control of such factors.[105] Taken together, then, this suggests that the $8.6 billion in yearly direct costs of adolescent childbearing, coupled with the web of social problems that it entails, could actually be costing America much, much more.

Finally, even after controlling for a range of other factors, teen motherhood is an important predictor of problems for the next generation, thereby perpetuating a cycle of low expectations, low performance, and misery. When the offspring of young mothers reach adolescence and young adulthood, they are at added risk for a number of troubling behaviors, including fighting, truancy, and early sexual activity.[106] And the daughters of adolescent mothers are much more likely themselves to become mothers before turning eighteen than are the daughters of older mothers.[107]

❧

Ultimately, it's impossible to quantify the tragic social, human, and economic price that Americans pay when the cycle of young, unmarried motherhood, with its attendant social ills, continues. We are all the poorer for it—and not simply in economic terms.

When a young girl's life is limited, damaged, or destroyed—physically, emotionally, or economically—as a result of having given too much, too soon, it's not just a great defeat for everyone who believes that each young life begins with special and unique promise. It's also an enormous loss to America as a whole.

9

DO-ME FEMINISTS AND
DOOM-ME FEMINISM

*If you're a successful single woman in this city, you have two
choices: You can beat your head against the wall trying to
find a relationship, or you can say "screw it" and just go out
and have sex like a man.*

Candace Bushnell, *Sex and the City*

The Old Forms of Courtship

For those born during the 1960s or after, it's sometimes hard to
believe that male–female relationships were once ordered much
differently than they are today. In fact, a significant proportion
of traditional courtship rituals have become as antiquated as
hoop skirts and velocipedes.

But once upon a time, about a century ago, in a land *not* so
far away, young men actually initiated relationships with young
women under conditions that the females set. They had to woo
girls by presenting themselves at the women's houses, opening
themselves to rejection by either the girl herself or by her family.

At least in theory, it was a man's responsibility to prove that he was worthy of a young woman's interest and affection.

By the 1930s and early 1940s, home-based courtship had been replaced by dating in public, where it was expected that a young man would actively seek out a young woman in advance for formal dates. In exchange for nothing more than the pleasure of her company, a boy would pay for dinner, dancing, or any other type of entertainment that he could afford. Popularity was defined by how many dates with how many members of the opposite sex a girl or boy had; the most socially successful dated a number of different people, while those less blessed contented themselves with a steady admirer or got by with no one at all.

After World War II, teens began marrying sooner. In fact, in 1959, almost half of brides were younger than nineteen.[1] Accordingly, dating began earlier, and going steady lost some of its earlier overtones of social undesirability. Even then, however, sexual mores remained fairly traditional, and premarital sex was almost universally condemned. It was only after the late 1960s and early 1970s, with the advent of the second wave of the women's liberation movement, that courtship as Americans had known it changed forever.

Women's "Liberation"

Today feminism[2] is prominently associated with an image of sexual liberation. But the link between promiscuity and women's rights is of relatively recent vintage, having come into being only in the wake of Betty Friedan's *The Feminine Mystique* in 1963.

The First Wave

The first wave of the women's rights movement in America was inaugurated by a women's rights convention in Seneca Falls, New York, in 1848. Elizabeth Cady Stanton and other women issued a

"Declaration of Sentiments," enumerating the grievances that its signatories asserted women had suffered at the hands of men.

But even as early feminists such as Susan B. Anthony and Elizabeth Cady Stanton offered a critique of marriage as it was practiced in the United States at the time, they were hardly champions of sexual promiscuity. In Article Nine of the "Declaration of Sentiments," Stanton wrote that men had "created a false public sentiment by giving to the world a different code of morals for men and women, by which the moral delinquencies which exclude women from society are not only tolerated, but deemed of little account in man." Even as Stanton denounced the injustice of a double standard, the crux of her objection rested less on the existence of moral standards than on their inequitable application between the sexes.

Women who advocated free love, such as anarchist Emma Goldman, were on the margins of first-wave feminism. After Victoria Woodhull proclaimed in 1871 that she was a "free lover," both Susan B. Anthony and Elizabeth Cady Stanton disavowed Woodhull and sought to disassociate her from their National Women's Suffrage Association. As Harvard Law professor Mary Ann Glendon has pointed out, the most prominent early feminists believed that free love (along with abortion and easy divorce) were nothing short of disastrous for women and children alike.[3]

The Second Wave

In contrast with the aim of the early women's rights movement, which focused primarily on obtaining political equality and redressing the most obvious gender-based inequities embedded in American law, the second wave of feminism was infinitely more ambitious. Not only did it push identical treatment for both sexes under the law, it likewise aspired fundamentally to change women's place in society.

"Women need men like fish need a bicycle," a famous 1970 quote attributed to it-girl feminist Gloria Steinem insisted. Along with exhorting women to seek jobs and fill roles that had traditionally been reserved for men, the second-wave feminists often devalued the unpaid work of mothers and wives, and encouraged women to renounce conventional romantic and family arrangements in ways that frequently seemed overtly hostile toward men.

One of the traditional female roles most emphatically rejected by second-wave feminists was a women's responsibility to serve as a sexual gatekeeper. Many feminists believed that any arrangement that made women accountable for restraining their sexual impulses (and men's, too) represented an unfair and sexist burden. Female sexual purity, they argued, had nothing to do with virtue—and wasn't so much about an effort on the part of men to protect women as it was a patriarchal attempt to stifle and control them and their sexuality.

As recently as 2005, left-leaning columnist Diane Glass expressed a typical second-wave feminist view toward sex when she wrote in *The Atlanta Journal-Constitution*: "Although the Christian modesty movement is the more subtle of female controls, it is still a romanticized form of control that persuades Christian women to take small pleasure in being lifelong babysitters to feeble-minded men . . . The modesty movement may seem like a wholesome trend, but it is probably one of the oldest forms of female control."[4]

In short, during feminism's second wave, chastity became almost as stigmatized as promiscuity had been in an earlier age, as writers like Erica Jong celebrated the "zipless" casual sexual encounter. Even though engaging in heterosexual sex could have been considered, in some sense, to be sleeping with the enemy, women who declined to engage in spontaneous sex were understood to be complicit in their own victimization by a control-hungry, male-dominated establishment. They had, their more "liberated" sisters insisted, adopted the false, sexist consciousness of their oppressors.

The Third Wave

With female chastity redefined by many second-wave feminists as an artificial social construct that had been foisted upon them by domineering and insecure men, it's hardly surprising that the idea of "free love"—antithetical to the original feminist thought of Stanton and Anthony—became an important part of the second wave of women's liberation. But along with all the "free love" came disquieting questions for at least some feminists. Noting that pornography was becoming increasingly mainstream with movies like *Deep Throat* and its successors, many of them pointed out that pornography was degrading to women in its content, and exploitative in its production.

Throughout the 1980s, prominent radical feminists such as Catharine MacKinnon and Andrea Dworkin campaigned against pornography in particular and, it seemed to many, against men in general. Thus, by the 1990s, some younger women had begun to see feminism as a puritanical theory that was fundamentally hostile both to males and to heterosexual sexual pleasure. It seemed that one couldn't be a committed feminist and still retain the prerogative to enjoy the traditional female indulgences—flattering male attention, sexual fulfillment with a man, and flirty, fun clothes—that the second wave seemed implicitly to denounce. This presented a problem for young, good-looking women who wanted to have their cake and eat it, too.

Accordingly, in the 1990s, a third wave of feminists redefined feminism's relationship to heterosexual sex, creating the phenomenon of what's been variously called "do-me feminism,"[5] "Ally McBeal feminism"[6] (after the lead character in the hugely successful 1990s television program *Ally McBeal*), "thong feminism,"[7] or "lipstick" or "girlie" feminism.[8] Its proponents insisted that women were entitled to be as sexually aggressive as their male counterparts, and that true empowerment consisted in their doing so. "Liberation" meant developing the capacity to separate sex from emotion in stereotypically male fashion.

Perhaps the earliest icon of the early do-me feminists was Madonna, extolled in a 1991 *New York Times* feature as "the most influential feminist of the day," for whom "feminism means the freedom to be sexy as well as sexual."[9] The feature noted a "feminist subtext" to a music video that included images of Madonna chained to a bed, and approvingly characterized her assertion that she'd chained herself instead of having a man chain her as "a distinction that any honest feminist would respect."[10]

More conventional feminists embraced Madonna's example. Third-wave poster girl Naomi Wolf fantasized about "wanting to be surrounded by adoring, nubile seventeen-year-old soccer players who long to do [her] every bidding," while novelist Mary Gaitskill insisted that "the pleasure of sexual violence is not something only men like" and writer Rene Denfeld asserted than she found *Penthouse* less offensive than *Little House on the Prairie.*[11] In her 1997 book *Promiscuities,* marketed as "a call to women of all ages to reclaim and celebrate their sexuality,"[12] Wolf likewise bemoaned the lack of healthy outlets for girls' sexual desires.

In a sense, the Clinton–Lewinsky affair simply reinforced the third-wave template glorifying women's sexual power. Many 1990s feminists used White House intern Monica Lewinsky's thong-snapping pursuit of Bill Clinton as a way to mitigate Clinton's guilt:[13] *She* was, in fact, the one in control! As the wife of one Clinton supporter asked, "When a woman is giving a man a blow job, who's in the position of power?"[14] Likewise, in a piece posted on Feminist.com, the author of advice column

"Ask Amy" accused a reader critical of pro-Clinton feminists of "underestimating the ability of Monica Lewinsky to decide for herself whether or not to have a sexual encounter with the President" and asserted, "My take is that both Monica and the President did decide for themselves."[15] For some, that was apparently all that mattered.

From its inception, much of third-wave feminism derided the concepts of chastity and self-restraint as relics of a less enlightened age, and glorified aggressive sexual behavior as a key source of female power, so long as the woman was "in control." Significantly, being in control was understood in stereotypically male terms as pursuing sexual pleasure unburdened by the constraints of commitment or emotion.

Do-Me Feminism Today

It didn't take long for do-me feminism, equating aggressive sexuality with empowerment, to trickle from the pages of *The New York Times* and the pens of elite feminists into the popular culture. If Madonna was an icon of do-me feminism in the late 1980s and early 1990s, its avatars in the late 1990s and beyond were the four protagonists of the popular HBO series *Sex and the City*. The program focused on four affluent, professional thirty-something young women living in Manhattan, reveling in a variety of sexual partners, and discussing their sexual experiences in graphic detail along the way. In fact, in the program's pilot episode, one main character resolved to begin having sex "like a man"—that is, without any feeling. Until the final season of the entire six-year run of the series, they pursued this course—with only an occasional digression into a relationship and, for one, a sexless marriage—while extravagantly indulging stereotypically feminine interests in flirting, fashion, shoes, and makeup.

Notably, *Sex and the City* made it clear that its four heroines were in control of their own sexuality (even as they stifled heartache along the way)—with the least sexually inhibited member of the foursome consistently presented as the most daring, courageous, and empowered. Showcasing heroines who shared the dual obsessions of sex and fashion, *Sex and the City* represented the apotheosis of do-me feminism and served as the model for what many young girls would consider today's sexually empowered feminist ideal.

But although it may have been groundbreaking in some ways, *Sex and the City* is far from unique in its message—in pop culture generally, it's become conventional wisdom that men and women are essentially the same when it comes to their sexual needs and desires. What's more, we're told, it's entirely possible, even desirable, for women to decouple sex from emotion, just as men do.

This principle has been reflected in everything from a popular Diet Coke ad featuring female office staff ogling a male construction worker to the *Girls Gone Wild* videos, complete with images of drunk college girls on spring break, tearing off their bikini tops for the television cameras on the beach. In 2005, the Washington State affiliate of NARAL Pro-Choice America (formerly the National Abortion Rights Action League) even promoted a "Screw Abstinence" party to professional men and women alike, with the exhortation to "Throw your hands up and say it loud: 'Screw Abstinence!'"[16]

Likewise, in 2006, *Jane*, a magazine aimed at women in their twenties and younger, featured a blog devoted entirely to the sad fate of an attractive single woman named Sarah who, tragically, was *still a virgin* at twenty-nine! Readers were encouraged to check the blog to track Sarah's progress toward finding a man with whom to have sex before her thirtieth birthday. Not only is a young woman's sexual status not a private matter, but ensuring that she has the opportunity to sleep around has apparently become something of a public concern. In an age of do-me feminism, to be fully liberated is to be as happily promiscuous as the most swinging bachelor.

What's worrisome is that the new messages about sexual empowerment are finding their way to younger and younger girls.

The New Sexual Aggressors

The concept of sexual liberation as a feminist statement popularized by Sex and the City has had an enormous impact on young girls. Interviewing a Manhattan psychologist, a piece in The New York Times discussed the phenomenon of the "macho girl" and noted, "[I]t is as if the habits of 'Sex and the City'–style dating have trickled down to teenagers: think of Samantha [the series' most sexually aggressive character] at 14, not at 40."[17]

In a New York Health Department study of smoking focusing on girls aged thirteen through eighteen at a New York private school, virtually all of them reported that the program, featuring a smoking heroine, had influenced them.[18] Given that smoking plays only the most incidental role in Sex and the City, it's likely that its messages about sex are even more powerful. Even popular teen star Lindsay Lohan has reported that Sex and the City inspired her "dating philosophy"—although she was only twelve when the program debuted.[19]

Not surprisingly in an era where overt displays of female sexuality are equated with empowerment, even younger girls have adopted the persona of sexual aggressors. Openly seductive behavior and double entendres are standard and routinely observable at malls and movie theaters throughout America. In one instance, a scantily clad girl of about fifteen, flirting with a boy she had run into at a suburban Los Angeles fast-food restaurant, thrust her chest forward and asked playfully, "Want some?" A moment later, she proffered a sip of her drink, as if that had been the subject of the come-on.[20] Another evening, a different young girl, accepting a cup of ice at a cinema concession stand, announced to male companions, "I love to suck." After a pregnant pause (no pun intended), she added, "On ice."[21]

Evidence of the trend is both anecdotal and statistical. A piece in the July 16, 2000, edition of *The Washington Post Magazine* documented "a trend of girls who openly pursue sex, brag about sex, lie about sex, boldly offer themselves as sexual objects."[22] And others have noticed that girls are "catcalling after guys, groping them in hallways, sitting on their laps and even propositioning them for sex."[23] Nor are written propositions uncommon.[24] A teacher in San Jacinto, California, reported that some girls call their male classmates at home to describe what sexual favors they'd provide.[25] Emily Limbaugh, coordinator of the Best Choice character and sex education program in St. Louis, notes that "When it comes to sex, girls are more aggressive than I've ever seen them before. It's almost like we're teaching them to behave like men, and it's sad."[26]

Dr. Adria O'Donnell believes some of the aggression is a coping mechanism. She notes, "You get classified as to whether you're a virgin or not. [Girls] feel pressure. What the girls do nowadays—instead of being nervous—they decide to be an aggressor. [They think] 'If I give it up, then I'm in control—nothing's being taken from me.' "

In fact, a 2004 survey of teen boys and girls sponsored by the National Campaign to Prevent Teen Pregnancy revealed that 57 percent of teen boys and 51 percent of teen girls felt that girls were as sexually aggressive as boys.[27] The December 2002 SexSmarts survey sponsored jointly by the Kaiser Family Foundation and *Seventeen* magazine found that 54 percent of girls (and the same percentage of boys) responded that "boys lose their girlfriends because they won't have sex" either "a lot" or "sometimes."[28] In other words, sexual pressure now runs both ways.

According to the most recent Youth Risk Behavior Surveillance study, more white female high school students had been sexually active in the three months preceding the survey than their male counterparts (33.1 versus 28.5 percent).[29] In the 2002 National Survey of Family Growth, for the first time since 1973, when the study began,[30] more girls (47 percent) than boys (46 percent) reported having sex.[31]

Another study noted the significant rise over time in parental approval for girls calling boys[32]—a behavior once deemed unacceptably forward because it suggested an element of female sexual aggression. Likewise, behavior that signals girls' receptiveness to spontaneous sexual activity is widely condoned. A survey of fifteen- through seventeen-year-old girls found that 79 percent believed that if a girl carries a condom with her, she looks "prepared"; 64 percent believed that it made her look "responsible."[33]

To the extent that girls have learned to ape boys' sexual aggressiveness, it's been as a result of cultural pressures rather than biological imperatives. After all, young women are much less fixated on sex in general than young men—males in their twenties think about sex every fifty-two seconds,[34] and their sex drives are considerably stronger, in general, than those of their female counterparts. Between nine and fifteen, boys' levels of testosterone (the hormone that engenders both lust and aggression) increase twenty-five-fold, while girls experience a meager five-fold increase.[35]

Clearly, do-me feminists have worked hard to dismantle the social conventions and sexual morality that have traditionally informed relationships between the sexes. As author and essayist Caitlin Flanagan has pointed out, the goals of contemporary American feminism have been "to encourage girls not to be shackled by the double standard and to abandon modesty as a goal, to erode patriarchal notions of how men ought to treat women, and to champion aggressiveness in girls."[36]

The question that's worth asking, however, is whether all the girls who have been "liberated" are really more powerful, or freer, or happier in this brave new world of female sexual aggression. When much of the media sends a message that a young girl's primary objective should be to elicit lustful reactions from men, is that really empowerment? When young girls are offering blow jobs to their male classmates in school bathrooms, gyms, and parking lots, is that really liberation?

A Longing for Times Past?

The cultural climate fostered by do-me feminism is reflected in the attitudes even of those who might be expected to know better. In a 2000 piece titled "The Face of Teenage Sex Grows Younger,"[37] focusing on the burgeoning oral sex practices of middle and high school students, a *New York Times* reporter quoted the director of the Wellesley College Center for Research on Women, who complained that "when it comes to oral sex, 'the boys are getting it, the girls no. It's the heterosexual script that entitles boys and disables girls.'" In other words, the problem with sexual activity among young boys and girls was not the fact that it was happening among middle schoolers, but rather the gender-based disparity in the amount of oral sex being practiced!

In such a world, it's not surprising that many young girls experience a sense of nostalgia for a more conventional style of courtship—in fact, that longing may underlie the recent upsurge in popularity of movies based on Jane Austen books. In Austen's Regency world, whatever the manifold disadvantages women confronted, there were prescribed rituals and courtesies that accompanied the dance of courtship, and everyone knew what was expected of her—or him.

Today, in contrast, young girls must navigate the complicated world of male–female relationships armed with little more than a mandate *not* to conform to traditional gender roles. As a result, on a typical Friday night at a California cineplex, it's the girls—dressed in body-baring fashions—who approach the boys, presenting themselves and signaling their availability through seductive gestures, flirtatious conversation, or even the initiation of physical contact. For their part, the boys sit back, look the girls over, and accept their advances with the practiced nonchalance of those accustomed to being sought out. Now it's the girls who risk humiliation and rejection by pursuing boys, and boys who exercise the power of choice that once belonged to their female counterparts.

This dynamic may explain why dating is virtually dead in the teen world. Planned one-on-one outings are now extremely rare; groups of girls and boys generally go out together, with each individual paying his or her own way. "Dates?" one lively, attractive high school senior asked. "Today, you just call a guy and kind of figure out where to meet. That other way must have been fun."[38] In today's landscape, girls and boys simply hang out and, perhaps, hook up—more than 60 percent of sexually active teens have had sex with someone they are not dating.[39] Accordingly, it's not necessary for boys to submit to the inconvenience of calling a particular girl and then committing to a day, time, and activity. The girls will be around (and available) and the boys know it.

It's worth asking whether the new arrangements are really superior to the dating conventions of yesteryear. Certainly girls have gained the ability to exercise the power of choice that traditionally was a boy's—but what, exactly, does she have the ability to choose? Which boy she's going to approach and desperately hopes to please? And even if a boy does, in fact, decide he "likes" her, what, exactly, does that mean? That he's willing to "hang out" with her? Or that he'll "hook up" with her?

In any case, once the hanging out or hooking up has taken place, it still falls to the girl and her friends to sort out what the entire interaction meant. Then she can wonder whether it's too much for her to call him, or she can just wait by the phone. Especially in the latter case, little seems to have changed since the fifties[40]—except, of course, that many girls have already said yes before the phone has ever rung.

Although it's noteworthy that the overwhelming majority of the effort to attract and please the opposite sex is coming from the girls, it's hardly surprising. As one seventeen-year-old boy told researchers, he was having sex in the context of a nondating arrangement with a female friend whom he simply didn't consider "girlfriend material."[41] Well, from his perspective, why not? With girls offering no-strings sex, why would boys invest any effort at all to court or please a young woman—or to commit to a relationship with her in even the smallest way?

When females vied for male attention in an earlier era, social success was defined by how much a particular girl could inspire a boy to pursue, woo, and do for her. Now girls compete for boys' attention on the basis of how much they, the girls, are willing to do for the boys, sexually and otherwise. What this dynamic means, as girls themselves have pointed out, is that the boys call the shots more than ever. Even boys who are involved in relationships are more frequently tempted to cheat, simply because of the sheer profusion of sexual offers they receive from a variety of girls.[42] Ironically, the new sexual landscape has resulted in a competition that is profoundly anti-feminist—and every (not-so-nice) man's dream.

Girls have certainly been told that they're now in control when it comes to their sexual relationships. But what they may not realize is that when it comes to uncommitted sex, with the attendant risks of heartbreak, pregnancy, and sexually transmitted disease, control is ultimately nothing more than an illusion.

What a Girl Wants

In a do-me feminist's perfect world, young women would be more like young men. A girl would be out doing her own thing with a posse of female friends, free to satisfy her sexual desires on her own terms. But it's hardly a revelation that this pipe dream doesn't comport with reality.

Whether the do-me feminists like it or not, girls and boys are different when it comes to their attitudes toward love and sex. Girls care more than boys about forming opposite-sex relationships that involve emotion and commitment. Boys, by contrast, care more than girls about sexual variety without commitment.[43] What's more, males in general are simply more focused on sex. A 1994 study from the University of Chicago found that 54 percent of men admitted they think about sex every day—or several times a day—compared with the 67 percent of women who think about it only a few times weekly or monthly.[44] In fact, on average, men have ten to one hundred times more testosterone (the lust hormone) than women.[45]

The old cliché that "men give love to get sex; women give sex to get love" was only reinforced by a 1994 study of teenage sexuality in an inner-city community. The author noted that the girls dreamed of being carried off by a Prince Charming who would love and provide for them, while the boys wanted to play a game where "sex is the prize."[46] As long as girls are innately more invested in relationships and emotions than boys are, they will be at a grave disadvantage in a sexual landscape where optional, emotion-free sex is deemed the ultimate in "coolness" and liberation—and often is the norm.

Loveline host Dr. Drew Pinsky reports how dramatically the responses of males and females differ when he speaks to college students about hooking up.[47] After being asked why they must be "loaded" (drunk) in order to hook up, the boys tell him, "I get loaded because it [easy sex] is out there, I want to do it, I got to do it, but it's hard to run the risk of being rejected."[48] In contrast, the women confide, "I get loaded just to tolerate this."[49]

The hookup culture makes it difficult for girls to get what they want most—and, sadly, many young women are reluctant even to admit what they're really seeking. In fact, many girls hook up with boys in the hope that physical intimacy will jump-start a real relationship.[50] When he asks the college students to describe the kind of social landscape they wish they had, Dr. Drew notes that the girls will answer only after significant hesitation. "They're embarrassed," he observes, "to say what they really want. They're ashamed." Finally, he reports, "a girl will say, 'Well, I just kind of wish someone would sit down and listen to me or talk to me.' The guys are like, 'What? What does *that* do?'"[51]

Ironically, the strictures of do-me feminism have made it more difficult for girls to find the attention, affection, and connection they want, even as it's become harder for them to refuse what many hormone-driven boys really want—sexual activity. By offering their bodies so quickly and so easily, girls have essentially surrendered their most effective means for securing the kind of male companionship that they most desire.

Dr. Adria O'Donnell observes, "All my girls say they loved the cuddling after [sexual activity]. It's sad because they're just lying or sitting there, and they're just being used for pleasure."

. . . And the Sex Isn't Even That Great

Even the sex young girls are having isn't likely to be that pleasurable—for them, at least. Dr. O'Donnell says that she tells young women, "Sex will not be fun for you. Sex will be fun for the boys." She notes, "Boys at this age have orgasms and girls at this age don't. Girls do not physically enjoy sex," she adds. "Girls' bodies aren't ready for sex. Their hips are small, so it's uncomfortable and the boys don't know what they're doing."

In fact, the circumstances most conducive to female sexual arousal and satisfaction are hard to come by in the impersonal, sex-act-driven landscape of the hookup culture. As Pfizer learned when it tried to create the female equivalent of Viagra, female sexuality isn't as much of a biological as it is a mental matter,[52] and an emotional one.

Fear and stress, for example, inhibit women from reaching orgasm.[53] Obviously, it's much easier for a girl or woman to be comfortable and relaxed with a trusted partner who cares about her as an individual, not primarily as a sex object—and is therefore interested in enhancing her sexual satisfaction, rather than being exclusively focused on his own. Such partners are found not in quick, furtive hookups or meaningless one-night stands, but in the context of a committed relationship like marriage.

Even common sense suggests that it's more difficult for a female to overcome orgasm-defeating fear and stress if she is having sex with a relative stranger; she confronts a potential threat of harm both physically, simply by virtue of a male's superior strength, and emotionally, as she risks rejection in the most intimate of contexts. Indeed, the trust factor may be why women in monogamous relationships enjoy vastly superior sex lives than the "liberated" girls who are engaging in sexual activity with a variety of males.[54]

The differences between men and women when it comes to sex—and the centrality of the heart and mind to female sexuality—manifest themselves in a variety of other ways. For example, women are sexually aroused by dramatically different stimuli than men are. As part of their sexual fantasies, women tend to think about a current romantic partner and are more likely to focus on his personal and emotional characteristics.[55] Their sexual triggers are more internally focused; they tend to concentrate on specific men that they care about or on romantic situations—both hard to come by in the context of a hookup.

In contrast, male sexual fantasies often center on physical characteristics and people with whom they are not involved.[56] Unlike women's more mental or emotional approach, men are frequently and readily stimulated by external factors: a woman in a provocative outfit, a titillating billboard—really, at times, almost anything female-related will do.

As Dr. Drew Pinsky puts it, "Women have drive activation—their sexual center—from intimate conversation, not from visual arousal. But men are visually aroused. Drive and arousal are connected in men; they're disconnected in women. [With women] you can have arousal and no drive; men drive immediately from arousal. Always. Always."[57]

Girls who wear sexy clothes to school and then assert that it's the boys' problem if they're distracted by the attire simply don't understand this fundamental difference between male and female sexuality.[58] Girls make a similar mistake when they buy into the idea that a boy is paying them a great compliment by hooking up with them. They mistakenly attribute to their male counterparts the mental and/or emotional judgments that precede their own decisions to engage in sexual activity, not understanding that—for a boy who's sexually aroused—almost any willing girl is good enough.

What signifies that a particular girl is special to a boy? Not simply a desire to have sex with her—for every teenage boy, awash in testosterone, there are *plenty* of girls who fall into that particular category. If a girl truly matters to him, a boy will want something more than just sex from her—he'll be interested in pursuing a real relationship. He'll be willing to invest time and emotional energy, without a girl having to "reward" him by engaging in sexual activity that isn't even likely to be all that pleasurable for her.

The Subtle Power of Virginity

It's worth asking: As a result of the much-vaunted freedoms that have sprung from the sexual revolution, are America's young girls really living happier, more wholesome lives? Are their thoughts, conversations, activities, and preoccupations more elevated? Are they healthier in body, mind, and spirit?

What's increasingly clear is that the advent of do-me feminism has undermined the quality of the interactions between young men and women. In *The Washington Post,* discussing a friend who hooked up with a boy she'd known for some time, a college girl noted, "She wants the guy to know she's using him as much as he's using her."[59] That, apparently, is what passes for a relationship in the do-me feminist culture.

For young girls, at least, there's only one way out of this sordid competition focusing on who's using whom for what: virginity. Contrary to the assertions of the jaded and the cynical who would claim it's nothing more than a power play by the frigid or manipulative, virginity actually represents an expression of respect for the awesome power of sexual passion—and a manifestation of fidelity to something higher than momentary desires. It is, as essayist Sarah E. Hinlicky has written, "a sexuality dedicated to hope, to the future, to marital love, to children, and to God."[60]

It's also an expression of self-respect. Girls who refuse to play the hookup game are asserting that they deserve something better than sexual fumbling either with boys who want them for nothing but their bodies, or with those who may claim to care about them—but not necessarily enough to commit to a formal relationship such as marriage (or to promise marriage should an unexpected pregnancy result). Being a virgin means being truly in control of oneself: body, heart, and soul. It's a way of determining which boys care about a girl for herself, rather than simply for her body. And although it's no guarantee against heartbreak, virginity *does* ensure that a girl will never know the bitter regret of having given part of herself to someone who was unworthy of the gift.

What's more, sexual self-restraint is also often a necessary condition for maintaining one's own self-respect. In fact, even some of the most sexually adventurous women apparently believe that "the number of guys they've had sex with . . . really does count"—and some will make up silly excuses ("it doesn't count if he might be gay") to avoid adding additional names to their list of past sexual partners if the total exceeds what they deem to be an acceptable number.[61]

Paradoxically, chastity also helps preserve the respect of men later in life. Although many males are perfectly willing to seek out sexually available girls for a good time, they often likewise believe that—as one successful documentary producer put it— "Those girls are fine until it's time to get married."[62] Even "liberated" women can find it difficult to confide an extensive sexual history to the men they eventually wed; even "liberated" men rarely welcome the news that their fiancées bring with them considerable sexual experience.

In fact, exercising the self-control implicit in virginity represents girls' best chance to find the loving, committed relationships that most dream of, not only during their teen years, but for a lifetime. As Leon Kass noted, "It is a woman's refusal of sexual importunings, coupled with hints or promises of later gratification, that is generally a necessary condition of transforming a man's lust into love."[63] Sex therapist Ian Kerner makes essentially the same point in his book *Be Honest—You're Not That into Him, Either.*[64]

A girl may try to train herself to enjoy sex without love, but biology and her own nature set her up for heartache and failure. If she offers sex in the hope of finding true love, ironically, she diminishes the chances of finding and keeping the love she's seeking. Virginity is the only foolproof way of truly escaping the catch-22 of do-me feminism.

Toward a New Sexual Feminism

Many of the feminists who have been exquisitely sensitive to the impact of traditional social pressures on young girls' behavior, aspirations, and self-esteem seem curiously impervious to the pernicious impact of the new sexual norms they have championed.

Certainly, the glorification of female sexual aggressiveness has made remaining a virgin more difficult than ever. Determined and constant devaluation of sexual innocence, so evident in almost every part of American culture, has deprived chaste girls of the social esteem that they once enjoyed. In an ironic inversion of the laws of the market, chastity is the one good that becomes less valuable with scarcity—at least during the teen years, when the prospect of marriage isn't even part of the equation.

That's because, when a variety of young girls are offering sexual activity to young boys, it becomes much more difficult for chaste girls to compete for male attention, much less to secure it for a period substantial enough for real relationships to grow. And when male attention can't be secured without it, sexiness begins to assume exaggerated importance—becoming nothing short of a female imperative. The logical culmination of such an obsession extends far beyond young girls propositioning their male classmates to bizarre manifestations of sexual desperation by females of all ages—like the older women enduring optional cosmetic surgery to enhance the appearance of their private parts.[65] Do-me feminism hasn't prevented women from being treated like sex objects—it just means that women themselves are doing the objectifying.

In fact, the do-me model of promiscuous, commitment-phobic sexuality has done nothing to make girls more truly independent of men or heedless of male opinion. Despite all its promises, do-me feminism has delivered nothing—not even the likelihood of real sexual pleasure. After years of liberated sexuality, empowered women are left more vulnerable than ever before. They confront the twin risks of sexually transmitted disease and unwanted pregnancy—as well as the prospect of a future spent alone, because it's become increasingly unnecessary for men to promise a lifetime of fidelity in order to have the privilege of depositing his genetic inheritance with a willing woman.

For their part, rather than being taught to value those who decline to engage in easy sex, boys are simply learning to avoid them; it's easier to seek out the girls who will meet their sexual needs while asking nothing in return. Over time, of course, such behavior breeds in men a lack of respect for women in general, and for their unique emotional and sexual needs in particular. Ultimately, it results in a selfish disregard—even contempt—for women, which erodes the chivalric impulses that have long been the hallmark of civilized societies. It's not just the characters, morals, and behavior of girls that do-me feminism has degraded.

In the name of all women, the do-me feminists demanded equal sexual power—and many men granted that request, all too willingly. Perhaps that's because the feminists, secure in their conviction that men and women are essentially the same, adopted a quintessentially male definition of what constitutes sexual "liberation"; as Dr. Drew Pinsky notes, "[Women] are coopting the system presented by men and taking it on as their own." English actress Dame Edith Evans once asked, "When a woman behaves like a man, why doesn't she behave like a nice man?" Indeed, the hookup culture's emphasis on the freedom to engage in commitment- and relationship-free sex adopts and glorifies the worst stereotypes of male sexual behavior.

In truth, although they are—and should be—considered equal before the law and in the eyes of the culture, men and women simply aren't the same. Instead of limiting their notion of equality to the insistence that girls have the prerogative to behave like boys when it comes to sex, feminists should be encouraging women to assert their right to demand that sex occur only in the context of loving, committed relationships with men who cherish them. Women have distinct preferences and desires when it comes to their hopes for intimate relationships—and a feminism more respectful of and true to their deepest longings would encourage women to develop a sexual ethic that meets *their* needs as well as men's.

Women's aspirations and longings cannot ultimately be ignored or denied, as even the creators of the do-me feminist fairy tale *Sex and the City* were ultimately forced to acknowledge. After six years of glorifying casual sex, the series concluded with what its legions of female fans would have considered the only truly happy ending. Of the four protagonists, two ended up happily married; a third was headed for the altar with the man of her dreams, and the last (and most promiscuous) finally found sexual and emotional contentment in the first stable, monogamous, and long-term relationship she had ever known.

Through their insistence on male-style sexual liberation, the do-me feminists have deprived women of the most powerful influence they have ever exercised over men. Only when sexual restraint is once again as celebrated as female sexual promiscuity has become will women finally reclaim their true power—the power to hold men to standards of behavior that honor the differences between the sexes, even as it recognizes their intrinsic equality.

10

FROM LIBERTY TO LICENTIOUSNESS

Men are qualified for freedom in exact proportion to their disposition to put moral chains on their own appetites. Society cannot exist unless a controlling power on will and appetite be placed somewhere, and the less of it there is within, the more there is without. It is ordained in the eternal constitution of things that men of intemperate minds cannot be free.

Edmund Burke

It's impossible to understand how America became so sexualized without taking a look at the various cultural forces that have driven this phenomenon. Do-me feminism has, of course, played a significant role in the sexing up of America. But it alone isn't to blame. Four specific developments have played a particularly important role in creating a culture where sex is a constant in the lives of young girls.

An Emphasis on Sexual Self-Expression Over Sexual Self-Restraint

For years, Americans have been told that sexuality is at the very heart of one's identity, and that the right to sexual self-expression constitutes a core freedom. Perhaps one of the most famous expressions of this view came from Justice Anthony Kennedy, who in 2003 authored a Supreme Court opinion striking down Texas's homosexual sodomy law. Kennedy opined that the right to engage in the sexual acts of one's choosing "involves the liberty of the person both in its spatial and more transcendent dimensions," noting, "At the heart of liberty is the right to define one's own concept of existence, of meaning, of the universe, and of the mystery of human life."[1]

Such an emphasis on the importance of sexual self-expression is of relatively recent vintage. For many years, self-restraint in all areas was deemed the indispensable mark of a civilized person; the ability to refrain from what was generally understood to be immoral or socially unacceptable activity of all kinds was considered an essential component of personal rectitude. Nowhere was this truer than in the area of sex; indeed, the term *virtue* was long understood to refer to the chastity of a woman.[2]

But the traditional understanding of sex began to erode in the 1940s. Penicillin became available to treat sexually transmitted diseases, which had previously meant certain death or infertility. And in 1948, Alfred Kinsey issued his *Sexual Behavior in the Human Male,* which purported to demonstrate that extramarital sexual activity was far more common than anyone had previously suspected. What's more, Kinsey's supposedly scientific approach and studiously nonjudgmental reporting suggested that morality itself was irrelevant to sex. Although much of Kinsey's data (and methods) have subsequently been discredited, his ideas were tremendously influential.[3]

Kinsey's amoral approach to sex was perfectly suited to the emerging social consensus of the 1960s, when the importance of self-expression was elevated over that of self-restraint in many areas of American life. Nowhere was the new emphasis on self-expression more vigorously embraced than in the sexual arena.

One of the clearest examples of this cultural shift came in Justice William O. Douglas's concurrence to a 1966 Supreme Court opinion finding that the erotic book *Fanny Hill: Memoirs of a Woman of Pleasure* was not obscene.[4] Justice Douglas's concurrence consisted of a December 1965 sermon by the Reverend John R. Graham of the First Universalist Church of Denver. In it, the Reverend Graham argued that the novel detailing the adventures of a prostitute "represents a more significant view of morality" than did Dr. Norman Vincent Peale's book *Sin, Sex and Self-Control*. Graham insisted that the Peale book was the one that was truly immoral, as self-restraint is the enemy of love and self-expression. The sexual discipline Peale advocated was deemed stultifying, part of a world "where life is predetermined and animal-like," in contrast with the "growth, spontaneity and expression" that were supposedly at the heart of Fanny Hill's way of life.

Certainly, most Americans were hardly aware of this sermon. But the view it represented—equating sexual promiscuity with self-expression, and identifying both as the distinguishing features of a truly joyful, meaningful existence—quickly gained cultural currency.

Sexual license became a central theme of the counterculture and the peace movement—exemplified by celebrities including John Lennon and Yoko Ono, who posed nude together for their *Unfinished Music No. 1: Two Virgins* album cover and famously staged a "bed-in" (refusing to leave their bed) for peace. The Woodstock music festival of 1969 was an orgy of sex and "free love." The age-old fear of pregnancy was dispelled by the advent of the Pill—which meant that women could express themselves sexually without concern for the quality of their relationships or the character of their partners. Throughout the 1970s, "do your own thing" and "love the one you're with" applied in particular to sexual behavior, where hitherto forbidden forms of exploration flourished—and were publicly discussed in terms that would have been previously unimaginable.

Long after the counterculture's heyday, its values have lingered. None has been more celebrated than the emphasis on sexual self-expression, which is now deemed virtually synonymous with freedom and authenticity. In large part, the virtues of sexual self-discipline and self-restraint have come to be understood as the stigmata of conformity and social subjugation. Any kind of repression—particularly when it comes to sex—is assumed to be somewhat suspect, even bizarre. As Katie Couric noted, addressing her fellow baby boomers in a televised special on teens and sex, "We swore we wouldn't be as uptight about sex as our own parents were."[5]

Indeed, "uptightness" is despised by much of elite culture. A San Francisco columnist wrote in 2005, "[S]omeone should really do a national, once-and-for-all study to back up what everyone already knows—which is, of course, that the more repressed and sanctimonious and uptight you are about sex and love and gender and religion, the more likely you are to be involved in secret kink, in deep perversion, illegal perversion . . ."[6] To some, the advocates of sexual restraint aren't simply repressed, they're actually closeted perverts.

Certainly, the moral and sexual freedom permitted by the emphasis on self-expression over self-discipline has held enormous superficial appeal. But many of its outcomes are undesirable. When self-restraint becomes conflated with repression and regarded as an unqualified evil, it becomes difficult to make a principled argument against girls "expressing themselves" through highly sexualized dress, reading choices, or behaviors, however inappropriate they might be. The end result is plenty of young people who feel justified in indulging their impulses, sexual and otherwise, without restraint—often with unfortunate consequences both for them personally and for society as a whole.

The Privatization of Religion and Sexual Morality

Early American laws forbade a wide range of consensual sexual behaviors, including sex outside of marriage, adultery, and prostitution.[7] And although those laws could be justified on secular social welfare grounds, the behavior they mandated was also reinforced by the Judeo-Christian religious heritage of early American society. In fact, the Founding Fathers welcomed the influence of religious belief, deeming it an essential influence on public morals and realizing that in a free society, where government doesn't regulate every aspect of citizens' lives, religion served as an important check on personal behavior. And though they understood the Constitution to forbid establishment of a particular, sectarian national religion, they did not believe that it required the government to separate itself from religion altogether.

In recent decades, however, the Supreme Court has reinterpreted the role of religion in American life, gradually excluding it from the public square. That's why even voluntary prayers are no longer allowed at high school graduations, and public displays at Christmastime must include Santa and his reindeer, along with the Baby Jesus, in order to be legal. Indeed, by 1994, Justice Sandra Day O'Connor was alluding to "a principle at the heart of the establishment clause, that government should not prefer one religion to another, *or religion to non-religion*"[8] (emphasis added). Agnosticism became the official position of a government that had inscribed IN GOD WE TRUST on its national currency in 1864, and then inserted the phrase *under God* into the Pledge of Allegiance ninety years later.

Even in a country where 80 to 90 percent of Americans answer affirmatively when asked if they, personally, believe in God,[9] the reinterpretation of the role of religion in American life has done a great deal to undermine traditional notions of sexual morality. Like the Founding Fathers, ardent secularists seem to believe that morality is inextricably intertwined with religion, at least when it comes to sex.[10] But because the government must be neutral about religious belief, they maintain, it therefore must remain neutral about sexual behavior.

One striking example of this phenomenon occurred in the spring of 2005, and focused on the 4Parents.gov Web site created by the Department of Health and Human Services, devoted to advising parents about how to talk to their children about sex. Because the site observed that "Abstinence is the healthiest choice for teens," groups including the ACLU, the Sexuality Information and Education Council, the National Education Association, and more than a hundred others demanded that it be taken down. They objected to the government "dictating values," as the Associated Press put it.[11]

Common sense confirms that Web site's assertion is, in fact, true even from a secular, scientific viewpoint—abstinence eliminates the possibility of AIDS, sexually transmitted diseases, unwanted pregnancies, and abortions. And it's doubtful that any critics would have condemned a government site informing parents that abstinence from smoking is the "healthiest choice." But when it comes to sex, "values" are equated with morality, and morality with religion. As a result, any governmental call for sexual restraint is deemed suspect, a constitutionally impermissible effort to establish religion.

Certainly, these perceived constraints on government technically do nothing to prevent nongovernmental entities or individual Americans from talking about sexual morality. But over time, the systematic elimination of religion from public life creates an impression that religion isn't just something impermissible for government to weigh in on—it's inappropriate for public discussion generally. As writer Rod Dreher has put it, "a believer may keep his or her quaint devotions, but is expected to have the decency to keep them in the closet."[12] When religion becomes something that can be discussed only in private, the ideas, opinions, and behaviors that are associated with it, such as chastity, will be increasingly perceived as marginal, too—something people may believe or act on privately, but have no right to say in public.

In American culture today, people of faith who break this unspoken rule are often treated with remarkable suspicion and contempt. In a 2005 *Rolling Stone* article cutely titled "The Young & the Sexless," Jeff Sharlet wrote that "Chastity is a new organizing principle of the Christian right, built on the notion that virgins are among God's last loyal defenders";[13] on his Web site, Sharlet opined that for Christian conservatives, "Pre-marital sex is the new communism, the new 'evil empire.'"[14] In other words, they are nothing more than religious freaks, fixated on what, in his view, is nothing more than paranoiac obsession.

Fictional portrayals likewise advance a stereotype that religiously observant advocates of chastity are repressed, sanctimonious religious zealots. A subplot of the popular drama *The West Wing* featured President Bartlett (Martin Sheen) berating a guest in the White House, a female radio talk-show host who had spoken out against homosexual behavior based on the tenets of her religion. He ends his tirade by condemning her as a member of "the Ignorant Tight-Ass Club."[15] Similarly, in the short-lived television series *The Book of Daniel,* the retired Episcopal bishop identified as an adherent of traditional sexual morality was portrayed as stiff and repressed—and hypocritical, given that he himself was conducting an adulterous affair.

Even without stigmatizing outspoken advocates of chastity as zealots, those who support a more flexible sexual ethic deploy a powerful American tradition in their favor by identifying sexual restraint as an exclusively religious matter. Given this country's long-standing tradition of religious tolerance, equating chastity with religion decreases the likelihood that people will outspokenly advocate it. If the topic is deemed to be freighted with religious overtones, Americans will be reluctant to outspokenly advocate chastity as the best choice for young girls, in much the same way they would refrain from proselytizing.

The successful effort to characterize advocacy of sexual restraint as the illegitimate imposition of religious values on society has resulted in the effective self-censorship of many chastity advocates. And that's troubling—because reticence is fatal to any effort to influence public morality in favor of sexual restraint. To be effective, informal messages about socially acceptable and unacceptable behaviors must be driven home repeatedly and explicitly—as advocates of hybrid cars and smoking bans alike would attest.

Ultimately, the marginalization of religious faith in public debate and the identification of chastity as nothing but a religious issue have one result: The pro-sex messages directed at young girls go largely unchallenged. When a moral defense of chastity is deemed inappropriate for public debate, rebuttal is limited to a discussion of the adverse health or economic consequences of giving too much, too soon. And such arguments are woefully incomplete.

The Rise of Moral Relativism and
the Death of Shame

When sexual morality is equated with religion and, as a result, declared unfit for discussion in the public square, the consensus about sexual morality that a society has shared will eventually erode. In its place, a new ethic of moral relativism arises, in which the primary evil becomes exercising judgment about the behavior of others.

In fact, the multiculturalism trend of recent years has fueled the rise of moral relativism. The multicultural mantra insists that different people in different places and times create different cultures. In this view, all of us are malleable creatures who are nothing more than the product of the culture that has supposedly created us and our values. In this formulation, cultures may differ dramatically, but there's no objective criterion for deeming any one culture superior to another; each culture is deemed to have different ways and different truths that are entitled to equal respect.

That argument has been extended to American culture itself. If there are different truths for different people in different cultures, then certainly there might be different truths for different people within the same culture. And what's right for *you*, the argument goes, might not be right for *me*—and who are you to have an opinion on what I do anyway, sexually or otherwise?

That attitude has trickled down into the very foundations of moral reasoning among American girls. One seventh grader began to object to the very skimpy outfits worn by one of her classmates, and then quickly caught herself: "But after all, who am I to say anything? It's her outfit, and I'm not the one that's got to wear it," she insisted.[16] Similarly, the founder of a project dedicated to supporting self-esteem in girls defended girls' rights to wear thongs to school, asking "Whose business is it?" In her view, the girls were entitled to sport the thongs because, as the *Seattle Post-Intelligencer* put it, "They might make her feel beautiful and give her an inner sense of her own sexuality."[17]

The same kind of reasoning is evident in the girls' novel *The Virginity Club* by Kate Brian. The book centers on four girls competing for a generous scholarship that requires "purity of soul and body" of its recipient. At the novel's climax, one of the competitors informs the scholarship committee, "I don't think it's right for you guys to make us prove to you how pure we are . . . What we do in our personal lives, that's our business. And you know what? Our definitions of purity are our own business, too."[18] The scholarship committee, composed of teachers, agrees with her.[19]

Likewise, talking with teens about sex, Katie Couric challenged the one girl who had advocated abstinence education by citing the opinion of another teen that sex was "an individual decision."[20] Even the feeble efforts of the Motion Picture Association of America to set some standards for sex on the screen have been harshly criticized. In a *Los Angeles Times* review of a film challenging the movie ratings system (revealingly titled "Sitting in Judgment of Those Who Judge"), the reviewer sympathizes with "anyone who has ever felt bullied by the mythical 'average American parent,' whose prudery seems matched only by tolerance for gore . . . What [the film] ultimately reveals is what has come to stand for morality; a morality divested of all reason and humanity, speciously reduced literally to counting hip thrusts and obscenities."[21]

Implicitly, the reviewer echoes the morally relativist line; *her* sexual morality certainly isn't the morality of the "average American parent." And in fact, the idea that everyone has his or her own, individual sexual morality—which no one else is entitled to challenge—has contributed immeasurably to the sexualization of American culture.

It's also contributed to the death of the concept of sexual shame, which is nothing more than an inner recognition that one has violated established standards of propriety, good taste, and morals. That's because, in a world dominated by moral relativism, it's unnecessary to have any sexual standards, and impermissible to criticize another for failing to. Even as members of the cultural elite, such as *The New York Times*'s Frank Rich, hail the triumph of "candor" over "ignorance and shame in the national conversation about sex,"[22] it's worth remembering that a healthy sense of sexual shame in the proper circumstances is beneficial both for individuals and for society. It inhibits people from engaging in behavior that will be detrimental to them or to their future children—and thereby reduces the chance that the government will have to pick up the slack for those who simply can't afford to bear the consequences of their behavior.

Ultimately, moral relativism can survive only because Americans have come to see moral judgment as residing exclusively in the subjective realm of values, rather than in the objective realm of facts. But there are, indeed, moral facts—valid for all people in all times. They include such truths as "All men are created equal" or "Slavery is wicked." The truthfulness of moral facts is independent of the number of people who believe them; they're true always and everywhere regardless of popular opinion. And the domination of sexual morality by moral relativism can be combated only by widespread recognition of two profound truths: first, that moral facts do exist—and second, that "sexual behavior that degrades girls is wrong" is one of them.

The Advent of the "Cool Mom"

An inadvertently revealing ad appeared in the March 13, 2006, edition of *Newsweek,* the March 9, 2006, edition of the *Los Angeles Times,* and elsewhere. It's a sad sign of the times when the government must offer a national reminder like the one sponsored by the Office of National Drug Control Policy, which reads: "It's a fine line between respecting your teen's privacy and doing your job as a parent. How far should you go? As far as you have to."

Even in a nation overwhelmingly dominated by caring, concerned parents, the ad highlighted the fact that, apparently, there are actually some adults who must be reminded by the government to "set clear rules" and "keep close tabs on [their] teens" when it comes to "drugs, drinking, tobacco, sex." The adults to whom these ads are directed are likely to be what writer Kay Hymowitz has dubbed "buddy adults" and "parent peers"—parents who seem more like their children's "housemates and friends than experienced adults guiding and shaping the young."[23]

Desperate for a good relationship with their children, these adults, mothers in particular, seem to believe that they can win their children's affection only by being "cool." Accordingly, they behave a lot like their children's peer and unquestioning advocate, offer generous and constant approval whether or not it's merited, toss discipline largely out the window, and pretend to be little older than their children.

Dr. Adria O'Donnell deplores the example that some mothers are setting. "Girls are being raised to be too sexy, too early," she says. "Moms come in [to her practice] and they've had breast augmentations . . . we're the Botox generation. Our girls are being raised that way, and it's everywhere."

The prototypical "cool mom" is the kind of woman parodied

by Amy Poehler in the movie *Mean Girls*. Dressed in a pink Juicy Couture sweat suit, she can't feel her pet dog gnawing her breast, presumably because of the plastic surgery she's undergone. The "cool mom" serves her high-school-aged daughter and her friends happy-hour drinks, and, when one girl asks if they contain alcohol, quickly replies, "Why, do you want a little?" before gushing "you girls keep me young, unhh, I love you *so much*." At the extreme, they're women like Silvia Johnson of Denver, who hosted teen parties where she provided alcohol and methamphetamine, and engaged in sexual activity with boys fifteen to seventeen years old because, she explained, she was a "cool mom" who was "feeling like one of the group."[24]

Either unable or unwilling to take charge of their children, they are parents who are committed above all to remaining popular with their own children. They're the moms who allow their daughters to wear inappropriately suggestive outfits, even when they disapprove of them.[25] Or those who insisted that a vice principal be demoted for ensuring that the girls who wore skirts to a school dance weren't wearing thong underwear, so that their bottoms would remain covered when they freak danced.[26]

And just as they are desperate to remain popular with their own children, they are likewise preoccupied with ensuring that their offspring are popular with their own peers—sometimes, of course, for their children's sake, but also often for their own. As a headmistress of a middle school in downtown Manhattan put it, "As for parents, their egos can get entangled. They want their kids to be liked, and if dating is what it requires, then they're for it."[27]

Elite culture is highly approving of these parent-peer relationships. As one *New York Times* Sunday Style section piece put it, "A generation of teenagers share CDs, fashion and politics with, of all people, their parents. How cool is that?"[28] For the parents, it's "cool," indeed. They are able to ignore the most difficult parts of parenting—setting an example, and assuming responsibility for supervising and disciplining their children—and enjoy all the fun of relating to them as friends.

But when mothers squander their moral authority, it's the daughters who ultimately suffer, because they are deprived of the wisdom, experience, and guidance of a mature adult. Girls who want to rebel are pushed to ever-more-extreme behaviors, because minor acts of defiance (such as provocative clothes or risk-taking behaviors) are tolerated, celebrated, or even, in extreme cases, emulated by adults who are supposed to know better. And given that mothers play a particularly influential role when it comes to sexual decision making,[29] the abdication of maternal responsibility is particularly damaging when it comes to sex.

Even as many of the parent peers act their daughters' age, they also end up treating their children as if they were little adults,[30] capable of making their own decisions with minimal instruction or supervision. Pop culture examples of parent-peer moms abound, including Susan Mayer (Teri Hatcher's character) on *Desperate Housewives* and Lorelei Gilmore on *The Gilmore Girls*.

Many girls with parent peers are allowed to function so autonomously that they alone decide even what morals they will embrace—which, in practice, may mean that peers, the culture, or others who may not have their best interests at heart are shaping girls' principles. One particularly revealing exchange in "The Lost Children of Rockdale County" includes the impotent mother of a young girl involved in the epidemic of group teen sex, who said, "I can give [my children] my opinion and tell them how I feel, but they have to decide for theirself [sic]."[31] Sadly, she reports that her daughter told her, "I wish you'd been more— you should have been more strict with me."[32]

In fact, today's young people are far more open to parental supervision and guidance than their parents often suspect. Dr. Drew Pinsky says, "Kids now see their parents as something to help them. They feel this generation is there to help them enter adulthood successfully. They're looking for them to do these things they're not doing." Pinsky advises parents to get over "this ambivalence about being a parent—for fear of being somehow seen the way you would have seen your parents had they done the same thing." Moms and dads, he notes, need to understand that "you are somebody else's parent now, in a different time, with a different set of needs. And they're asking you to do these things. They look to you to do it."

Why It Matters

The four developments discussed above—the elevation of self-expression over self-restraint, the privatization of religion and sexual morality, the rise of moral relativism, and the advent of the "cool mom"—are central to understanding how America has developed a culture that has normalized, and even celebrated, sexual promiscuity among young girls. That's because all four of them share one common trait: They undermine private, informal, nongovernmental controls on human sexual behavior—whether the controls are internal (springing from one's personal convictions) or external (resulting from a desire to avoid censure by society as a whole, or one's parents in particular). The result is detrimental—not just to young girls, but to American society in general.

That's because a society that celebrates self-expression as an unqualified good risks creating a citizenry that will become less capable of exercising self-discipline of all kinds, even when it's necessary. A culture that marginalizes religion will lose the social benefits that accrue when people voluntarily seek to behave well without government coercion. A society that denies the validity of any sexual morality because of an ethic of moral relativism ultimately loses the capacity to compel decent public behavior even through the heavy hand of government. And a culture that condones parenting that offers children no moral compass can eventually find itself dominated by a generation that understands neither the necessity nor the importance of ethics of any sort.

When cultural forces combine to encourage the indulgence of a people's appetites while eroding any competing constraints on them, it becomes increasingly likely that people will eventually become ruled by their passions. That, without more, is deeply inimical to the flourishing of a truly free society—for when people cannot control themselves, ever more government intrusion into the private sphere becomes necessary to avoid a descent into disorder or even chaos.

Indeed, without sexual self-restraint, the private realm cannot remain truly private. With indiscriminate sexual activity comes a host of ills that ultimately require the government to intrude into the most intimate realms of its citizens' lives—from the agencies devoted to extracting child support payments from unmarried, deadbeat fathers to the armies of social workers employed to check on the well-being of children born to unmarried teen mothers who, too often, are completely unable to provide them with the loving, stable homes they deserve.

It's ironic that sexual liberation—and all the cultural forces that support it—actually end up making a society *less* free. But as the Founding Fathers recognized, liberty and self-government are impossible without a nation of citizens willing both to cultivate personal self-discipline and to establish informal social institutions that reinforce behaviors that help a society flourish with minimal government control.

As John Adams wrote in 1789: "We have no government armed with power capable of contending with human passions unbridled by morality and religion . . . Our Constitution was made only for a moral and religious people. It is wholly inadequate to the government of any other."

11

STEMMING THE TIDE

As a guy, I find the self-respect, beauty and dignity of a modest girl to be irresistibly attractive. And the girls most personally attractive are the ones who know how to live happily without a guy, but want out of generosity to give of themselves in a relationship. The less self-mastery they have (the more sexualized the culture) the less they meet this ideal.

Sherif Girgis, Princeton '08
President, Anscombe Society

Despite the many negative elements of America's sex-saturated culture, it's worth remembering that there is some good news when it comes to teen sex. Teen pregnancy declined by 36 percent between 1990 and 2002,[1] and the teen birth rate decreased by 33 percent between 1991 and 2004.[2] Between 1994 and 2000, the number of abortions among girls fifteen to seventeen declined by 39 percent.[3] What's more, overall rates of sexual intercourse for girls between fifteen and seventeen were reduced by 16 percent (and by 15 percent among fourteen-through sixteen-year-olds) between 1991 and 2000.[4]

And it seems that some teens' attitudes reflect a heartening cultural conservatism that's not always evident in their behavior. According to a survey from the National Campaign to Prevent Teen Pregnancy, 69 percent of all teens and 85 percent of those twelve through fourteen do not "think it's okay for high school teens to have sexual intercourse."[5] A whopping 92 percent of teens agreed that it's important "for teens to be given a strong message from society that they should not have sex until they are at least out of high school."[6]

Dr. Drew Pinsky states, "I am little more optimistic than I've been in the past . . . There's a growing distance between how kids expect to behave, perceive their peers behaving, and what [the standards of behavior] are. Norms have actually gotten better over time." Cultural observers such as *City Journal*'s Kay Hymowitz have theorized that "it's morning after in America," noting that "Americans are looking more favorably on old-fashioned virtues like caution, self-restraint, commitment, and personal responsibility."[7] And columnist David Brooks has argued that teens privately are more sexually self-restrained than appearances would suggest, concluding, "America's social fabric is in the middle of an amazing moment of improvement and repair."[8]

Any and all improvement in the cultural climate is welcome. Even so, it's clear that plenty of work remains to be done—whether it's instilling sexual standards or merely closing the gap between how girls know they should behave and what they actually do.

Certainly, finding meaningful ways to convince young people to abstain from sex is optimal. As Peter Bearman, director of the Institute for Social and Economic Research and Policy at Columbia University, and Hannah Bruckner, then of Yale, concluded in an influential 2001 study: "In general, if adolescents do say no thank you [to sex], they are better off. They have fewer health risks, and they feel better about themselves. Programs that work to delay first intercourse make a contribution to adolescent health. Even if we did otherwise, and even if some adolescents feel that they ought to do otherwise, they are better off waiting. This is especially true for girls . . ."[9] What's more difficult, however, is figuring out the best approach to helping young people understand why waiting is so important.

There are many innovative programs aimed at reducing teen pregnancy. One of the most novel, Baby Think It Over, provided teens with a lifelike seven-pound doll programmed to cry like an infant at random intervals ranging from fifteen minutes to four hours, around the clock. The idea was to expose young girls to one of the challenges they would face as single mothers. But a study conducted on the program concluded that there was little evidence that teens equated caring for the doll with real infant care, or that the way they felt about caring for the doll affected their desire to avoid having a child.[10]

Perhaps that result isn't surprising. Although animals may respond well to rudimentary cause–effect training (where undesirable behaviors are deterred by the threat of punishment), it's likely that human beings need something more than fears of specific negative consequences to fortify a commitment to chastity.[11] In fact, the explosion of oral sex could, in fact, be a rational response to a certain kind of sex education. To the extent that the twin threats of unwanted pregnancy and sexually transmitted disease are presented as the only real disadvantages of sexual activity, the appeal of oral sex is enhanced—30 percent of girls aged fifteen through seventeen (and 47 percent of boys the same age) consider it safer than intercourse.[12]

Many young girls, when asked to discuss their own experiences with and views on the sexualized culture, are able to rattle off a host of bad effects that could result from early uncommitted sex. They explain that sexual decision making is about "having life choices and STDs," or "not getting pregnant." Plenty of girls have apparently adopted the catchphrase, "Sex is a few minutes, but a baby is forever." Significantly fewer girls, however, seem able to articulate any deeper moral or ethical basis for sexual restraint. They define sexual choices in terms of economics or their health—and, most often, leave it at that.

Perhaps it's worth exploring whether most programs and enterprises might do more than simply highlight the punishing effects of bad sexual choices, given teens' well-known sense that nothing bad will ever happen to them. Could defining intimate sexual contact (oral or vaginal) as a moral issue *and* a health-risk-based one be more effective in driving down the incidence of teen sex? Perhaps girls and boys need something deeper and more transcendent than just the physical threats of unwanted pregnancy or sexually transmitted disease to support their efforts to remain chaste—especially in a society that so often celebrates teen sex.[13]

The Commission on Children at Risk, a panel of thirty-three children's doctors, neuroscientists, research scholars, and youth services professionals, has reported that children are hardwired for enduring connections to others, and for moral and spiritual meaning.[14] If the same principle holds true for teens as well, it would suggest that organizations that foster both individual character and a sense of connectedness to a larger community of caring adults have the best chance to influence the sexual behavior of young people.

There are many programs across the United States that do seek to assist in the formation of character generally, and sound sexual decision making in particular. They come in all shapes and sizes, but their goals—and how they're attaining them—offer great insight about the best way to help young women live up to their highest and best ideals.

Smart & Good High Schools: A Blueprint

In "Report to the Nation: Smart & Good High Schools," Dr. Thomas Lickona and co-author Matthew Davidson offer a blueprint for high schools to help their students become responsible sexual decision makers in the context of developing adolescent character. Presenting a host of best practices that can be integrated into school curricula, the report is backed by site visits to twenty-four diverse high schools that had received external recognition and guidance from a national experts panel and a student leaders panel. It advises approaching sex education "holistically, as an opportunity to develop good character and a future orientation." "Chastity," Lickona notes, "is one of a constellation of virtues that make up good character. The virtues support each other."[15]

"To exercise sexual wisdom in today's sexual culture," according to Lickona, "young people need three things: (1) internally held convictions of conscience about why it makes sense to save sexual intimacy for a truly committed relationship—a vision of what they're 'waiting for'; (2) the strengths of character—such as good judgment, self-control, genuine respect for self and others, modesty, and the courage to resist sexual pressures—needed to live out this choice; and (3) support systems for living a chaste lifestyle, including, ideally, support from their families, faith communities, schools, and at least one friend who has made the decision to wait."[16]

In the report, rather than treating sex with what they characterize as a " 'preventing problems' mindset," Lickona and Davidson counsel promoting a more positive outlook in which sexual desires are treated as one more opportunity for developing character. Instead of relying on fear of an STD or unwanted pregnancy to motivate students, Lickona and Davidson's approach to sex education emphasizes the centrality of character to the achievement of a number of desirable life goals such as happiness (including sexual self-fulfillment), self-respect, economic stability, and strong marriages and families.

"About sex," Lickona and Davidson conclude, "our core message to young people must be this: Self-discipline in the sexual domain of your life can be very challenging but very rewarding—to you, to those you love and those that love you, and to society in general."

Best Friends/Diamond Girls

In the "Smart & Good High Schools" report, Lickona and Davidson point to Best Friends as a model youth development program. Founded by Elayne Bennett in 1987, it offers a character-building curriculum through schools that choose to participate. The program combines an emphasis on chastity with peer support and adult guidance. Girls begin the Best Friends program in the sixth grade, while those in grades nine through twelve are part of the Diamond Girl Leadership program. The program has spread nationwide; there are Best Friends and Diamond Girl chapters in a variety of locations including Los Angeles, San Diego, Milwaukee, Texas, North Carolina, and Newark.

Discussing the Best Friends approach to character education, Elayne Bennett, the program's president and founder, observed, "If you just want to make sure that kids don't get pregnant and protect themselves, you're going to have a whole lot more sexual activity. Adolescents need guidelines and standards of behavior. They want it, it gives them a sense of security, and it gives them a sense of well-being."

In fact, Best Friends girls learn about much more than sexual abstinence. They set educational goals and discuss a variety of character-related topics, including decision making, self-respect, alcohol and drug abuse, and love and dating. Along with peer dialogue, there's adult guidance. The girls meet with an adult mentor (a member of the school faculty) for thirty to forty-five minutes weekly, and hear from distinguished women in their communities at least twice yearly. In addition, they participate in fitness and nutrition classes and engage in at least one community service project each year.

The program likewise includes opportunities for cultural enrichment and a "music not madness" program—an outreach effort to extend the Best Friends message about risk behaviors to the school's entire student body. Elayne Bennett noted that the program is "a long term commitment . . . with activities [that] have to do with inspiring and enriching one's life overall, and then also things like selecting music that's uplifting and doesn't degrade."

Overall, participants engage in at least 110 hours of instruction, mentoring, and group activities in the course of a year. According to a study of the program released in 2005, participants in the Best Friends program were nearly six and a half times more likely to refrain from sex, compared with peers in the DC public schools.[17] They were also significantly less likely to engage in other risk behaviors like alcohol and drug use, as well as smoking.

The Best Friends program makes time for fun, too. Each year culminates in an Annual Family and School Recognition Ceremony honoring Best Friends girls, Diamond Girls, mentors, and parents. There are also special events like dance parties, where certain standards for dress (no revealing attire) and behavior (no raunchy dancing) are expected. "Kids don't really have a good time when they're crossing the line," Bennett observed. Discussing one of the dances, she recalled, "Kids had a great time, they were happy, the joy was lovely to behold."

Best Friends and its founder emphasize the importance of offering young people wholesome activities. "If we give our children our best," Elayne Bennett said, summarizing Best Friends' credo, "then they will surely give us their best."

Information on starting a Best Friends chapter is available through the program's Web site, www.bestfriendsfoundation.org.

PALS (Program for Academic and Leadership Skills)

Located in Washington, DC, and operating under the aegis of the Youth Leadership Foundation, PALS (For Girls) offers girls an academic program that also focuses on character development. During the school year, participants, ranging in age from seventh grade through high school, meet weekly on Saturdays. The girls attending the program tend to be from underprivileged, African American households, many headed by a single parent.

One component of the program focuses on sexual morality. Liz Fisher, a volunteer with the program who discusses this issue with the participants, notes that girls as young as the seventh grade are being pressured to have oral sex. Volunteers with the program highlight the differences between male and female sexuality in an effort to teach the girls "self-respect, respect for your own sexuality, and respect for the differences between male and female sexuality," Fisher notes.

PALS seeks to fill the holes in girls' academic and moral education. Participants, Fisher reports, resent being mistreated (or "disrespected") by boys. She says, "No one teaches these girls about modesty. A lot of the girls don't like negative attention, and are glad to find ways to avoid it." She recalls one little girl observing that "by wearing clothing that doesn't reveal too much, they'll look at my face and see that I'm pretty."

Contrary to stereotypes about a lot of teen girls, those in the PALS program make it clear that they don't want to be seen as sexually loose, and resent cultural elements—from dress to rap lyrics—that degrade women. And although the program has a religious (Roman Catholic) element, its teachings work for those of other faiths, and of no faith at all. Fisher points out, "How is someone supposed to make important moral decisions if she's never heard she has a soul as well as a body? Many of these girls don't hear the message—which denies them the opportunity to agree or disagree with it."

The program also attempts to provide participants with a role model. Rashida Jolley, a former Miss DC and a rhythm and blues singer, stresses to the girls the importance of having goals—and the difference that good decisions make in being able to achieve them. Ultimately, Fisher says, the PALS program is about offering the girls an opportunity to develop the character that will serve them well in making life choices, sexual and otherwise. "We're giving them the tools to have a sense of self-awareness and self-respect—a sense that their body and health are precious gifts not to be shared with just anyone."

Best Choice

In contrast to many of the programs that provide sex education to teens, Best Choice emphasizes character—specifically, "sexual integrity." As coordinator of the Best Choice program, Emily Limbaugh conducts training programs across the entire St. Louis region to public and private high schools, middle schools, youth groups, and churches.

Limbaugh believes that many young people see the term *abstinence* as focusing on "what they *can't* do," which is why she emphasizes the concept of integrity: "The idea is that you can never have too much integrity," she notes. "We've taken the term *abstinence* out of it to prevent the door from being slammed in our face because kids think, 'We've already heard about that.'"

Limbaugh is critical of the physical focus of so much teen sexual education: "We're trying to say as a society that sex is more than physical, but then we just reinforce how you don't get a physical disease or get pregnant." Accordingly, Best Choice goes far beyond discussing the physical ramifications of sexual activity. When she enters a classroom, Limbaugh says, "Teens want to know: 'Are you just going to talk about STDs and teen pregnancy, because I've already heard about that?'"

Hardly. One of the key components of Best Choice is instilling the understanding that sex is much more than physical. "The first day [of the program], the kids think I'm half crazy," Limbaugh says. "I ask, 'What is sex?' and when they answer, it's clear they're just thinking about two bodies slapping together." Instead, Limbaugh explains that there's much more to it, outlining the five components of sexual activity: physical, emotional, intellectual, social, and spiritual.

"The lightbulbs seem to turn on once the students understand that beyond STDs and teen pregnancy, the most destructive thing sex outside of marriage does is mess with their emotions," Limbaugh observes. The goal of Best Choice isn't to manipulate teens or force-feed teens handpicked statistics. Rather, Limbaugh continues, "We're trying to swing the pendulum inside them—we want them to decide that 'even if I can get away with this [unharmed], I don't want to.'"

Teens seem to embrace her message, Limbaugh says. On evaluation forms, 75 percent of the teens who noted that they had been sexually active express the intention either to "wait until marriage" or "wait until later in life" before having sex again. And even if they don't all adhere to their newly made resolutions, Limbaugh notes, some of the comments suggest that the program makes a profound impact.

On her evaluation form, one girl stated, "I was planning on losing my virginity tonight, but now I realize I'm too special and I want to wait for my husband. Thank you." And perhaps most poignantly, a young woman wrote, "This message changed my life. You actually probably saved my life."

The Anscombe Society

The Anscombe Society was founded as a student organization at Princeton University to promote and support traditional sexual values—including chastity. In fact, the very existence of a pro-chastity group at an elite and highly sought-after university sends an important message to younger students. One of the group's founders, Cassandra DeBenedetto (Princeton '07) notes that numerous youth groups, clubs, and schools have contacted society members about speaking to young girls and boys.

When the Anscombe Society was established in the autumn of 2004, it was the first group at an Ivy League university defending traditional sexual mores. The society's 2006–07 president, Sherif Girgis, recalls what prompted him and fellow students to found the group. "The biggest factor for most of us was either experiencing firsthand or seeing in friends the brokenness that results from an anything-goes attitude," he says. "We're the generation with the best evidence of the damage the sexual revolution has done."

Girgis's commitment to chastity was reinforced by his own observations. "Of all the relationships I've witnessed among my friends," he notes, "the unchaste ones have been by far the most tumultuous, with the worst longevity, the hardest breakups, and the most difficult transitions between relationships because of the way they stunt people's ability to live happy, independent lives."

Although the group is named for Elizabeth Anscombe, a Cambridge philosopher who defended the Catholic Church's sexual teachings, it's not a religious group.

Rather, its purpose is twofold: to offer social support to those who believe that the proper context for sex is within marriage, and to offer an intellectual counterweight to the unthinking acceptance of sexual activity on campus.

The debate the society's members offer isn't restricted to moral or philosophical arguments; they employ sociological data and medical research to make their points, as well. Speakers have included Professor Steven J. Rhoads, author of *Taking Sex Differences Seriously,* and writer and commentator Maggie Gallagher, author of several books including *The Case for Marriage.*

Like other members of the society, Girgis is unapologetic in defending chastity. "It's the best, and in some ways the only, way to enjoy love and sex to the fullest. Anything so powerful, so closely connected to our highest powers . . . has *got* to be respected, and respect means appropriate use, which in turn means limits."

DeBenedetto insists that being "out there" (in the dating world) as a young woman "is not as difficult as some people might think. The key is not being apologetic for my beliefs. I try to live them with confidence and grace, not pushing them in anyone's face, but not shying away from talking about them, either." Girgis concedes that some of his fellow students consider him and other members of the society somewhat strange. "But," he adds, "there's also a certain secret curiosity—'Can these guys really be smart, well adjusted, and chaste? What's their motivation?'"

And despite his admission that "relationships without a sexual element are pretty rare" on the Princeton campus, Girgis is optimistic. "The irreverence for sex isn't as pervasive as it seems," he says. "There's a quiet but growing group on campus coming to see the problem with hookups and with serial but unserious relationships . . . [I]f the tide is changing at all, it's in the direction of reconsidering chastity . . . as a way to restore sanity to the dating scene."

It's worth wondering whether attitudes like those expressed by Anscombe Society members will, in fact, trickle down to the high school level. "After all," DeBenedetto says, "we certainly recognize how important it is that those younger than we have a good example set for them."

∞

Although these programs differ in how or where they're carried out, each strives both to buck the tide of a sexually permissive culture and to emphasize the centrality of intellect, heart, and spirit to the cause of chastity. Each engages transcendent values in an effort to affirm that human sexuality involves more than momentary physical pleasure and the avoidance of sexually transmitted disease or unwanted pregnancy.

Certainly, there's something a little poignant in the fact that character-building groups that emphasize the importance of chastity are needed as early as middle school. That alone is a sign of how entrenched the concept of sexual permissiveness has become. But the fact that these ideas and programs are flourishing is a promising sign that many Americans are rethinking the mindless sexual permissiveness that's come to dominate the culture.

Dr. Thomas Lickona has commented that "trying to get kids to abstain without developing their character is like coaching someone to run a marathon without having them train for the course."[18] The best kinds of chastity programs "train" young people's characters, hearts, and souls to equip them with the endurance that will help them finish the race with dignity and strength.

CHAPTER 12

PROUDLY, A PRUDE

So-called sexual freedom is really just proclaiming oneself to be available for free, and therefore without value. To "choose" such freedom is tantamount to saying that one is worth nothing.

Sarah E. Hinlicky, "Subversive Virginity"[1]

When it comes to any kind of risky behavior—whether it's smoking, alcohol, drugs, or even imprudent driving—the joy and optimism of youth often mean that young people carry with them a sense of personal invulnerability, a sense that nothing bad can ever happen to them. Certainly, all the difficulties that attend trying to convince young people not to experiment with smoking, drugs, alcohol, or risky driving are only exacerbated when it comes to sex. That's because, unlike the other behaviors, sex in and of itself isn't dangerous—in fact, at the right time and with the right person, it's lots of fun and one of life's greatest blessings.

In a culture that too often glamorizes teen sex, it's more difficult than ever to convince young women of the dangers of giving too much, too soon. With sex, guiding teens isn't as simple as teaching them to "just say no"; it's also helping them understand when, why, how, and with whom it's finally right to say yes.

Many (including 47 percent of parents with children seventeen or younger[2]) believe that the right time for sex doesn't come until after marriage. Others believe sex is acceptable only in the context of a committed relationship, and/or once a girl has reached maturity—variously defined as reaching the age of eighteen, graduating from college, becoming self-supporting, or passing one of life's other milestones. But surely almost every American can agree that girls between twelve and seventeen are, quite simply, too young to be engaging in sexual activity.[3] Even those who are ready physically aren't equipped for the intense feelings that accompany sexual relationships, or the psychological and emotional aftermath.

Many adults and most parents know this instinctively. That's why they do what they can to protect young girls from a culture that often teaches them that early sexual activity isn't just okay—it's right, normal, and "cool," and those who aren't participating are missing out on a wonderful (and typical) teen experience.

It's not easy to figure out how to restore the notion of sexual innocence to girlhood. It's discouraging to live in a world where porn stars publish best-selling autobiographies and pole dancing, stripper style, is touted as a "hot" new form of aerobic exercise. It's demoralizing to find that a government panel is recommending that eleven-year-old girls (and even those as young as nine, at a doctor's discretion) receive vaccinations for a cervical cancer that results from sexually transmitted diseases.[4] It's unthinkable that a high school newspaper would publish a "sex edition," including a quiz question about anal sex, an interview with a custodian who found a vibrator in the girls' shower, and a photograph of two women kissing headlined "Why men love women who love women."[5] The fact that someone at a Florida Hooters thought, even for a minute, that it would be a good idea to hold a "Little Miss Hooters" contest for girls five years old and under[6]—competitors to be dressed in orange spandex shorts and clingy HOOTERS T-shirts—boggles the mind.

But in a country like America, where we are free to live, think, speak, and act as we wish, none of us is powerless. There are real steps that all of us can take to do our part in restoring a more wholesome, decent culture for young girls—and plenty that we can keep in mind, including the following:

1. We Are Not Alone

In a culture where cheap and easy sex is presented as the norm, it's easy to start believing that sort of behavior *is* the norm. All of a sudden, it seems we are the ones who are hopelessly old-fashioned, out-of-step, unhip—that we're *prudes*.

But it's not true. As I began to work on this book, I thought I was a voice in the wilderness. Amazingly, though, when people of widely varying political stripes, races, religions, and socio-economic backgrounds heard about this project, the overwhelming majority expressed strong support and admitted that they, too, were both appalled at how degraded the culture had become and shocked at the kind of behavior that has been condoned by the leaders of popular culture.

The fact is that millions of Americans—perhaps, even, the majority—distrust and dislike the culture's attitude toward teen sex, whether it's being casually accepted or actually celebrated. The greatest problem isn't that most ordinary people agree with the way sex is currently portrayed in America—it's that the elites who have anointed themselves the gatekeepers of cultural attitudes don't share their commonsense values.

Relatively small groups of out-of-touch cultural arbiters in New York and Los Angeles have an influence on how *normal* is defined that's totally disproportionate to their numbers. The values embodied in the reading, movies, television programs, fashions, and music that come from the coasts don't reflect the beliefs of normal Americans. Rather, they present a warped version of them.

Sadly, over time, with prolonged exposure to this distorted reflection, normal Americans start to doubt themselves, becoming convinced that *they* are the outliers. Without realizing it, we all begin to defer to the "hip," creative people on the coasts who are toasted by the mass media and wear their cultural confidence as if it were a crown of divine right.

It's easy to fall into self-doubt and then begin to believe that the elite's sexually permissive attitudes, which would sound laughably ridiculous if put forward at a neighborhood barbecue or weekend cocktail party, have become an accurate reflection of reality. It's easy to become convinced that the world has changed—that it's our responsibility to make the best of it we can, or else withdraw into cloisters where there are neither the opportunities nor the threats that come with experiencing and engaging mainstream culture.

But none of that is true. All across America, in the heartland, the South, the industrial North—and yes, even on the coasts— there are plenty of people who still believe in traditional morality, still believe it's important to exercise the same kind of judgment about sex as we do about everything else, and are still committed to creating a culture that will permit young people to grow, flourish, and thrive in relative innocence.

When cultural sophisticates tell us that we have no right to exercise our own judgment about what's suitable for the public square—and that we must simply avert our eyes to avoid the crass sexualization of too much American culture—they're suggesting that we are the ones who are out of touch. They are wrong. And they deserve to be ignored.

You are not alone.

2. It Is Possible to Change the Culture

Looking at the extent to which sex has permeated almost every aspect of youth culture, it's difficult to believe that anything ever could be different. Perceived social norms about teen sex constitute an important factor influencing teens' decisions to engage in sex—and right now, the culture certainly condones, even approves of, sexual behavior on the part of teens. Could there really come a day when it's considered wrong to glorify irresponsible sexual behavior on the part of young people?

Absolutely—as the history of other efforts to change the culture demonstrate. Take drinking and driving, for instance. Mothers Against Drunk Driving (MADD) was established in 1980, after founder Candy Lightner's thirteen-year-old daughter was killed by a drunk driver. From those modest beginnings, a gigantic movement mushroomed, and attitudes about the acceptability of drinking and driving changed radically. In stark contrast to the days when it was relatively acceptable to get behind the wheel after "having a few," even alcohol advertisements now encourage viewers to "drink responsibly" and find a "designated driver."

Another heartening example involves the enormous change in American attitudes toward cigarette smoking over the past thirty years. Back in the 1940s, '50s, and '60s, cigarette smoking was considered the hallmark of glamour and sophistication, and featured prominently in classic films such as *Now, Voyager; Casablanca;* and *Breakfast at Tiffany's.* During the 1950s and 1960s, smoking was so widely accepted that cigarette makers frequently sponsored television shows, including *I've Got a*

Secret and *To Tell the Truth*. The Marlboro Man became an American icon, and jingles like "You get a lot to like with a Marlboro" and "Winston tastes good like a cigarette should" were part of the American vernacular. Almost every living room in America included ashtrays prominently displayed on side tables and placed at every setting at elegant dinner parties. From 1950 until 1997, Joe Camel made smoking attractive to the younger set—a 1991 study found that more five- and six-year-olds could recognize the Camel cigarette mascot than Mickey Mouse or Fred Flintstone.[7]

Like teen sex today, smoking was seemingly ubiquitous—not only tolerated but almost celebrated. Even so, all that changed, and relatively quickly, too. Smoking is now banned in public areas ranging from airports to restaurants all across the United States. Over the space of just a few decades, it became socially unacceptable. How did this happen?

It wasn't because of government regulation, which, in most cases, conformed to public opinion rather than shaping it. Social attitudes about smoking changed because Americans came to realize that smoking—like drunk driving—was a problem, not just for smokers themselves but also for innocent bystanders and society as a whole. We simply decided that it exacted an unacceptably heavy toll on Americans in terms of both health and money.

The same argument can be applied to promiscuous underage sex. Certainly, not every smoker develops lung cancer, not every drunk driver injures someone, and not every sexually active young girl is going to contract a sexually transmitted disease. But when one out of four sexually active teenagers are infected with a sexually transmitted disease,[8] that has a real impact on public health both in terms of the infected teens' present and future sexual partners, as well as the burden of the significant added costs to the health care system for treatment. Teenage pregnancy likewise exacts a heavy social price that's spread across American society—and that's without adding the incalculable toll that abortion can take on those who choose it. And even though the psychological and emotional costs of giving too much too soon are intangible, they, too, are real, and they merit society's compassion and concern.

It's true that those who doubt the extent of the culture's impact on young girls' choices are often tempted to adopt a libertarian view. It makes great intuitive sense to argue, in effect: "Don't want your daughter to experience that television program/music/lifestyle? Don't let her see it/hear about it/do it." After all, Americans prize personal responsibility—and certainly the primary responsibility for a girl's well-being rests with her parents.

For their part, given the coarseness and vulgarity that infects so much of the culture, parents could be forgiven for wanting to lock their daughters away from the television, the music, the fashions—and so much more—that send the destructive dual message: Sexiness is all that matters, and chastity is for losers.

But both impulses are terminally flawed, and for the same reason. In effect, they assume that it would, in fact, be possible for girls to be entirely isolated from the prevailing culture. And that's nothing more than wishful thinking. After all, even if a girl is forbidden to see particular television programs or movies, or to read certain books, or to visit certain Internet sites, or to wear certain fashions, those prohibitions alone could never be effective. They don't prevent her from being exposed to other girls who are allowed to watch, wear, and read what they please—and who will model the behaviors and usages that they learn about from doing so. And they won't curb a girl's natural desire to be able to watch, wear, and read what her friends do.

What's more, just as secondhand smoke can injure non-smokers, a culture in which promiscuous sexual activity is accepted and even condoned is harmful to innocent bystanders. It hurts the young people who are themselves trying to refrain from engaging in sexual behavior. It teaches them that their sexual restraint is somehow abnormal, and puts chaste girls at a disadvantage compared with those who dress or behave less modestly. And girls themselves realize it. An eighth grader at a private school in the Midwest said that she felt "really annoyed about girls who give sex to get male attention." Another, a public school freshman in California, confided, "Sometimes [other girls' behavior] does bother me. Like I'll be down at the movies with friends, and we're talking to our other guy friends . . . and two or three girls will walk down with their shirts showing up to their bellies or past their bellies, and really short skirts. They do it to get attention from the guys, and . . . it makes me mad."

But worst of all, a sex-saturated culture encourages girls to have sex when they otherwise might have waited to do so. In other words, it pressures them to make decisions that are neither wise nor healthy for them.

Of course, the "sexification" of American life, and the resulting impact on young girls, isn't a problem that can (or should) be addressed through government censorship, which is unacceptable even in light of the offensive sexual content so prevalent in today's mass culture. Nor is it a matter of what Americans choose to see, read, or consume in their own homes.

Rather, the issue is one that must be resolved informally through a social consensus both that the harm is real and that it outweighs the rights of those who enjoy the highly sexualized popular culture—just as the rights of nonsmokers and other drivers or pedestrians outweigh the rights of those who want to smoke, or drink and drive. Ultimately, the question boils down to what Americans believe is appropriate content for the atmosphere that all of us share. It isn't a matter of what one does in the sanctity of one's home; it's what's put "on display"—in terms of public dress, culture, discussion—that Americans need to confront.

Change can (and will) come, but only when a critical mass of Americans decide that the tangible and intangible costs imposed by gratuitous sex in the public square are unacceptably high, and that it's more important to protect young people's innocence than it is to exercise our right to be exposed in public to titillating words and images.

3. Give Girls Great Expectations, and Break the Vicious Cycle

Cassandra DeBenedetto, the Princeton student who helped found the university's Anscombe Society, believes that girls fall into sexual relationships because they believe that's all there is. She notes, "Girls lose hope that there exists a decent guy who is genuinely interested in getting to know them and in potentially having a deep relationship with them . . . and so they settle."

When girls believe that boys are unwilling to or incapable of establishing relationships that aren't based on sex, it becomes infinitely harder for them to resist the temptation to flaunt their sexuality. And that behavior itself helps to establish a vicious cycle. As DeBenedetto puts it, "A man's expectations often reflect a woman's behavior. So guys . . . expect to sleep or go far with girls who dress immodestly (advertising their sexuality) and flirt a lot. If girls' dress, attitude, and behavior say 'I'm easy and interested,' then they will attract guys looking for 'easy' girls." In turn, believing that nothing but shallow men are available, the girls' behavior becomes even more degraded.

Young women need to realize that their own behavior determines the quality of the guys they will attract. Sleazy behavior appeals to sleazy guys. It's important for girls to understand that there *are* fine, wholesome guys who are looking for something more than cheap thrills—and admire girls who dress modestly and behave with self-respect. For every "pig" out there, there's likewise a good, decent man who's hoping to find the woman of his dreams. And marry her.

Convincing girls to have high expectations—both for men and for their relationships—may not be as difficult as it sounds, for at least some teen girls already suspect that the new order of ubiquitous, taken-for-granted, no-strings sex isn't all it's been cracked up to be. A female student's commentary for the Phillips Academy (Andover) high school newspaper captures perfectly the undercurrent of wistfulness that tinges even the permissive attitudes toward sex so prevalent among young women today:

> People are having sex. Some are doing it on campus. Great. Wonderful. Amazing. (Use protection!!!) But where are the dates? The couples we are supposed to see walking each other to class from conference period? The holding hands, kissing, hugging, etc., that actually amounts to something, other than, "We're just really good friends"? (For all of you rolling your eyes right now, it is actually pretty cool to have a person care about you like that.) Where are the relationships? Where is the intimacy?[9]

Despite what seem like the best efforts of an oversexed culture, relationships and intimacy remain important to young women, even though—as with traditional morality—they're playing a smaller role in teen girls' sexual experiences. They want more than they're getting from the hookup culture—and that's a yearning that should be respected and encouraged. Ultimately, it signifies that there's hope, both for them and even for the culture itself.

4. Don't Forget the Boys

This book has concentrated on the sexualization of young girls and the cultural forces that encourage it. But that focus doesn't mean that boys and their attitudes toward the opposite sex (and sex itself) are any less important.

Certainly boys and girls are different in many ways when it comes to their sexual development and urges. But just because boys have a greater sex drive, and girls—who risk more with promiscuous sex—have traditionally been the sexual gatekeepers, young men aren't absolved of the responsibility to behave properly and treat girls respectfully.

As human sexuality educator Deborah Roffman has pointed out, the notion that "boys will be boys" offers young men nothing but a "corrupting set of expectations"—specifically, the opportunity to behave badly without any accountability for wrongdoing, sexual or otherwise.[10] Much public indignation has properly been directed at the North Carolina prosecutor who sought to prosecute several Duke University lacrosse players wrongly accused of raping a stripper in spring 2006. But amid the justifiable outrage against the apparent and egregious prosecutorial abuse, too few adults have pointed out that privileged young men at a prestigious private university really had no business cavorting with strippers in the first place. Setting aside the issue of whether their behavior was legal, it certainly wasn't *right,* or appropriate, or manly.

Indeed, in an age where too many young girls have decided that flaunting their sexuality is the only way to attract male attention, it's important that the boys learn that real men, manly men, don't exploit women—even if a female invites them to. Real men don't call girls "bitches" and "ho's" and "sluts" and "hoochies"; they honor women, and treat them the way they hope their mothers and sisters (and, someday, their daughters) will be treated.

Making sure boys understand these concepts is important—not only for them, but for the girls, too. When boys admire modest girls, and avoid those who are willing to barter themselves and their sexuality in exchange for male attention, it becomes easier for girls to behave in a way that preserves their own self-respect. What's more, it becomes possible for boys and girls alike once again to enjoy the innocent joys of teen romance without the conflicts, worries, and pressures that arise when sex becomes part of a relationship.

Ultimately, boys need to understand that their decisions about the kind of women they'll pursue say more about their own characters than those of the women. Becoming a real man—a gentleman—is about more than learning to appreciate women with standards. It's about boys setting high standards for themselves, too, and having the guts to stick with them, even in the midst of trouble, difficulty, and temptation.

It's comforting to know that even in a culture that condones easy sex, there are plenty of fine, decent boys who understand this already. As one seventeen-year-old girl remarked, discussing hooking up and oral sex, "I know many guys who are opposed to it. They think it degrades the girls."

5. Chastity Isn't Just a Religious Matter

There are, of course, those who neither understand nor share many Americans' objections to the sexualization of the culture. In fact, they resent efforts to reintroduce the twin notions of self-restraint in sexual behavior and reticence when it comes to public discussion of sex. For some, these efforts seem like little more than an attempt to repress healthy sexual self-expression. As one diarist on liberal Web site Daily Kos wrote, "If sex is good, why don't we talk about it more? Are we all buying into some right-wing conspiracy of silence?"[11]

Hardly. In fact, these days, self-censorship is more closely associated with spiritual matters—think of the increasing reluctance to identify Christmas as an explicitly religious holiday—than sexual ones.[12] But many of those who applaud the sexual openness in the culture likewise seek to define chastity as something relevant only to the overtly religious. The Kos diarist above condemns the "sustained attack on sexual freedom" by "the religious right," and argues that "conservatives have been able to get away with this only because they have employed and sometimes misused concepts of morality and religious dogma."[13]

Certainly, some of the most powerful and beautiful arguments for sexual self-restraint—and a culture that supports it—have religious underpinnings. People of faith believe, for example, that their bodies don't belong to themselves alone; they belong, as well, to the God who created them. As such, it's wrong to misuse or abuse one's body by engaging in promiscuous sex, without love or commitment.

That doesn't mean, however, that the concept of sexual restraint is good, true, or valid only for those who are part of a faith tradition that embraces chastity. The physical, emotional, and psychological effects of giving too much, too soon—and the self-confidence and self-respect that result from living up to high standards and exercising self-restraint—aren't limited to religious girls and their parents.

Contrary to the suggestions of the sexual libertines, conflict over the sexualization of American culture is more than a debate between religious fanatics and everyone else. One needn't be overtly religious (or even religious at all) to recognize and deplore the corrosive effects on young people of a sex-obsessed culture. It's natural for parents of every religious stripe (or none) to want to protect their daughters from the undesirable outcomes that result from giving too much, too soon.

And those who attempt to marginalize the concept of sexual

purity by making it an exclusively religious matter ignore the fact that agnostics and atheists can suffer from broken hearts, depression, unwanted pregnancies, and STDs, too.

6. Take a Stand Against Lowest-Common-Denominator Capitalism

It's tempting to blame the free market for the sex-saturated movies, ads, television shows, magazines, books, and Internet content that have deformed America's cultural landscape. The market wants to appeal to the greatest possible number, the argument goes, and thus caters to the lowest common denominator. Sex sells, so sex is marketed, early and often.

But that argument is too easy. In fact, the beauty of capitalism is that it gives consumers free choice, thereby empowering all of us. The profit motive guarantees that if a critical mass begins to object to the oversexualized content of what's being marketed to young girls, alternatives will emerge. American girls (and Americans generally) can decide to bypass the sexy clothes, raunchy books, coarse magazines, and vulgar music—the power of free markets guarantees that more wholesome content will quickly be made available to them. It's all a matter of free will and human choice.

Certainly, it's not an easy sell to convince those accustomed to the easy vulgarity of popular culture to demand something better. But if Americans are committed to preserving young people's innocence, it's up to them to call to account those who have been profiting from the sexy and exploitative music, fashions, books, magazines, movies, Internet content, and TV shows aimed at teens.

In fact, young people themselves can be encouraged to take the lead in making their wishes known to the purveyors of pop culture. It's empowering for girls, in particular, to realize

that they wield a good deal of consumer clout, and, if orga-
nized properly, they have the power to force real change—like
eleven-year-old Ella Gunderson did when, simply by writing
a letter of complaint about the absence of anything but low-
cut pants and clingy tops, she convinced Nordstrom to stock
more modest fashions.[14] As for college students, some of the
idealism and activism that's been directed toward stopping
abuses perpetrated by third-world sweatshops could be just as
effectively employed in protecting their younger brothers and
sisters from inappropriate and offensive products or marketing pitches.

When young people join their elders in demanding a more
wholesome culture and rejecting the sex-saturated excesses of
the hookup culture, the market will respond. When a critical
mass of American consumers decides that the common good—
and the protection of the innocent—is more important than
being able to enjoy sexy products in public, and then direct their
dollars accordingly, purveyors will follow their lead. When the
American public begins to regard inappropriate sexual content
promoted to the young with the same abhorrence that would
greet any new sales overtures by Joe Camel, the market will
respond.

7. Set the Example, Bit by Bit

At the beginning of her reign as America's most influential television talk-show host, Oprah Winfrey covered many of the same
sorts of sensationalistic stories as her rivals. But after a while, she
decided that she didn't want shows about cross-dressers, polyga-
mists, and sexually active priests to be her legacy. So she changed
her focus. For years, her show has brought positive and uplifting
messages about spirituality and self-improvement to millions of
women across America, all in a spirit of camaraderie and good

fun. Oprah proved that television doesn't have to be vulgar or titillating to attract an audience—hers is the longest-running daytime talk show in American history, enormously popular in the United States and around the world.

Few of us are as powerful as Oprah Winfrey. But all of us can, in our own way, set an example for ourselves and those who look to us—whether they are daughters, nieces, sisters, younger class-mates, or others. Girls depend on mature women they admire to model what it means to be a real woman. That's why moms who want young girls to dress appropriately help achieve that end when they themselves don't wear skimpy workout attire to drop their daughters off at school—and even, perhaps, explain to their daughters why they object to the women who do. Aunts or big sisters who want little girls to love *Little Women* rather than *Gossip Girl* need to take the time to explain that great en-tertainment doesn't have to rely on sensationalism—that sleaze is, in fact, the cheap and easy way out for the lazy and the untal-ented. Every time anyone makes it clear that over-the-top sexual dialogue or images aren't acceptable for public consumption, she strikes a small but meaningful blow for a cleaner, more whole-some culture.

Setting standards and then refusing to apologize for them reintroduces the notion that it's okay to have standards when it comes to sex, just as Americans have when it comes to any other topic. And every time that a woman whom teen girls respect sets and holds to her own standards, it sends a message. Girls learn that having standards is, in fact, a sign of respect for oneself and others. They see that being confident in one's own values is what's truly "cool"—and that confident people set their own rules for their conduct, without looking to others in their peer group or the culture to lead the way.

Mother Teresa observed, "We can do no great things, only small things with great love." Taken alone, any individual act may seem insignificant. Together, however, they have a real and lasting power on every woman's circle of influence.

8. Equal Doesn't Have to Mean the Same

Over the past forty years, women have made great and welcome strides in overcoming legal and institutional discrimination in educational and employment prospects. The sweeping changes we've seen in access and opportunity for girls and women over a relatively short time is testimony to the basic commitment to fair play and equality that's characteristic of the American people.

Certainly, in an era when virtually every professional option is open to young women, they should be encouraged to become ambitious, assertive individuals. Accordingly, the 1990s witnessed the birth of "girl power"—defined in 2001 in the *Oxford English Dictionary* online as "a self-reliant attitude among girls and young women manifested in ambition, assertiveness and individualism."[15]

But somewhere along the line, the same girl power that was intended to motivate young women to compete and excel in academics and sports became the standard for female behavior in other contexts. The aggressiveness that became emblematic of the girl-power approach to the world may account for rising rates of drinking[16] and drug use[17] among girls relative to boys—and of course, for more pronounced sexual aggression on the part of young women. As Caitlin Flanagan puts it, "It was very possible for a girl in the nineties to have her well-intentioned parents buy her a CD in which she was urged to [have oral sex and intercourse], and to have a well-intentioned teacher (I was one such) tell her to be as intellectually and verbally aggressive as she could—that aggression for its own sake was a good thing, because it leveled the playing field in a male-dominated world."[18]

But especially when it comes to sex, American culture has

done girls a great disservice by teaching them that in order to be equal to boys, they must be the same—just as promiscuous, just as uncommitted. This attitude has led to what historian Robert McElvaine has dubbed the "Masculine Mystique: If it has long been a man's world, whatever men have done is what everyone should do."[19] The problem, as McElvaine points out, is that no one ever considers the converse: If there are certain behaviors that are too objectionable, crass, or wrong to merit women's participation, why, exactly, should men engage in them? If women don't do it, why should men?

Even as American culture has succeeded in empowering girls, it's failed to teach them how to use that power responsibly. As Dr. Drew Pinsky puts it, "Girl power has become 'uncontained aggression is your right.'" Ironically, as girls have been encouraged to adopt male attitudes toward sex, they've been taught to deny, denigrate, or ignore the needs and desires that define them as female. They've learned that, at least in the eyes of the culture, male attitudes toward sex are the only ones that have true value. In short, they've been taught that it's more important to have sex in the *same* way as a man than it is to claim an *equal* right to satisfying interactions with the opposite sex.

And even as girls have been taught to flaunt the sexual power they can wield over their male counterparts, they've been deprived of the sweeter, more wholesome experience of discovering they have the power to influence men for good—when it comes to sexual behavior and even more generally. "Men are very compliant," says Dr. Drew Pinsky. "If you tell us 'it's this way,' that's the way we go. If you told us this [hookup culture] has to stop immediately, that this is hurting people, it would stop.

"Women do, in fact, have the power," Dr. Pinsky continues. "They just have to assert it properly, rather than relinquishing it to the males—or co-opting it, pretending it's theirs when it's actually still the males'."

When in the film *As Good as It Gets,* Jack Nicholson's character tells Helen Hunt's that "You make me want to be a better man," she responds that it's the "best compliment of [her] life." It's likely many women would agree. In the hookup culture, however, a comment like "nice tits"[20] passes for a compliment (and an opening line) in some circles. No doubt condoning, engaging in, and responding to such vulgarity all make girls more similar to boys. But how, exactly, does this make them more equal?

9. Our Culture Isn't Just an American Matter

It's becoming ever more obvious that the quality of our culture has resonance far beyond our nation's borders. In an era characterized by increasing globalization, the messages that American entertainment sends abroad have an impact on attitudes toward the United States across the world. As Joseph Nye pointed out in 2000, "some Iranian officials say that to understand what they mean by 'the great Satan,' one need merely watch MTV."[21] In 2004 alone, a soap advertisement in Jerusalem featuring *Sex and the City* star Sarah Jessica Parker was considered inappropriately revealing; the Chinese responded to a revealing poster of *Baywatch*'s Pamela Anderson with displeasure; and Janet Jackson's "wardrobe malfunction" was beamed around the world.[22] It's not hard to imagine the disgust with which some of the world's more traditional societies view certain aspects of US pop culture.

Certainly, Americans' decisions about what to think, say, or embrace should never be subject to a global test. And make no mistake—terrorism and other aggression visited on the United States is the fault only of those who perpetrate it. But many of the same voices expressing profound concern about our nation's moral authority when it comes to America's efforts to defend itself in the war on terror fall suspiciously silent when the topic shifts from war to culture. It's remarkable that those so exquisitely sensitive to world opinion in other contexts remain so insensitive to the impact that crass, vulgar entertainment has on the world's perception of America and its values.

"Winning hearts and minds" is an important step toward maintaining America's status in the world in general, and achieving victory in the war on terror in particular. Surely those objectives are undermined when the messages in our culture seem sharply at odds with the values we profess to uphold. Efforts to secure legal rights and protections for women in the Middle East are hardly advanced by movies that portray American girls as sex-hungry floozies. And it must be confusing for emerging Middle East democracies to hear Americans insist, on the one hand, that women be given the vote and treated with respect, while, on the other, our culture celebrates, enriches, and rewards artists who routinely refer to them as "bitches," "ho's," and "skanks."

Proudly, a Prude

As those in recovery programs often state: The first step is realizing that there is a problem.

For those who seem unconvinced, it's worth asking: Have the sexual revolution and do-me feminism allowed America's young girls to really live happier, more wholesome lives? Are their thoughts, conversations, activities, and preoccupations more elevated? Are they healthier in body, mind, and spirit? The answer is obvious.

Even so, those can be difficult questions to ask. That's because there is a widespread perception that anyone who practices chastity, or objects to others' moral or sexual choices, is somehow a prude—a sexual Puritan who, in H. L. Mencken's famous formulation, suffers from a priggish, "haunting fear that someone, somewhere is having a good time." It's hard for anyone (and especially healthy, normal young people who very much want to have a good time) to endure the kind of ridicule that often greets those who champion chastity.

But there is a price for our collective unwillingness to confront a culture dominated by sexual libertines. From our silence, young people can infer consent, drawing the mistaken conclusion that adults believe what's happening today is just fine. Worse yet, our reticence can lead to abdication of the right—and the responsibility—to exercise judgment in the area of sex, as we do in almost every other facet of our communal life. And exercising that judgment is crucial to the happiness, health, and well-being of young people, boys and girls alike.

The hypersexualization of American culture—and its impact on young girls—is a collective problem that must be addressed cooperatively. As with pollution or man-made global warming or terrorism, even innocent bystanders can't be entirely insulated from the damaging environment created by the destructive behavior of others.

Unless we are willing to speak out and work for change, the danger remains that the problem will only grow worse, for with culture, there is always a slippery slope. Every time looser standards for dress or behavior become socially sanctioned, it becomes more difficult to retrench—and twice as difficult to resist the next step toward the vulgar or extreme on the cultural continuum.

We can do better—and we must. It's time that Americans feel empowered to object to cultural trends and behaviors that are degrading—not only to young women, but to all of us. It's never too late to enlist in the struggle to protect America's future by insisting on a culture that honors sexual morality, protects young people, and champions our highest ideals.

NOTES

CHAPTER 1: THE NEW SCARLET LETTER

1. Elena Kagan, address at the Association of the Bar of the City of New York, November 17, 2005.

2. "More Women than Men Seek Entry to US Medical Schools," *Medical News Today,* November 27, 2003, accessed at www.medicalnews today.com/medicalnews.php?newsid=4744.

3. Peg Tyre, "The Trouble with Boys," *Newsweek,* January 30, 2006.

4. Meadows, S.O., Land, K.C., and Lamb, V.I., "Assessing *Gilligan vs. Sommers:* Gender-Specific Trends in Child and Youth Well-Being in the United States 1985–2001," *Social Indicators Research* 70 (2005), pp. 1–52; Glenn Sacks, "Boys or Girls—Pick Your Victim," *Los Angeles Times,* March 20, 2005.

5. Tyre, "The Trouble with Boys."

6. Meadows, Land, and Lamb, "Assessing *Gilligan vs. Sommers.*"

7. Alex Morris, "The Cuddle Puddle of Stuyvesant High School," *New York Magazine,* February 6, 2006.

8. Wells, B.E., and Twenge, J.M., "Changes in Young People's Sexual Behavior and Attitudes, 1943–1999: A Cross-Temporal Meta-Analysis," *Review of General Psychology* 9, No. 3 (2005), pp. 249–261.

9. News release, San Diego State University, "Landmark New Report on Teenage Sex in America Tracks Dramatic Changes Over Last Five Decades," October 3, 2005.

10. "Sexy Foods," *Food & Wine Magazine,* accessed at www.food andwine.com/slideshows/sexyfoods.

11. Chuck Anderson, "Cooking with Tyler Florence: Sexy Chef Talks About the Art of Food," *Santa Cruz Sentinel,* January 14, 2004, accessed at www.santacruzsentinel.com/archive/2004/January/14/style/stories/01style.htm.

12. Martha Hindes, "2004 Sexy Car Buyer's Guide," *Road & Travel,* accessed at www.roadandtravel.com/roadtests/buyersguides/2004buyersguide/sexysportscars/2004sexysportscars.htm.

13. Damian Koh, "Can Cameras Be Sexy?" *CNet Asia Reviews,* November 16, 2005, accessed at http://asia.cnet.com/reviews/techbuzz/digital_eye/0,39041402,39291259,00.htm.

14. Hetal Bhatt, "Sex Sells Politics," *Daily Illini,* September 28, 2004, accessed at http://media.www.dailyillini.com/media/storage/paper736/news/2004/09/28/News/Sex-Sells.Politics-733291.shtml?sourcedomain=www.dailyillini.com&MIIHost=media.collegepublisher.com.

15. Robin Givhan, "Condoleezza Rice's Commanding Clothes," *Washington Post,* February 25, 2005.

16. Josh Grossburg, "Zahn Spot Too Hot for CNN," E! Online News, January 8, 2002, accessed at http://cache-origin.eonline.com/News/Items/0,1,9343,00.html.

17. Lee Siegel, "Against 'Sucks,' " *New Republic Online,* April 28, 2006, accessed at http://cache-origin.eonline.com/News/Items/0,1,9343,00.html.

18. "Buying into Sexy: The Sexing Up of Tweens," CBC Marketplace, January 9, 2005, accessed at www.cbc.ca/consumers/market/files/money/sexy.

19. For an excellent piece pointing out that America's "chief source of inequality" is the marriage gap between college-educated women and the less educated, see Kay S. Hymowitz, "Marriage and Caste," *City Journal,* winter 2006. Hymowitz points out that, as of 1960, even the percentage of high school dropouts who had children out of wedlock was barely 1 percent.

20. Gillmore, M.R., Archibald, M.E., Morrison, D.M., Wilsdon, A., Wells, E.A., Hoppe, M.J., Nahom, D., and Murowchick, E., "Teen Sexual Behavior: Applicability of the Theory of Reasoned Action," *Journal of Marriage and Family* 64, No. 4 (2002), pp. 885–897.

21. Robin Shamburg, "Be a Slut! Be a Slut! Be a Slut!" Salon.com, May 2, 2001, accessed at www.cbc.ca/consumers/market/files/money/sexy.

22. Liz Smith, "Fabulous Tom Ford Tells All," *New York Post*, November 1, 2004.

23. Stephanie Rosenbloom, "The Taming of the Slur," *New York Times,* July 13, 2006.

24. Letter, "What Is a Prude?" *Go Ask Alice!,* January 29, 1999, accessed at www.goaskalice.columbia.edu/1435.html.

25. Personal interview, September 20, 2006.

CHAPTER 2: DEFINING DECENCY DOWN

1. Kaiser Family Foundation and *Seventeen* magazine, SexSmarts Survey, "Relationships," July 2002, accessed at www.kff.org/entpartnerships/upload/Relationships-Summary-of-Findings.pdf.

2. "The Lost Children of Rockdale County," produced by Rachel Dretzin Goodman and Barak Goodman, PBS *Frontline,* October 19, 1999.

3. Liza Mundy, "Sex & Sensibility," *Washington Post Magazine,* July 16, 2000, p. W16.

4. Laura Sessions Stepp, "Unsettling New Fad Alarms Parents: Middle School Oral Sex," *Washington Post,* July 8, 1999.

5. Marsha Low, "Casual Sex Becomes Subject for Middle Schoolers," *Detroit Free Press,* June 11, 2002.

6. Ibid.

7. Michael Fisher, Linda Lou, and Iona Patringenaru, "Youthful Sexuality Worries Adults," *(Inland Southern California) Press-Enterprise,* December 10, 2003.

8. Kim Painter, "Sexual Revolution Hits Junior High," *USA Today,* March 14, 2002.

9. Low, "Casual Sex."

10. Associated Press, "Judge Upholds Suspension of Girl for Sex Act on Bus," October 3, 2003.

11. Jane Elizabeth and Mackenzie Carpenter, "More Kids Are Having Sex, and They're Having It Younger," *Pittsburgh Post-Gazette,* September 14, 2003.

12. Associated Press, "Kids Allegedly Had Sex in Classroom During Assembly About Killing," March 30, 2007.

13. Ruth Padawer, "Relax, Your Kids Probably Aren't Having Sex," *(Bergen County, NJ) Record,* March 30, 2005.

14. First Coast News, Jacksonville, FL, "Students Arrested for Oral Sex in Classroom," December 13, 2005, accessed at www.firstcoastnews.com/news/topstories/news-article.aspx?storyid=48816.

15. Tara Bahrampour and Ian Shapira, "Sex at School Increasing, Some Educators Say," *Washington Post,* November 6, 2005.

16. Ibid.

17. Jerry Jordan, "Ozen Coach/Teacher's Aide and Former Student Indicted," *(Southwest Texas) Examiner,* August 13, 2006.

18. Marianne Garvey and Carl Campanile, "Kids' Cuff Kink," *New York Post,* May 23, 2004.

19. NBC Channel 10, Philadelphia, "Sex Bracelets Cause for Parental Concern," November 7, 2003, accessed at www.nbc10.com/news/2619696/detail.html.

20. NBC4-TV, Washington, DC, "Jelly Bracelets Linked to Sex Game," November 13, 2003, accessed at www.nbc4.com/family/2634926/detail.html.

21. Douane James, "Principal Puts Ban on 'Sex Bracelets,'" *Gainesville Sun,* October 18, 2003.

22. WEWS NewsChannel 5, Cleveland, "Principal Bans Jelly Bracelets for Sexual Innuendo," November 4, 2003, accessed at www.newsnet5.com/news/2611103/detail.html.

23. Alexa Aguilar and Kaitlin Bell, "Rumors Swirl Linking Bracelets to Sex Game," *St. Louis Post-Dispatch,* November 18, 2003.

24. NBC5, Dallas, "Bracelets with Rumored Sexual Meaning Worry Parents," November 18, 2003, accessed at www.nbc5i.com/news/2645629/detail.html.

25. *Time* magazine likewise ran a piece. Jeffrey Ressner, "Parents: Brace Yourselves," *Time,* October 27, 2003.

26. Garvey and Campanile, "Kids' Cuff Kink."

27. Elizabeth and Carpenter, "More Kids Are Having Sex."

28. Personal interview, September 18, 2006.

29. Personal interview, September 20, 2006.

30. Personal interview, September 20, 2006.

31. Personal interview, September 20, 2006.

32. 2002 National Survey of Family Growth, September 15, 2005, accessed at www.cdc.gov/nchs/data/ad/ad362.pdf.

33. Youth Risk Behavior Surveillance—United States 2005, 55(SS05) (June 9, 2006), pp. 1–108, accessed at www.cdc.gov/mmwr/preview/mmwrhtml/ss5505a1.htm#tab44.

34. Abma, J.C., Martinez, G.M., Mosher, W.D., and Dawson, B.S., "Teenagers in the United States: Sexual Activity, Contraceptive Use, and Childbearing, 2002," *National Center for Health Statistics* 23, No. 24, pp. 1–48; Abma, J.C., and Sonenstein, F.L., "Sexual Activity and Contraceptive Practices Among Teenagers in the United States, 1988 and 1995," *National Center for Health Statistics* 23, No. 21.

35. Youth Risk Behavior Surveillance.

36. Child Trends, *Facts at a Glance,* Publication 2005-02, March 2005, accessed July 30, 2006, at www.childtrends.org/Files/Facts_2005.pdf (citing 2002 National Survey of Family Growth).

37. Kaiser Family Foundation and *Seventeen* magazine, SexSmarts Survey, "Are You Ready for Sex?" accessed at www.seventeen.com/health/smarts/articles/0,,625884_698323,00.html.

38. Personal interview, September 18, 2006.

39. 2002 National Survey of Family Growth, Advance Data No. 362, September 15, 2005, accessed at www.cdc.gov/nchs/data/ad/ad362.pdf.

40. 2002 National Survey of Family Growth, September 15, 2005, accessed at www.cdc.gov/nchs/data/ad/ad362.pdf.

41. Boekeloo, B.O., and Howard, D.E., "Oral Sexual Experience Among Young Adolescents Receiving General Health Examinations," *American Journal of Health Behavior* 26, No. 4 (2002), pp. 306–314 at 310. The researchers point out that the lower frequency of oral sex among the youngest adolescents in the study render analyses of them exploratory rather than dispositive.

42. Ibid.

43. NBC News, "NBC News, People Magazine Commission Landmark National Poll," January 31, 2005, accessed September 25, 2006 at www.msnbc.msn.com/id/6839072.

44. Megan Rausher, "Oral and Anal Sex Increasing Among Teens," Reuters, May 9, 2006.

45. Figure 4, "Among Teens 15–19 Who Have Not Had Sexual Intercourse, Percentage of Males and Females Who Have Any Oral Sex Experience, by Age, 2002," Child Trends Data Bank, "Oral Sex" (analyses of the 2002 National Survey of Family Growth), accessed at www.childtrends databank.org/figures/95-Figure-4.gif. What's likewise noteworthy is that while there was no overall increase in oral sex experience among never-married boys aged fifteen through nineteen between 1995 and 2002, there was an increase in the proportion of those who were engaging in oral sex without ever having had intercourse. Trend data was not available for girls.

46. Halpern-Felsher, B.L., Cornell, J.L., Kropp, R.Y., and Tschann, J.M., "Oral Versus Vaginal Sex Among Adolescents: Perceptions, Attitudes, and Behavior," *Pediatrics* 155, No. 4 (2005), pp. 845–851 at 847.

47. Ibid.

48. Boekeloo and Howard, "Oral Sexual Experience Among Young Adolescents."

49. *Contraceptive Technology Update* 22, No. 5 (May 2001).

50. "The 411: Teens & Sex, Part 1: Are TV, Movies and Music to Blame?" Katie Couric, NBC *Today Show*, January 31, 2005, accessed at www.msnbc.msn.com/id/6872269.

51. Low, "Casual Sex" (quoting Lisa Remez of the Alan Guttmacher Institute); Lisa Remez, "Oral Sex Among Adolescents: Is It Sex or Is It Abstinence?" *Family Planning Perspectives* 32, No. 6 (2000) (quoting Deborah Roffman).

52. Cornell, J.L., and Halpern-Felsher, B.L., "Adolescents Tell Us Why Teens Have Oral Sex," *Adolescent Health* 38 (2006), pp. 299–301, at 300.

53. NBC News, "NBC News, People Magazine Commission Landmark National Poll."

54. "The 411: Teens & Sex, Part 2: Oral Sex and 'Friends with Benefits,'" Katie Couric, NBC *Today Show*, January 31, 2005, accessed at www.msnbc.msn.com/id/6872484.

55. Hoff, T., Greene, L., Davis, J., *National Survey of Adolescents and Young Adults: Sexual Health Knowledge, Attitudes and Experiences* (Menlo Park, CA: Kaiser Family Foundation, 2003), at 16, accessed at www.kff.org/youthhivstds/upload/National-Survey-of-Adolescents-and -Young-Adults.pdf.

56. Halpern-Felsher, Cornell, Kropp, and Tschann, "Oral Versus Vaginal Sex Among Adolescents," at 848. In another survey of 519 adolescents aged twelve to seventeen, 21 percent considered oral sex to be "safe sex." Kaiser Family Foundation and *Seventeen* magazine, SexSmarts Survey, "Safer Sex, Condoms and 'the Pill,'" November 2000, p. 2, accessed at www.kff.org/entpartnerships/upload/SexSmarts-Survey-Safer-Sex-Con doms-and-the-Pill-Summary.pdf.

57. Halpern-Felsher, Cornell, Kropp, and Tschann, "Oral Versus Vaginal Sex Among Adolescents," at 848.

58. Ibid., at 849.

59. Kaiser Family Foundation and *Seventeen* magazine, SexSmarts Survey, Questionnaire, and Detailed Results, "Virginity and the First Time," October 2003, p. 1, accessed at www.kff.org/mediapartnerships/loader .cfm?url=/commonspot/security/getfile.cfm&PageID=15491.

60. Hoff, Greene, and Davis, *National Survey of Adolescents and Young Adults,* at 12.

61. Kaiser Family Foundation and *Seventeen* magazine, SexSmarts Survey, "Are You Ready for Sex?"

62. Anna Mulrine, "Risky Business," *U.S. News & World Report,* May 27, 2002.

63. Personal interview, October 18, 2006.

64. The percentage of ninth- through twelfth-grade students claiming to have had sex with four or more partners fell from 18.8 percent in 1993

to 14.3 percent in 2005. Centers for Disease Control, "Percentage of Students Who Had Sexual Intercourse with More Than Four People During Their Life," Youth Risk Behavior Surveillance, Comprehensive Results, accessed January 24, 2007, at http://apps.nccd.cdc.gov/yrbss/QuestYear Table.asp?cat=4&quest=Q59&loc=XX&year=Trend.

65. The number of girls who have had sex before the age of thirteen decreased from 5.1 percent in 1993 to 3.7 percent in 2005. Centers for Disease Control, "Percentage of Students Who Had Sexual Intercourse for the First Time Before Age 13 Years," Youth Risk Behavior Surveillance, Comprehensive Results, accessed January 24, 2007, at http://apps.nccd.cdc.gov/yrbss/QuestYearTable.asp?cat=4&quest=Q58&loc=XX&year=Trend.

66. National Campaign to Prevent Teen Pregnancy, *National Teen Pregnancy and Birth Data: General Facts and Stats,* updated November 2006, accessed at www.teenpregnancy.org/resources/data/genlfact.asp.

67. Anne Jarrell, "The Face of Teenage Sex Grows Younger," *New York Times,* April 2, 2000.

68. "The 411: Teens & Sex, Part 2."

69. Seventeen.com, "2006 Hookup Survey," accessed at www.seventeen.com/health/smarts/articles/0,,625884_694391,00.html.

70. Personal interview, September 20, 2006.

71. Laura Sessions Stepp, "The Buddy System," *Washington Post,* January 19, 2003.

72. Ibid.; Benoit Denizet-Lewis, "Friends, Friends with Benefits and the Benefits of the Local Mall," *New York Times Magazine,* May 30, 2004.

73. Cornell and Halpern-Felsher, "Adolescents Tell Us Why Teens Have Oral Sex." This study of ninth-grade adolescents found that girls were far more likely than boys—24.5 versus 5.5 percent—to believe that improving a relationship was a reason to engage in oral sex.

74. Personal interview, September 20, 2006.

75. Manning, W.D., Longmore, M.A., and Giordano, P.C., "Adolescents' Involvement in Non-Romantic Sexual Activity," *Social Science Research* 34 (2005), pp. 384–407 at 398.

76. A survey from the Kaiser Family Foundation pointed out, "The widely held opinion that oral sex is somehow less important or intimate than intercourse, may suggest that the behavior is going on more frequently than survey respondents are reporting." Hoff, Greene, and Davis, *National Survey of Adolescents and Young Adults,* at 16.

77. Denizet-Lewis, "Friends, Friends with Benefits."

78. Liza Mundy, "Sex & Sensibility," *Washington Post Magazine*, July 16, 2000.

79. Personal interview, October 18, 2006.

80. "Potomac Confidential: Live Discussion with *Post* Metro Columnist Marc Fisher," *Washington Post*, November 3, 2005, accessed at www.washingtonpost.com/wp-dyn/content/discussion/2005/10/28/DI2005102801494.html?nav=left.

81. *The Oprah Winfrey Show* (ABC television broadcast, March 18, 2004).

82. Personal interview, October 18, 2006.

83. Kaiser Family Foundation and *Seventeen* magazine, SexSmarts Survey, "Virginity and the First Time."

84. Interview with Dr. Eddie Newman, director ROP, adult education, high school academies, Pasadena Unified School District, January 17, 2006.

85. Ott, M.A., Millstein, S.G., Ofner, S., and Halpern-Fisher, B.L., "Greater Expectations: Adolescents' Positive Motivations for Sex," *Perspectives on Sexual and Reproductive Health* 38, No. 2 (2006), pp. 84–89 at 86–87.

86. Ibid., at 87.

87. Prinstein, M.J., Meade, C.S., and Cohen, G.L., "Adolescent Oral Sex, Peer Popularity, and Perception of Best Friends' Sexual Behavior," *Journal of Pediatric Psychology* 28, No. 4 (2003), pp. 243–249 at 247.

88. Ibid.

89. Personal interview, September 20, 2006.

90. Fully 89 percent of girls aged fifteen through seventeen reported a lot of or some pressure to have sex, and 84 percent of girls, along with 73 percent of boys, said that "girls lose their boyfriends because they won't have sex" either a lot or sometimes. Kaiser Family Foundation and *Seventeen* magazine, SexSmarts Survey, "Gender Roles," December 2002, pp. 3–4, accessed at www.kff.org/entpartnerships/upload/Gender-Rolls-Summary.pdf.

91. Fully 91 percent of girls aged fifteen through seventeen agreed either "strongly" or "somewhat" with the proposition that "girls are often pressured to have sex before they are ready." Kaiser Family Foundation and *Seventeen* magazine, SexSmarts Survey, "Virginity and the First Time," at 2.

92. The study also found that a more modest (but still significant) 23 percent of females between fifteen and seventeen had "personally" felt a

lot or some pressure to have sex; 23 percent of thirteen- and fourteen-year-old girls had experienced the same pressure, and 54 percent responded that there was pressure to have sex by a certain age. Hoff, Greene, and Davis, *National Survey of Adolescents and Young Adults,* at 8, 39.

93. Kaiser Family Foundation and *Seventeen* magazine, SexSmarts Survey, "Gender Roles," at 4. Of the girls aged fifteen through seventeen who responded to the survey, 53 percent said that there was "a lot" or "some" pressure from other girls to engage in sex.

94. In the National Center for Health Statistics survey, approximately 11 percent of girls aged fifteen through nineteen reported same-sex experiences, almost the same percentage as those aged fifteen through forty-four—suggesting that more girls are experimenting with one another at younger ages. 2002 National Survey of Family Growth, Advance Data No. 362, September 15, 2005, accessed at www.cdc.gov/nchs/data/ad/ad362 .pdf. Of girls fifteen through nineteen, 10.6 percent had engaged in same-sex sexual contact compared with 11.5 percent of those eighteen through forty-four.

95. Laura Sessions Stepp, "Partway Gay?" *Washington Post,* January 4, 2004.

96. Ibid.

97. Alex Morris, "The Cuddle Puddle of Stuyvesant High School," *New York,* February 6, 2006.

98. Ibid.

99. Ibid.

100. Personal interview, October 11, 2006. Certainly, all the experimentation isn't necessarily serious. In a 2006 ABC report on teen sexuality, one girl reported that, at parties, boys will often ask girls to make out, and the girls comply. ABC News, "What Parents Don't Know About Their Teen Daughters' Sex Lives," May 18, 2006, accessed at http://abcnews .go.com/Primetime/Health/story?id=1974232&page=1.

101. "The Lost Children of Rockdale County," produced by Rachel Dretzin Goodman and Barak Goodman, PBS *Frontline,* October 19, 1999.

102. A 2003 survey by the Kaiser Family Foundation found that 60 percent of girls between fifteen and seventeen—and 56 percent of thirteen- and fourteen-year-old girls—believe that "Waiting to have sex is a nice idea but nobody really does." Hoff, Greene, and Davis, *National Survey of Adolescents and Young Adults,* at 12, 39. In a poll of thirteen- through sixteen-year-olds conducted for NBC News/*People* magazine and released

in 2005, 66 percent of respondents agreed (along with 85 percent of their parents!). See NBC News, "NBC News, *People* Magazine Commission Landmark National Poll."

CHAPTER 3: HOOKED IN, HOOKED UP

1. "Help Me Heather," gURL.com, accessed July 3, 2006, at www .gurl.com/findout/hmh/0,,605394-1,00.html?t=605394&x=10&y=6.

2. Hugh Hewitt, *Blog* (Nashville, TN: Nelson Books, 2005), pp. 47–59.

3. Roberts, F., Foehr, U.G., and Rideout, V., *Generation M: Media in the Lives of 8–18 Year-Olds* (Menlo Park, CA: Kaiser Family Foundation, 2005), at 30.

4. Robyn Greenspan, "Online Teens Shape Trends," ClickZ.com, May 6, 2004, accessed at www.clickz.com/news/article.php/3350571.

5. Lenhart, A., Madden, M., and Hitlin, P., *Teens and Technology: Youth Are Leading the Transition to a Fully Wired and Mobile Nation* (Washington, DC: Pew Internet & American Life Project, July 27, 2005), at 1.

6. Escobar-Chaves, S.L., Tortelo, S.R., Markham, C.M., Low, B.J., Eitel, P., and Thickstun, P., "Impact of the Media on Adolescent Sexual Attitudes and Behaviors," *Pediatrics* 116, No. 1 (2005), pp. 303–326 at 319.

7. Lenhart, Madden, and Hitlin, *Teens and Technology,* at 37.

8. Ibid.

9. Ibid., at 42.

10. Rideout, V., *Generation Rx.com: How Young People Use the Internet for Health Information* (Menlo Park, CA: Kaiser Family Foundation, 2001), at 7.

11. Borzekowski, D.L.G., and Rickert, V.I., "Adolescent Cybersurfing for Health Information," *Archives of Pediatric and Adolescent Medicine* 155, No. 7 (2001), pp. 813–817 at 816.

12. Suzuki, L.K., and Calzo, J.P., "The Search for Peer Advice in Cyberspace: An Examination of Online Teen Bulletin Boards About Health and Sexuality," *Applied Developmental Psychology* 25, No. 6 (2004), pp. 685–698 at 686.

13. See www.webmd.com/search/search_results/default.aspx?query= sex&x=38&y=11, accessed July 3, 2006.

14. See www4.plannedparenthood.org/pp2/portal/medicalinfo/teen sexualhealth/;jsessionid=A5CC4B34F7E3E13C51977DA7CABA58E9, accessed January 18, 2007.

15. See www.plannedparenthood.org/birth-control-pregnancy/birth-control/outercourse.htm, accessed January 18, 2007.

16. www.teenwire.com/ask/2006/as-20060707p1305-test.php, accessed July 10, 2006.

17. Eric Johnson, "Friends with Benefits: The Perfect Solution or Risky Venture?" accessed January 30, 2006, at www.sexetc.org/story/2184.

18. Ibid.

19. See www.sexetc.org/topic/birth_control, accessed July 5, 2006.

20. Acacia Stevens, "Abstinence Is Foolproof? Think Again!" Sex, Etc., accessed July 5, 2006, at www.sexetc.org/story/2043.

21. See www.gurl.com/about/help/pages/0,,621911,00.html, accessed July 5, 2006.

22. See ibid.

23. See www.gurl.com/about/help/pages/0,,629823,00.html, accessed July 5, 2006.

24. "Help Me Heather," gURL.com, accessed February 9, 2006.

25. See www.gurl.com/findout/fastfacts/0,,623854,00.html, accessed July 5, 2006.

26. See www.gurl.com/findout/fastfacts/pages/0,,622676,00.html, accessed July 5, 2006.

27. Special thanks to eMarketer, Inc., for making the information from Nielsen/NetRatings available during a phone interview on July 6, 2006.

28. See www.memegen.net/popularmemeweek.pl, accessed July 5, 2006.

29. Special thanks to eMarketer, Inc., for making the information from Nielsen/NetRatings available during a phone interview on July 6, 2006.

30. See www.flooble.com/fun/gayquiz.php, accessed July 5, 2006.

31. See www.misterpoll.com/cat210_new.html, accessed July 5, 2006.

32. www.cosmogirl.com, accessed February 6, 2006.

33. See www.seventeen.com/health/smarts/articles/0,,625884_630872,00.html, accessed July 5, 2006.

34. See www.seventeen.com/health/smarts/articles/0,,625884_630868,00.html, accessed July 5, 2006.

35. See www.seventeen.com/health/smarts/articles/0,,625884_630610,00.html, accessed July 5, 2006.

36. See www.seventeen.com/health/smarts/articles/0,,625884_630869,00.html, accessed July 5, 2006.

37. See www.seventeen.com/health/smarts/articles/0,,625884_630605,00.html, accessed July 5, 2006.

38. Top Ten Reviews, Inc., "Internet Filter Review: Internet Pornography Statistics 2007," Blockbuster Online, accessed at http://internet-filter-review.toptenreviews.com/internet-pornography-statistics.html.

39. Greenfield, P.M., "Inadvertent Exposure to Pornography on the Internet: Implications of Peer-to-Peer File-Sharing Networks for Child Development and Families," *Journal of Applied Developmental Psychology* 25 (2004), pp. 741–750 at 745. The article notes that "A 1998 dissertation found that 48% of third through eighth graders reported having visited Internet sites with various types of 'adult' content." Ibid., at 745–746 (citing Kahn and Egan, 1998).

40. Sarah Gains, "Why Sex Still Leads the Net," *Guardian*, February 28, 2002 (citing a January 2002 study conducted by the London School of Economics).

41. "Protecting Kids Online," editorial, *Washington Post*, July 1, 2004.

42. "Internet Safety: Realistic Strategies & Messages for Kids Taking More and More Risks Online," (Petaluma, CA: Polly Klaas Foundation, 2005), at 8.

43. Roban, W., "The Net Effect: Girls and the New Media" (New York: Girl Scout Research Institute, 2002), at 11.

44. A lengthy discussion of the various subterfuges pornographers may adopt in order to obtain traffic is available in Committee to Study Tools and Strategies for Protecting Kids from Pornography and Their Applicability to Other Inappropriate Internet Content, *Youth, Pornography and the Internet,* edited by Dick Thornburgh and Herbert S. Lin (Washington, DC: National Academies Press, 2002).

45. See www.google.com/search?hl=en&lr=&ie=ISO-8859-1&c2coff =1&q=%22teen+girls%22, accessed July 6, 2006.

46. See www.google.com/search?hl=en&lr=&ie=ISO-8859-1&c2coff =1&q=%22teen+girls%22+AND+%22sexy+clothes%22.

47. Mitchell, K.J., Finkelhor D., and Wolak J., "The Exposure of Youth to Unwanted Sexual Material on the Internet," *Youth & Society* 34, No. 3 (2003), pp. 330–358 at 340.

48. The 2001 Kaiser study reported that 45 percent of its subject group—online youths between ages fifteen and seventeen—had been upset by the experience of unintentionally accessing pornography online. Rideout, V., *Generation Rx.com: How Young People Use the Internet for Health Information* (Menlo Park, CA: Kaiser Family Foundation, 2001).

49. Mitchell, Finkelhor, and Wolak, "The Exposure of Youth to Un-

wanted Sexual Material on the Internet," *Youth and Society 34*, No. 3 (2003), at 346.

50. Roban, "The Net Effect."

51. Mitchell, Finkelhor, and Wolak, "The Exposure of Youth to Unwanted Sexual Material on the Internet," at 352.

52. Rideout, *Generation Rx.com.*

53. Cantor, J., Mares, M.L., and Hyde, J.S., "Autobiographical Memories of Exposure to Sexual Media Content," *Media Psychology 5* (2003), pp. 1–31.

54. Ibid., at 19.

55. Ibid., at 25.

56. Lenhart, A., and Madden, M., *Summary of Findings: Teen Content Creators and Consumers* (Washington, DC: Pew Internet & American Life Project, November 2, 2005), at i.

57. Ibid., at 4.

58. Ibid., at 6.

59. Ibid., at 3.

60. Gross, E.F., "Adolescent Internet Use: What We Expect, What Teens Report," *Journal of Applied Developmental Psychology 25*, No. 6 (2004), pp. 633–649 at 641.

61. Ibid., at 642.

62. "Internet Safety: Realistic Strategies & Messages," at 5.

63. Gross, "Adolescent Internet Use," at 642.

64. Subrahmanyam, K., Greenfield, P.M., and Tynes, B., "Constructing Sexuality and Identity in an Online Teen Chat Room," *Journal of Applied Developmental Psychology 25*, No. 6 (2004), pp. 651–666; Suzuki, L.K., and Calzo, J.P., "The Search for Peer Advice in Cyberspace: An Examination of Online Teen Bulletin Boards About Health and Sexuality," *Journal of Applied Developmental Psychology 25*, No. 6 (2004), pp. 685–698.

65. Subrahmanyam, Greenfield, and Tynes, "Constructing Sexuality and Identity," at 659.

66. Lenhart, A., Rainie, L., and Lewis, O., *Teenage Life Online* (Washington, DC: Pew Internet & American Life Project, June 20, 2001), at 18.

67. See www.teenspot.com/boards/index.html?s=h55n7db425fdmbss kejs8jhpr5, accessed January 20, 2007.

68. See www.teenspot.com/boards/showthread.html?t=315913, accessed January 20, 2007.

69. See www.teenspot.com/boards/showthread.html?t=315643, accessed January 20, 2007.

70. See www.teenspot.com/boards/showthread.html?t=315977, accessed July 8, 2006.

71. See www.teenspot.com/boards/showthread.html?t=315496, accessed January 20, 2007.

72. Suzuki and Calzo, "The Search for Peer Advice in Cyberspace," at 695.

73. Ibid.

74. Ibid., at 694.

75. Greenfield, P.M., and Subrahmanyam, K., "Online Discourse in a Teen Chatroom: New Codes and New Modes of Coherence in a Visual Medium," *Journal of Applied Developmental Psychology* 24, No. 6 (2003), pp. 713–738 at 736.

76. "Internet Safety: Realistic Strategies & Messages for Kids," at 5.

77. Roban, "The Net Effect," at 19.

78. Subrahmanyam, Greenfield, and Tynes, "Constructing Sexuality and Identity," at 662 (citing Rodino, 1997).

79. Benoit Denizet-Lewis, "Friends, Friends with Benefits and the Benefits of the Local Mall," *New York Times Magazine,* May 30, 2004.

80. Associated Press, "Dutch Study: A Quarter of Boys, 20% of Girls Claim to Have Cyber Sex," June 2, 2006, accessed at www.smh.com.au/news/Technology/Dutch-study-A-quarter-of-boys-20-percent-of-girls-claim-to-have-cyber-sex/2006/06/02/1148956492604.html.

81. "Internet Safety: Realistic Strategies & Messages for Kids," at 3.

82. See, e.g., Mitchell, K.J., Finkelhor, D., and Wolak, J., "The Exposure of Youth to Unwanted Sexual Material on the Internet," *Youth & Society* 34, No. 3 (2003), pp. 330–358.

83. Mitchell, K.J., Finkelhor, D., and Wolak, J., "Risk Factors for and Impact of Online Sexual Solicitation of Youth," *Journal of the American Medical Association* 285, No. 23 (2001), pp. 3011–3014 at 3012.

84. Top Ten Reviews, Inc., "Internet Filter Review."

85. This personal experience is similar to that described in academic research. See Greenfield, P.M., "Developmental Considerations for Determining Appropriate Internet Use Guidelines for Children and Adolescents," *Journal of Applied Developmental Psychology* 25 (2004), pp. 751–762.

86. Roberts, Foehr, and Rideout, *Generation M,* at 95.

87. "Internet Safety: Realistic Strategies & Messages for Kids," at 9. It's worth noting that, as early as 2001, 11 percent of girls aged twelve

through seventeen said they had lied about their age in order to access a Web site (compared with 19 percent of boys). Lenhart, A., Rainie, L., and Lewis, O., *Teenage Life Online* (Washington, DC: Pew Internet & American Life Project, 2001), at 33.

88. Gross, "Adolescent Internet Use," at 643.

89. Ibid.

90. Roban, "The Net Effect," at 15.

91. Berson, M.J., and Ferron, J.M, "The Computer Can't See You Blush," *Kappa Delta Pi Record* 36, No. 4 (2000).

92. Press release, "New Study Reveals 14% of Teens Have Had Face-to-Face Meetings with People They've Met on the Internet," National Center for Missing & Exploited Children, May 11, 2006, accessed at http://us.missingkids.com/missingkids/servlet/NewsEventServlet?LanguageCountry=en_US&PageId=2383.

93. Reuters, "MySpace Gains Top Ranking of U.S. Web Sites," July 11, 2006, accessed July 12, 2006, at http://today.reuters.com/news/newsArticle.aspx?type=technologyNews&storyID=2006-07-11T154250Z_01_N11382172_RTRUKOC_0_US-MEDIA-MYSPACE.xml.

94. Blair Meeks, "MySpace: Predator's Playground," WXIA Atlanta, March 22, 2006, accessed July 7, 2006, at www.11alive.com/news/news_article.aspx?storyid=77615.

95. ABC News, "What Are Teens Hiding on MySpace," May 18, 2006, accessed at http://abcnews.go.com/Primetime/story?id=1975086&page=1.

96. Associated Press, "Two Teens Face Child Pornography Charges," March 29, 2006, accessed at www.boston.com/news/local/rhode_island/articles/2006/03/29/two_teens_face_child_pornography_charges. Likewise, in 2003, police got involved when young people posted pictures featuring topless girls and drunken parties near Mount Lebanon, Pennsylvania. Jane Elizabeth and Mackenzie Carpenter, "More Kids Are Having Sex, and They're Having It Younger," *Pittsburgh Post-Gazette*, September 14, 2003.

97. Katharine Mieszkowski, "Candy from Strangers," Salon.com, August 13, 2001, accessed at http://archive.salon.com/tech/feature/2001/08/13/cam_girls/index.html; Mark Frauenfelder, "Cam Girls," *Yahoo Internet Life*, June 2002, accessed at http://boingboing.net/camgirls.html.

98. It's worth noting that the practice isn't restricted exclusively to girls. In April 2006, a boy who had starred in Web cam child pornography for five years criticized the Justice Department for not moving quickly enough to round up the fifteen hundred pedophiles whose information he had surrendered. Associated Press, "Child Porn Victim Says

Justice Did Not Protect Him," April 5, 2006, accessed at www.usatoday.com/news/washington/2006-04-04-child-porn_x.htm.

99. "Internet Safety: Realistic Strategies & Messages for Kids," at 1.

100. Ibid., at 5.

101. Ibid., at 7.

102. Tamekia Reece, "She Had an Online Stalker," *Seventeen,* October 2004, p. 104.

103. Chris Hansen, "Dangers Children Face Online: *Dateline* Hidden Camera Investigation Turns Spotlight on Internet Predators," MSNBC.com, November 11, 2004, accessed at www.msnbc.msn.com/id/6083442.

104. Sara Lin, "13 Charged in Sting Aiming for Molesters," *Los Angeles Times,* February 23, 2006.

105. Jason Szep, "Massachusetts Wants MySpace Crackdown on Predators," Reuters, May 2, 2006, accessed July 9, 2006, at http://ca.news.yahoo.com/s/02052006/6/n-technology-massachusetts-wants-myspace-crackdown-predators.html.

106. KCBD (Lubbock, TX), "Teenage Victim's Father Speaks Out About Daughter Being Solicited Online," March 22, 2006, accessed at www.kcbd.com/Global/story.asp?S=4669694&nav=CcXH.

107. Rod Antone, "Another Isle Man Allegedly Baits Teen Victim on MySpace," *Honolulu Star-Bulletin,* March 9, 2006.

108. CBS4 (Boston), "Man Accused of Using MySpace.com to Seduce Teen," February 27, 2006, accessed at http://cbs4boston.com/topstories/local_story_058193246.html.

109. Brian Stanley, "Police Accuse Man of Soliciting Child," *(Chicago) Herald News,* June 11, 2006, accessed at www.suburbanchicagonews.com/heraldnews/city/4_1_JO11_MYSPACE_S1.htm.

110. "Internet Safety: Realistic Strategies & Messages for Kids," at 5.

111. Hansen, "Dangers Children Face Online."

112. There are two characteristics common to most girls who do form close online relationships: high parent–child conflict and being highly troubled. Wolak, J., Mitchell, K.J., and Finkelhor, D., "Escaping or Connecting? Characteristics of Youth Who Form Close Online Relationships," *Journal of Adolescence* 26, No. 1 (2003), pp. 105–119.

113. "Internet Safety: Realistic Strategies & Messages for Kids," at 8.

114. Suzuki and Calzo, "The Search for Peer advice in Cyberspace," at 687 (citing Hassan and Creatsas, 2000).

115. Committee to Study Tools and Strategies for Protecting Kids

from Pornography and Their Applicability to Other Inappropriate Internet Content, *Youth, Pornography and the Internet,* section 5.3.

116. Mitchell, Finkelhor, and Wolak, "The Exposure of Youth to Unwanted Sexual Material," at 333–334.

117. Greenfield, "Inadvertent Exposure to Pornography on the Internet," at 748.

118. Corne, S., Briere, J., and Esses, L.M., "Women's Attitudes and Fantasies About Rape as a Function of Early Exposure to Pornography," *Journal of Interpersonal Violence* 7, No. 4 (1992), pp. 454–461.

119. Rideout, *Generation Rx.com,* at 12.

120. Pepper Schwartz, "Child and Adolescent Sexuality and the Internet," notes for presentation to the National Academy of Sciences, accessed July 10, 2006, at www7.nationalacademies.org/itas/Pepper_schwartz.html.

121. Ibid.

122. Greenfield, "Developmental Considerations for Determining Appropriate Internet Use Guidelines," at 754.

123. Ibid., at 755.

124. Ibid.

125. Lenhart, A., *Protecting Teens Online* (Washington, DC: Pew Internet & American Life Project, 2005), at 7.

126. Mitchell, Finkelhor, and Wolak, "The Exposure of Youth to Unwanted Sexual Material," at 347.

127. Elizabeth and Carpenter, "More Kids Are Having Sex."

CHAPTER 4: BETWEEN THE COVERS

1. Sally Beatty, "Young Girls Reading—Isn't That Wholesome?" *Wall Street Journal,* August 2, 2005.

2. Ibid.

3. Janet Shamlian, "New Trend in Teen Fiction: Racy Reads," NBC News, August 15, 2005, accessed at www.msnbc.msn.com/id/8962686.

4. Paul Ruditis, *Rainbow Party* (New York: Simon & Schuster, 2005), at 197.

5. Carol Memmott, "Controversy Colors Teen Book," *USA Today,* May 22, 2005.

6. Joy Bean, "Raining on the 'Rainbow Party,'" *Publishers Weekly,* April 25, 2005, accessed at www.publishersweekly.com/article/CA526624 .html?pubdate=4/25/2005&display=current.

7. Ibid.

8. Memmott, "Controversy Colors Teen Book."

9. Tania Padgett, "Sex and the Teenage Girl," *(New York) Newsday,* April 4, 2006.

10. R. A. Nelson, *Teach Me* (New York: Penguin Group, 2005), at 73.

11. Ibid., at 93.

12. Cecily von Ziegesar, *Nothing Can Keep Us Together* (New York: Little, Brown, 2005), at 80.

13. Ibid., at 56.

14. Ibid., at 136.

15. Ibid., at 166–167.

16. Ibid., at 210–211.

17. Ibid., at 218.

18. Shamlian, "New Trend in Teen Fiction."

19. Heather Salerno, "Racy Books Increasingly Target Teens and Tweens," *(Westchester, NY) Journal News,* July 27, 2005.

20. Shamlian, "New Trend in Teen Fiction."

21. Cecily von Ziegesar, *The It Girl* (New York: Little, Brown, 2005), at 33.

22. Lori Matsukawa, "Parents Shocked at Racy Teen Books," King 5 News (Seattle), November 17, 2005.

23. Ibid.

24. Shamlian, "New Trend in Teen Fiction."

25. Matsukawa, "Parents Shocked at Racy Teen Books."

26. SmartGirl.org, "Summary of Major Findings," Teen Read Week Survey (A Partnership of SmartGirl and the American Library Association), October 1999, accessed at www.smartgirl.org/speakout/archives/ trw1999/trwsummary.html.

27. There are other perceptive critiques of the magazines targeted at even younger girls. See, for example, Meghan Cox Gurdon, "It's, Like, So Totally Cool or Whatever," *Wall Street Journal,* August 19, 2005.

28. Girls represent 22.9 percent of the market for women's magazines. Kaiser Family Foundation, *Key Facts: Tweens, Teens, and Magazines,* fall 2004, accessed at www.kff.org/entmedia/upload/ Tweens-Teens-and-Magazines-Fact-Sheet.pdf (citing Larry Dobrow, "Simmons Measures Teen Readers," MediaPost's MediaDailyNews, June 18, 2003).

29. SmartGirl.org, "Summary of Major Findings."

30. Kaiser Family Foundation, *Key Facts: Tweens, Teens, and Magazines.*

31. Ibid. (citing Lisa Duke and Peggy Kreshel, "Negotiating Feminin-

ity: Girls in Early Adolescence Read Teen Magazines," *Journal of Communication Inquiry* 22, No. 1 [1998], pp. 48–72).

32. Ibid. (citing the Taylor Research & Consulting Group, "Taylor Kids Pulse: Where the Wired Things Are").

33. Along with *Teen People, Seventeen* and *Cosmo GIRL!* boast about six million readers combined. Rebecca Grace, "Teen Magazines Send Mixed Messages," *Religion News,* October 17, 2005 (citing Christine E. Virgin, editor and co-publisher of *Realiteen* magazine).

34. In 2003, *Seventeen* had the highest circulation of any teen-interest magazine at 2,372,261. Magazine Publishers of America, "Teen Market Profile," 2004, p. 15, accessed at www.magazine.org/content/files/teen profile04.pdf.

35. Peg Tyre, "No Longer Most Likely to Succeed: In an Overcrowded Market, Teen Magazines Fight for Their Lives," *Newsweek,* April 19, 2004.

36. According to the Audit Bureau of Circulation, in 2003, when the teen market generally was experiencing circulation losses compared with the previous year, the circulation of *Cosmo GIRL!* increased by 18.5 percent. Its total paid circulation that year was 1,258,881. Magazine Publishers of America, *Fact Sheet: Circulation,* 2003, accessed March 16, 2006, at www.magazine.org/content/Files/2003allabccirc.xls, at 16. By comparison, *Cosmo GIRL!* competitor *Seventeen* was down by 3 percent that year. Ibid.

37. Tyre, "No Longer Most Likely to Succeed."

38. Ibid. (quoting Carolyn Bivens, president of Initiatives, a media buying group).

39. Signorelli, N., "A Content Analysis: Reflections of Girls in the Media" (Menlo Park, CA: Kaiser Family Foundation and Children Now, 1997), table 18, accessed at www.kff.org/entmedia/1260-gendr6 .cfm#mag.

40. Marina Khidekel, "Guys Confess: Bust-ed!" *Cosmo GIRL!,* April 2005, p. 82.

41. Marina Khidekel, "Guys Confess: Say What?" *Cosmo GIRL!,* March 2005, p. 71.

42. "Love Stories: The Crazy Things You've Done in the Name of Love!," *Cosmo GIRL!,* June–July 2004, p. 74.

43. Ibid., p. 62.

44. *Cosmo GIRL!,* March 2006.

45. *Cosmo GIRL!,* March 2006.

46. *Cosmo GIRL!,* October 2004.

47. "Global Love Survey," *Cosmo GIRL!,* May 2005, pp. 130–131.

48. Laura Berman and Jennifer Berman, "10 Questions You Can't Ask Anyone," *Cosmo GIRL!,* May 2005, pp. 98–99.

49. Vanessa Silva, as told to Maura Kelly, "I Had an Affair with My Coach," *Cosmo GIRL!,* August 2004, p. 110.

50. "*Cosmo GIRL!*s Gone Wild!: All About . . . the Wildboyz," *Cosmo GIRL!,* April 2004, p. 53.

51. Karen Brodman-Grimm, MD, "Your Body Questions Answered," *Seventeen,* October 2005, p. 83.

52. "Your Body Questions Answered," *Seventeen,* February 2005, p. 65.

53. "Sex Survey: The Truth About Sexual Pressure," *Seventeen,* September 2005, p. 133.

54. "Sex Survey: Do You Trust Him Too Much?" *Seventeen,* August 2005, p. 131.

55. "Health Alert: Stop! Read This Before You Have Sex," *Seventeen,* July 2005, pp. 86–88.

56. "Guys' Love & Sex Secrets," *Seventeen,* February 2005, pp. 66–67.

57. Melanie Abrahams, "Guys Talk: Dating Older Guys," *Seventeen,* May 2005, p. 106.

58. Melanie Abrahams, "Guys Talk: 'Why I Cheated on My Girlfriend,'" *Seventeen,* June 2005, p. 103.

59. "Sarah," "Saving Himself," *Seventeen,* August 2005, p. 161.

60. "Anna," "Virginity Lost," *Seventeen,* March 2006, p. 138.

61. Rebecca Raphael, "He Won't Let Them Freak-Dance," *Seventeen,* October 2005, p. 89.

62. "Principal Bans Teen Magazine from School for Sex Content," *Media Report to Women* 26, No. 2 (1998), accessed at www.mediareport towomen.com/issues/262.htm. The other two banned magazines were *YM* and the now defunct *Teen.*

63. "The Big Question: Does Your Faith Affect Your Love Life?" *Seventeen,* February 2005, p. 69.

64. "The Art of Modesty," *Seventeen,* June 2004, p. 127.

65. Ruditis, *Rainbow Party,* at 23–24.

66. von Ziegesar, *The It Girl,* at 57.

CHAPTER 5: TRULY THE "BOOB" TUBE

1. Parents Television Council, "It's Just Harmless Entertainment," Parentstv.org, 2005, accessed at www.parentstv.org/PTC/facts/mediafacts .asp (citing Nielsen television rankings).

2. Parents Television Council, "The 2001–2002 Top 10 Best and Worst Shows on Network TV," at 5–6, accessed at www.parentstv.org/PTC/ publications/reports/top10bestandworst/2002/top10bestandworst.pdf.

3. Paul Davidson, "Indecent or Not? TV, Radio Walk Fuzzy Line," *USA Today,* June 2, 2005.

4. Parents Television Council, "The 2001–2002 Top 10 Best and Worst Shows."

5. TV.com, *Will & Grace:* The Hospital Show (NBC television broadcast, March 28, 2000), accessed at www.tv.com/will-and-grace/the-hospi tal-show/episode/1970/summary.html.

6. *Will & Grace:* Hey La, Hey La, My Ex-Boyfriend's Back (NBC television broadcast, March 14, 2000).

7. *One Tree Hill:* You Gotta Go There to Come Back (WB television broadcast, November 10, 2004).

8. *One Tree Hill:* Are You True? (WB television broadcast, October 7, 2003).

9. *One Tree Hill:* The Search for Something More (WB television broadcast, November 11, 2003).

10. *One Tree Hill:* A Multitude of Casualties (WB television broadcast, November 2, 2005).

11. *One Tree Hill:* Life in a Glass House (WB television broadcast, November 14, 2003).

12. *The O.C.:* The Road Warrior (Fox television broadcast, March 9, 2006).

13. *The O.C.:* Pilot (Fox television broadcast, August 5, 2003).

14. *The O.C.:* The Undertow (Fox television broadcast, March 24, 2006).

15. *The O.C.:* The College Try (Fox television broadcast, April 20, 2006).

16. Parents Television Council, "It's Just Harmless Entertainment" (citing Nielsen television rankings).

17. *That '70s Show:* Happy Jack (Fox television broadcast, March 24, 2004).

18. *Veronica Mars* official Web site, accessed at www2.warnerbros .com/television/tvShows/veronicamars.

19. *Friends:* The One with the Free Porn (NBC television broadcast, March 26, 1998).

20. *Sex and the City:* Politically Erect (HBO cable television broadcast, June 1, 2000).

21. *Sex and the City:* Three's a Crowd (HBO cable television broadcast, July 26, 1998).

22. *Sex and the City:* What's Sex Got to Do with It? (HBO cable television broadcast, June 17, 2001).

23. *Sex and the City:* Valley of the Twenty-Something Guys (HBO cable television broadcast, June 28, 1998).

24. *Sex and the City:* Easy Come, Easy Go (HBO cable television broadcast, August 6, 2000).

25. *Sex and the City:* Time and Punishment (HBO cable television broadcast, July 8, 2001).

26. *Sex and the City:* Baby, Talk Is Cheap (HBO cable television broadcast, July 1, 2001).

27. Parents Television Council, "Harsh Reality: Unscripted TV Reality Shows Offensive to Families," 2002, accessed at www.parentstv.org/PTC/publications/reports/realitytv/main.asp.

28. Davis, S., and Mares, M.L., "Effects of Talk Show Viewing on Adolescents," *Journal of Communication* 48, No. 3 (summer 1998), pp. 69–86 at 78.

29. Collins, R., Elliott, M., Berry, S., Kanouse, D., Kunkel, D., Hunter, S., and Miu, A., "Watching Sex on Television Predicts Adolescent Initiation of Sexual Behavior," *Pediatrics* 114, No. 3 (2004), pp. 280–289 at 287.

30. The 70 percent figure represents a 96 percent increase in the number of sexual scenes in the study's sample since the study began in 1997–98. Kunkel, D., Eyal, K., Finnerty, K., Biely, E., and Donnerstein, E., *Sex on TV 4* (Menlo Park, CA: Kaiser Family Foundation, 2005), at 58. The study sample excluded daily newscasts, sports events, and children's shows. According to the study, 35 percent of all programs sampled included depictions of sexual behavior, and 68 percent featured talk about sex. Ibid., at 68.

31. The 77 percent figure exceeds the 67 percent found in 1998. Ibid., at 50.

32. Ward, L.M., "Talking About Sex: Common Themes About Sexuality in the Prime-Time Television Programs Children and Adolescents View Most," *Journal of Youth and Adolescence* 24, No. 5 (1995), pp. 595–615 at 602.

33. According to the Kaiser study, sexual content appeared (in shows containing it) in an average of 5.0 scenes per hour, up from 3.2 in 1998 and 4.4 in 2002. Kunkel, Eyal, Finnerty, Biely, and Donnerstein, *Sex on TV 4*, at 57–58. The study notes that the increased percentage of shows with sexual content, taken together with the greater number of sexual scenes per program, accounts for the dramatic increase in the sexual content on television.

34. Ibid., at 51. The figure exceeds the overall average of sexual content appearing in 5.0 scenes per hour. Although depictions of oral sex on television are still relatively rare, the Kaiser study likewise noted that fully 45 percent of the programs most frequently watched by teens include some portrayal of sexual behavior (versus 35 percent of the programs in the overall study sample). Ibid. And although only 8 percent of the shows most often watched by teens include portrayals of sexual intercourse, the teen programs that do show it contain about twice as many scenes of intercourse per hour as the overall television sample. Ibid., at 52.

35. Fact Sheet, "Teens and Sex: The Role of Popular TV," Kaiser Family Foundation (July 2001), accessed at www.kff.org/entmedia/loader .cfm?url=/commonspot/security/getfile.cfm&PageID=13556.

36. Roberts, F., Foehr, U.G., and Rideout, V., *Generation M: Media in the Lives of 8–18 Year-Olds* (Menlo Park, CA: Kaiser Family Foundation, 2005), at 10.

37. Ibid.

38. Ibid.

39. Ibid., at 24.

40. Ibid.

41. Roberts, D.F., "Media and Youth: Access, Exposure and Privatization," *Journal of Adolescent Health* 27, No. 2 (2000) (2 suppl), pp. 8–14.

42. Ibid.

43. Roberts, Foehr, and Rideout, *Generation M*, at 15.

44. Peterson, J.L., Moore, K.A., and Furstenberg, F.F. Jr., "Television Viewing and Early Initiation of Sexual Intercourse: Is There a Link?" *Journal of Homosexuality* 21, No. 1–2 (1991), pp. 93–118.

45. Ibid.

46. Moore, K.A., Peterson, J.L., and Furstenberg, F.F., "Parental Attitudes and the Occurrence of Early Sexual Activity," *Journal of Marriage and the Family* 48 (November 1986), pp. 777–782 at 781.

47. "Parents, Media and Public Policy," Kaiser Family Foundation Survey (fall 2004), at 7, accessed at www.kff.org/entmedia/upload/Parents

-Media-and-Public-Policy-A-Kaiser-Family-Foundation-Survey-Report
.pdf.

48. Ward, L., "Does Television Exposure Affect Emerging Adults' Attitudes and Assumptions About Sexual Relationships? Correlational and Experimental Confirmation," *Journal of Youth and Adolescence* 31, No. 1 (2002), at 12. This study was of undergraduates aged eighteen through twenty-two.

49. Ward, "Talking About Sex," at 607.

50. Ibid., at 608.

51. Ibid., at 597.

52. Teresa Wiltz, "TV's Rare Bird: Networks Don't Know What to Do with Functional Families, Except Ignore Them," *Washington Post,* May 21, 2006. According to the study referenced in the piece, one-fifth of the scenes of intercourse involve characters who aren't in a committed relationship, and another 15 percent show characters having sex when they've just met.

53. Ward, "Talking About Sex," at 610.

54. Ibid.

55. Kunkel, D., Cope, K., Farinola, W., Biely, E., Rollin, E., and Donnerstein, E., "Sexual Messages on Entertainment TV in the USA," in *Children in the New Media Landscape,* edited by C. von Feilitzen and U. Carlsson (Goteborg, Sweden: UNESCO International Clearinghouse on Children and Violence on the Screen, 2000), pp. 155–158 at 157.

56. Kunkel, Eyal, Finnerty, Biely, and Donnerstein, *Sex on TV 4,* at 7.

57. Ibid., at 54.

58. Ward, "Talking About Sex," at 605.

59. Margo Maine, *Body Wars: Making Peace with Women's Bodies* (Carlsbad, CA: Gurze Books, 2000).

60. Kunkel, Eyal, Finnerty, Biely, and Donnerstein, *Sex on TV 4,* at 49. Movies broadcast on television during prime time featured discussion about sex in 100 percent of the sample and included sexual behavior in 83 percent of the sample.

61. Diane Brady, "Hollywood: Now It's a Girl Thing," *BusinessWeek,* May 24, 2004, accessed at www.businessweek.com/magazine/content/04 _21/b3884132.htm.

62. Roger Ebert, "Mean Girls," *Chicago Sun-Times,* April 30, 2004.

63. Mick LaSalle, "It's Yet Another High School Comedy, but 'Mean Girls' Has a Talented Cast and a Wickedly Intelligent Script," *San Francisco Chronicle,* April 30, 2004.

64. Ann Hornaday, "Mean Girls," *Washington Post,* April 30, 2004.

65. Paul Hyman, "Games Industry Battles New Legislation," *Hollywood Reporter,* April 21, 2006, accessed at www.hollywoodreporter.com/hr/search/article_display.jsp?vnu_content_id=1002384376.

66. *Family Entertainment Protection Act,* S. 2126, 109th Cong., 1st Sess. (2005).

67. Sargent, J.D., Beach, M.L., Dalton, M.A., Ernstoff, L.T., Gibson, J.J., Tickle, J.J., and Heatherton, T.F., "Effect of Parental R-Rated Movie Restriction on Adolescent Smoking Initiation: A Prospective Study," *Pediatrics* 114, No. 1 (2004), pp. 149–156 at 151.

68. Martin F. Kohn, "Ratings Let More Raunch Reach Teens," *Detroit Free Press,* February 25, 2005.

69. Press release, "Study Finds 'Ratings Creep': Movie Ratings Categories Contain More Violence, Sex, Profanity Than Decade Ago," Harvard School of Public Health, July 2004 (quoting Kimberly Thompson, associate professor in the Department of Health Policy and Management at Harvard School of Public Health and director of the Kids at Risk Project), accessed at www.hsph.harvard.edu/press/releases/press07132004.html.

70. Thompson, K.M., and Yokota, F., "Violence, Sex, and Profanity in Films: Correlation of Movie Ratings with Content," *Medscape General Medicine* 6, No. 3 (2004).

71. John Horn, "The Science of Comedy," *Los Angeles Times,* August 14, 2005.

72. Ibid.

73. Associated Press, "Class Watches '40 Year Old Virgin' Movie," January 26, 2006.

74. Wiltz, "TV's Rare Bird."

75. Dempsey, J.M., and Reichert, T., "Portrayal of Married Sex in the Movies," *Journal of Sexuality and Culture* 4, No. 3 (2000), pp. 21–36.

76. According to a statement from the American Academy of Pediatrics, "The conclusion of the public health community, based on over 30 years of research, is that viewing entertainment violence can lead to increases in aggressive attitudes, values and behavior, particularly in children." American Academy of Pediatrics, "Joint Statement on the Impact of Entertainment Violence on Children," Congressional Public Health Summit, July 26, 2000, accessed at www.aap.org/advocacy/releases/jstmtevc.htm.

77. Distefan, J.M., Pierce, J., and Gilpin, E., "Do Favorite Movie Stars Influence Adolescent Smoking Initiation?" *American Journal of Public Health* 94, No. 7 (2004), pp. 1239–1244 at 1241.

78. Ward, L., and Friedman, K., "Using TV as a Guide: Associations Be-

tween Television Viewing and Adolescents' Sexual Attitudes and Behavior," *Journal of Research on Adolescence* 16, No. 1 (2006), pp. 133–156 at 146.

79. Ward, L., and Rivadeneyra, R., "Contributions of Entertainment Television to Adolescents' Sexual Attitudes and Expectations: The Role of Viewing Amount Versus Viewer Involvement," *Journal of Sex Research* 36, No. 3 (1999), pp. 237–249 at 243.

80. Bryant, J., and Rockwell, S.C., "Effects of Massive Exposure to Sexually-Oriented Primetime Television Programming on Adolescents' Moral Judgment," in *Media, Children, and the Family: Social Scientific, Psychodynamic and Clinical Perspectives,* edited by J. Zillman, J. Bryant, and A.C. Huston (Hillsdale, NJ: Lawrence Erlbaum Associates, 1994), at 183–195.

81. Ward, "Does Television Exposure Affect Emerging Adults' Attitudes and Assumptions." This study was of undergraduates aged eighteen through twenty-two.

82. Ward and Friedman, "Using TV as a Guide," at 151.

83. Ward and Rivadeneyra, "Contributions of Entertainment Television to Adolescents' Sexual Attitudes and Expectations," at 244.

84. Ward and Friedman, "Using TV as a Guide," at 150.

85. See generally Davis and Mares, "Effects of Talk Show Viewing on Adolescents"; Ward, "Does Television Exposure Affect Emerging Adults' Attitudes and Assumptions" (studying undergraduates aged eighteen through twenty-two).

86. Ward and Rivadeneyra, "Contributions of Entertainment Television to Adolescents' Sexual Attitudes and Expectations," at 244.

87. Ibid.

88. Davis and Mares, "Effects of Talk Show Viewing on Adolescents," at 80.

89. Wingood, G., DiClemente, R., Harrington, K., Davies, S., Hook, E., and Oh, M.K., "Exposure to X-Rated Movies and Adolescents' Sexual and Contraceptive-Related Attitudes and Behaviors," *Pediatrics* 107, No. 5 (2001), pp. 1116–1119. The study focused on black girls between fourteen and eighteen.

90. Collins, Elliott, Berry, Kanouse, Kunkel, Hunter, and Miu, "Watching Sex on Television."

91. Ibid., at 285.

92. L'Engle, K.L., Brown, J.D., and Kenneavy, K., "The Mass Media Are an Important Context for Adolescent Sexual Behavior," *Journal of Adolescent Health* 38 (2006), pp. 186–192 at 422.

93. "The Lost Children of Rockdale County," produced by Rachel Dretzin Goodman and Barak Goodman, PBS *Frontline,* October 19, 1999.

94. Collins, Elliott, Berry, Kanouse, Kunkel, Hunter, and Miu, "Watching Sex on Television."

95. Research Highlight, *Does Watching Sex on Television Influence Teens' Sexual Activity?* (Santa Monica, CA: RAND, 2004), at 2, accessed at www.rand.org/pubs/research_briefs/2005/RB9068.pdf.

96. Kunkel, Eyal, Finnerty, Biely, and Donnerstein, *Sex on TV 4,* at 2.

97. Press release, "Admiration and Envy: The Star-Power List," Teen Research Unlimited, March 15, 2005, accessed at www.teenresearch.com/PRview.cfm?edit_id=370.

98. Associated Press, "Lindsay Lohan Says She's 'Appalled' by 'Vanity Fair' Article," *USA Today,* January 10, 2006.

99. Richard Johnson, "Perfect Gent," *New York Post,* March 15, 2006.

100. Richard Johnson, "Lindsay Gets Bedroom Shock," *New York Post,* May 1, 2006.

101. Jeanette Walls, "Paris Poses for *Playboy* . . . or Does She?" MSNBC, February 9, 2005, accessed at www.msnbc.msn.com/id/6908973.

102. ContactMusic.com, "Stone Advocates Oral Sex," March 28, 2006, accessed at www3.contactmusic.com/news/index34.htm.

103. Marilyn Elias, "TV Might Rush Teens into Sex," *USA Today,* September 6, 2004.

104. Ward, "Talking About Sex," at 610.

105. Kunkel, Eyal, Finnerty, Biely, and Donnerstein, *Sex on TV 4,* at 58. This figure denotes the fact that 70 percent of the programs in the study's sample included some kind of sexual content.

106. Collins, Elliott, Berry, Kanouse, Kunkel, Hunter, and Miu, "Watching Sex on Television," at 281.

107. Hal Marcovitz, *Teens & Sex, The Gallup Youth Survey: Major Issues and Trends* (Broomall, PA : Mason Crest, 2004), at 63.

108. Wartella, E., Scantlin, R., Kotler, J., Huston, A., and Donnerstein, E., "Effects of Sexual Content in the Media on Children and Adolescents," in *Children in the New Media Landscape,* edited by C. von Feilitzen and U. Carlsson, pp. 141–153 at 147.

109. Greenberg, B.S., Linsangan, R., and Soderman, A., "Adolescents' Reactions to Television Sex," in *Media, Sex and the Adolescent,* edited by B. S. Greenberg, J. D. Brown, and N. L. Buerkel-Rothfuss (Cresskill, NJ: Hampton Press, 1993), pp. 196–224.

110. Granello, D.H., "Using 'Beverly Hills, 90210' to Explore Develop-

mental Issues in Female Adolescents," *Youth & Society* 29, No. 1 (1997), pp. 24–53 at 38.

111. See, for instance, Amonker, R.G., "What Do Teens Know About the Facts of Life?" *Journal of School Health* 50, No. 9 (1980), pp. 527–530; Andre, T., Frevert, R.L., and Schuchmann, D., "From Whom Have College Students Learned What About Sex?" *Youth & Society* 20, No. 3 (1989), pp. 241–248.

112. Wartella, Scantlin, Kotler, Huston, and Donnerstein, "Effects of Sexual Content in the Media," at 148.

CHAPTER 6: AURAL SEX

1. Strouse, J.S., Buerkel-Rothfuss, N., and Long, E.C.J., "Gender and Family as Moderators of the Relationship Between Music Video Exposure and Adolescent Sexual Permissiveness," *Journal of Adolescence* 30, No. 119 (fall 1995), pp. 506–521.

2. Dawn Anfuso, "Tiffany Buys More Britney Than Boys Do," iMedia Connection, February 19, 2004, accessed at www.imediaconnection.com/content/2830.asp.

3. Ibid.

4. Robyn Greenspan, "Teen Girls Rule as Music Influencers, Spenders," ClickZ, February 9, 2004, accessed at www.clickz.com/showPage.html?page=3310371.

5. Rouner, D., "Rock Music Use as a Socializing Function," *Popular Music and Society* 14, No. 1 (1990), pp. 97–107.

6. Roberts, D.F., Christenson, P.G., and Gentile, D.A., "The Effects of Violent Music on Children and Adolescents," in *Media Violence and Children,* edited by D. A. Gentile (Westport, CT: Praeger, 2003), pp. 153–170 at 156.

7. Personal interview, October 18, 2006.

8. "Tunes 'n Tudes," *USA Weekend Magazine,* May 5, 2002, accessed at www.usaweekend.com/02_issues/020505/020505teenmusicresults.html.

9. Ibid.

10. Roberts, F., Foehr, U.G., and Rideout, V., *Generation M: Media in the Lives of 8–18 Year-Olds* (Menlo Park, CA: Kaiser Family Foundation, 2005), at 29.

11. Roberts, Christenson, and Gentile, "The Effects of Violent Music on Children and Adolescents," at 159.

12. American Association of Pediatrics Committee on Communica-

tions, "Impact of Music Lyrics and Music Videos on Children and Youth," *Pediatrics* 98, No. 6 (1996), pp. 1219–1221 at 1219.

13. Dan DeLuca, "Madonna the Mature: Who'd Have Thought?" *Philadelphia Inquirer,* July 15, 2001.

14. Strawberry Saroyan, "Oops, She's Doing It Again," Salon.com, May 22, 2000, accessed online at http://archive.salon.com/ent/feature/2000/05/22/britney/index.html.

15. W magazine, August 2003; see also Reuters, "I'm No Virgin, Admits Britney," July 9, 2003, accessed at www.smh.com.au/articles/2003/07/09/1057430243141.html.

16. *Rolling Stone,* October 2, 2003.

17. *Esquire,* November 2003.

18. Sean Piccoli, "Porn: It's Everywhere You Look, and Some Places You Wouldn't Think To," *South Florida Sun-Sentinel,* April 29, 2004.

19. *Primetime* (ABC News television broadcast, November 13, 2003).

20. "Christina Aguilera," Billboard.com, accessed June 5, 2006, at www.billboard.com/bbcom/bio/index.jsp?JSESSIONID=G2cFQSJrQ9LkG2xxgBJYgHYj1j31JsXnPCmb7HdJ1XC4wWmpCt71!-532578819&pid=325726.

21. "'Dirrty' by Christina Aguilera," Songfacts.com, accessed at www.songfacts.com/detail.php?id=2336.

22. Michelle Malkin, "Look Mama—She's Naked!" *Jewish World Review,* November 15, 2002.

23. "Sexy Dress and Sassy Rap Make Lil' Kim a Big Star," *Jet,* August 21, 2000.

24. "When Sex Goes Pop: Not That Innocent" (MTV cable television broadcast, December 9, 2000).

25. Hendren, R.L., and Strasburger, V.C., "Rock Music and Music Videos," in *Adolescents and the Media* 4, No. 3, edited by V. Strasburger and G. Comstock (Philadelphia: Hanley & Belfus, 1993), pp. 577–587, at 580.

26. Accessed at www.misterpoll.com/602593920.html.

27. Sesame Research, "A View from the Middle: Life Through the Eyes of Middle Childhood," Sesame Workshop, accessed at www.sesameworkshop.org/research/kidsview/summary.php.

28. Arnett, J.J., "The Sounds of Sex: Sex in Teens' Music and Music Videos," in *Sexual Teens, Sexual Media,* edited by J. D. Brown, J. R. Steele, and K. Walsh-Childers (Mahwah, NJ: Lawrence Erlbaum Associates,

2000), pp. 253–264 at 254; Roberts, Christenson, and Gentile, "The Effects of Violent Music," at 159.

29. Associated Press, "California Radio Station Changes Format from God to Sex," July 27, 2006.

30. www.seventeen.com, accessed June 3, 2006.

31. Chris Lee, "Attack of the Dolls," *Los Angeles Times,* August 1, 2006.

32. Gentile, D.A., *Teen-Oriented Radio and CD Sexual Content Analysis* (Minneapolis: National Institute on Media and the Family, 1999), at 11, accessed at www.mediafamily.org/research/report_radiocontentanaly sis.pdf.

33. Ibid.

34. Ibid., at 12.

35. Ibid.

36. Roberts, Christenson, and Gentile, "The Effects of Violent Music on Children and Adolescents," at 158.

37. Hansen, C.J., and Hansen, R.D., "Schematic Information Processing of Heavy Metal Lyrics," *Communication Research* 18, No. 3 (1991), pp. 373–411.

38. Roberts, Christenson, and Gentile, "The Effects of Violent Music on Children and Adolescents," at 159.

39. Greeson, L.E., and Williams, R.A., "Social Implications of Music Videos for Youth: An Analysis of the Content and Effects of MTV," *Youth & Society* 18, No. 2 (1986), pp. 177–189 at 179.

40. Tapper, J., Thorson, F., and Black, D., "Variations in Music Videos as a Function of Their Musical Genre," *Journal of Broadcasting and Electronic Media* 38, No. 1 (1994), pp. 103–113.

41. Wartella, E., Scantlin, R., Kotler, J., Huston, A., and Donnerstein, E., "Effects of Sexual Content in the Media on Children and Adolescents," in *Children in the New Media Landscape,* edited by C. von Feilitzen and U. Carlsson (Goteborg, Sweden: UNESCO International Clearinghouse on Children and Violence on the Screen, 2000), pp. 141–153 at 143.

42. Ibid.

43. Rich, M., Woods, E., Goodman, E., Emans, J., and DuRant, R., "Aggressors or Victims: Gender and Race in Music Video Violence," *Pediatrics* 101, No. 4 (1998), pp. 669–674 at 670.

44. Sun, S., and Lull, J., "The Adolescent Audience for Music Videos and Why They Watch," *Journal of Communication* 36, No. 1 (1986), pp. 115–25 at 117.

45. Rich, Woods, Goodman, Emans, and DuRant, "Aggressors or Victims," at 670.

46. Ibid.

47. Strouse, Buerkel-Rothfuss, and Long, "Gender and Family as Moderators," at 512.

48. Office of National Drug Control Policy, "Substance Abuse in Popular Prime Time Television, Appendix B: Adolescents and Television," October 2002 (citing Saatchi & Saatchi, SmartGirl Internette, and Teenage Research Unlimited; Kidscreen, August 1998), accessed at www.mediacampaign.org/publications/primetime/tv_appb.html.

49. Sun and Lull, "The Adolescent Audience for Music Videos," at 123.

50. Abt, D., "Music Video: Impact of the Visual Dimension," in *Popular Music and Communication,* edited by J. Lull (Beverly Hills, CA: Sage, 1987), pp. 96–111.

51. American Association of Pediatrics Committee on Communications, "Impact of Music Lyrics and Music Videos on Children and Youth," *Pediatrics* 98, No. 6 (1996), pp. 1219–1221 at 1220.

52. Hendren and Strasburger, "Rock Music and Music Videos," at 579.

53. Strouse, Buerkel-Rothfuss, and Long, "Gender and Family as Moderators," at 507.

54. Roberts, Christenson, and Gentile, "The Effects of Violent Music on Children and Adolescents," at 167.

55. American Association of Pediatrics Committee on Communications, "Impact of Music Lyrics," at 1220.

56. Sun and Lull, "The Adolescent Audience for Music Videos," at 121.

57. Strouse, Buerkel-Rothfuss, and Long, "Gender and Family as Moderators," at 509.

58. Casey Williams, "MTV Smut Peddlers: Targeting Kids with Sex, Drugs and Alcohol" (Los Angeles: Parents Television Council, 2004), accessed at www.parentstv.org/PTC/publications/reports/mtv2005/main.asp.

59. Campaign for a Commercial-Free Childhood, "Marketing Sex to Children," Fact Sheet (undated) (citing S. R. Lichter et al., *Sexual Imagery in Popular Culture* [Washington, DC: Center for Media and Public Affairs, 2000]).

60. DuRant, R., Rome, E., Rich, M., Allred, E., Emans, S.J., and Woods, E., "Tobacco and Alcohol Use Behaviors Portrayed in Music Vid-

eos: A Content Analysis," *American Journal of Public Health* 87, No. 7 (1997), pp. 1131–1135 at 1134.

61. Greeson and Williams, "Social Implications of Music Videos for Youth," at 183.

62. Baxter, R.L., De Riemer, C., Landini, A., Leslie, L., and Singletary, M.W., "A Content Analysis of Music Videos," *Journal of Broadcasting and Electronic Media* 29, No. 3 (1985), pp. 333–340 at 387.

63. Sherman, B.L., and Dominick, J.R., "Violence and Sex in Music Videos: TV and Rock 'n' Roll," *Journal of Communication* 36, No. 1 (1986), pp. 79–93 at 91.

64. Gregory Dark has also directed music videos for Linkin Park and Snoop Dog.

65. Tiggeman, M., and Pickering, A.S., "Role of Television in Adolescent Women's Body Dissatisfaction and Drive for Thinness," *International Journal of Eating Disorders* 20, No. 2 (1996), pp. 199–203.

66. Seidman, S.A., "Revisiting Sex-Role Stereotyping in MTV Videos," *International Journal of Instructional Media* 26, No. 1 (1999), pp. 11–22 at 16. Among Caucasians, women were portrayed as more sexually aggressive than men.

67. Among whites shown in the music videos studied, women were victimized in 78 percent of the violent acts portrayed. Rich, Woods, Goodman, Emans, and DuRant, "Aggressors or Victims," at 671. Overall, 46.3 percent of the victims were women. Ibid.

68. Lawrence Downes, "Middle School Girls Gone Wild," *New York Times,* December 29, 2006.

69. Sandy Cohen, "MTV Movie Awards Celebrate Fun of Films," Associated Press, June 5, 2006, accessed at http://news.aol.com/entertainment/movies/articles/_a/mtv-movie-awards-celebrate-fun-of-films/20060605071109990001.

70. Greeson and Williams, "Social Implications of Music Videos for Youth," at 185.

71. Calfin, M.S., Carroll, J.L., and Schmidt, J., "Viewing Music-Video Tapes Before Taking a Test of Premarital Sexual Attitudes," *Psychological Reports* 72 (1993), pp. 475–481.

72. Strouse, Buerkel-Rothfuss, and Long, "Gender and Family as Moderators," at 515.

73. Strouse, J.S., and Buerkel-Rothfuss, N.L., "Media Exposure and the Sexual Attitudes and Behaviors of College Students," *Journal of Sex Education and Therapy* 13, No. 2 (1987), pp. 43–51.

74. Strouse, Buerkel-Rothfuss, and Long, "Gender and Family as Moderators," at 515.

75. Ibid.; see also Hansen, C.H., and Hansen, R.D., "Music and Music Videos," in *Media Entertainment: The Psychology of Its Appeal,* edited by D. Zillman and P. Vorderer (Mahwah, NJ: Lawrence Erlbaum Associates, 2000), pp. 175–196.

76. In fact, one study reported a stronger association between exposure to music videos and permissive sexual behavior and attitudes for females than for males. Strouse, Buerkel-Rothfuss, and Long, "Gender and Family as Moderators."

77. Wingood, G.M., DeClemente, R.J., Bernhardt, J.M., Harrington, K., Davies, S.L., Robillard, A., and Hook, E.W., "A Prospective Study of Exposure to Rap Music Videos and African American Adolescent Health," *American Journal of Public Health* 93, No. 3 (2003), pp. 437–439 at 438.

78. Ward, L.M., Hansbrough, E., and Walker, E., "Contributions of Music Video Exposure to Black Adolescents' Gender and Sexual Schemas," *Journal of Adolescent Research* 20, No. 2 (2005), pp. 143–166 at 159.

79. Johnson, J., Adams, M., Ashburn, L., and Reed, W., "Differential Gender Effects of Exposure to Rap Music on Black Adolescents' Acceptance of Teen Dating Violence," *Sex Roles* 33, No. 7–8, pp. 597–605 at 602.

80. Kalof, L., "The Effects of Gender and Music Video Imagery on Sexual Attitudes," *Journal of Social Psychology* 139, No. 3 (1999), pp. 378–385 at 383.

81. Alexandra Marks, "Central Park Attacks on Women—Is MTV to Blame?" *Christian Science Monitor,* June 19, 2000.

82. Peter Christenson and Donald Roberts, *It's Not Only Rock & Roll: Popular Music in the Lives of Adolescents* (Cresskill, NJ: Hampton Press, 1998), at 110–111. Christenson and Roberts note that rap has crossover appeal to black and white girls alike, despite its often misogynist lyrics, because they deem it to be good dance music. Ibid., at 94.

83. Seema Mehta, "Teens' Dancing Is Freaking Out the Adults," *Los Angeles Times,* October 17, 2006.

84. Nurith C. Aizenman, "Sexy Dancing Has Schools on Prom Patrol: Teens' Gyrations a Bit Too Risque," *Washington Post,* May 17, 2002.

85. Strouse, Buerkel-Rothfuss, and Long, "Gender and Family as Moderators," at 517.

86. Roberts, Christenson, and Gentile, "The Effects of Violent Music on Children and Adolescents," at 160.

87. Strasburger, V.C., and Donnerstein, E., "Children, Adolescents and the Media: Issues and Solutions," *Pediatrics* 103, No. 1 (1999), pp. 129–139 at 131 (citing Peterson, R.A., and Kahn, J.R., "Media Preferences of Sexually Active Teens," paper presented at the meeting of the American Psychological Association, Toronto, Canada, August 26, 2004).

88. Roberts, Christenson, and Gentile, D.A., "The Effects of Violent Music on Children and Adolescents," at 159. ("[I]t is difficult to deny that music has become more aggressive and edgy over the decades.")

89. Sommers-Flanagan, R., Sommers-Flanagan, J., and Davis, B., "What's Happening on Music Television? A Gender Role Content Analysis," *Sex Roles* 28, No. 11–12 (1993), pp. 745–753.

90. Ibid., at 752.

91. Dana Williams, "Hip Hop's Bad Rap?" Tolerance.org, February 28, 2003, accessed at www.tolerance.org/news/article_hate.jsp?id=720.

92. "When Sex Goes Pop: Not That Innocent" (MTV cable television broadcast, December 9, 2000).

93. Jim DeRogatis, "My Britney Problem—and Yours," Salon .com, December 3, 2001, accessed at http://archive.salon.com/ent/music/feature/2001/12/03/britney_spears/index.html.

94. "The 411: Teens & Sex, Part 1: Are TV, Movies and Music to Blame?" Katie Couric, NBC *Today Show,* January 31, 2005, accessed at www.msnbc.msn.com/id/6872269.

95. Nolan Strong, "Nelly's Pimp Juice Cracks a Million in Three Months," AllHipHop News, January 28, 2004, accessed at www.allhiphop .com/hiphopnews/?ID=2805.

96. Army Archerd, "It's Hard Out Here for a Censor," Variety.com blog, February 23, 2006, accessed at www.armyarcherd.com/2006/02/its_hard_out_he.html.

97. *Primetime* (ABC News television broadcast, November 13, 2003).

98. "Nelly: 'I'm Not a Role Model,'" TeenMusic.com, January 12, 2005, accessed at www.teenmusic.com/d.asp?r=88517&cat=1020.

99. Christenson and Roberts, *It's Not Only Rock & Roll*, at 7. The authors note that members of the music industry who "deny any possibility that their products might influence America's hip, sophisticated young consumers ignore the fact that most human learning is incidental . . ." Ibid.

100. *The Oprah Winfrey Show* (ABC television broadcast, April 10, 2006).

CHAPTER 7: BARELY THERE

1. Bob Garfield, "Top 100 Advertising Campaigns of the Century," *Advertising Age,* accessed June 20, 2006, at www.adage.com/century/campaigns.html.

2. Christina McCarroll, "Parents Gird for Midriff Wars with Preteen Set," *Christian Science Monitor,* August 15, 2001.

3. Thongs came about when New York Mayor Fiorello La Guardia insisted that nude dancers cover their private parts for the World's Fair in 1939. Alison Pollet and Page Hurwitz, "Strip Till You Drop," *The Nation* 278, No. 2 (January 12, 2004), pp. 20–25.

4. Joanne Ramos, "For Adults Only?: Maybe Not, as Marketing of Sexy Products Reaches Kids," ABCNews.com, June 12, 2002, accessed at www.prisonplanet.com/for_adults_only.html.

5. Vikki Ortiz, "Parents Say Kid's Thong Is Just Plain Wrong," *Milwaukee Journal Sentinel,* May 17, 2002.

6. Joe Kovacs, "Trick or Treat 2004: 'Pimp and Ho' Kids," WorldNet Daily, August 25, 2004, accessed at www.worldnetdaily.com/news/article.asp?ARTICLE_ID=40152.

7. Bella English, "The Disappearing Tween Years," *Boston Globe,* March 12, 2005.

8. Kelly Smith, "Sexy Halloween Costumes Rile Parents," *Albany Times Union,* October 16, 2006. *The New York Times* observed that many grown women have likewise been embracing the trend of revealing Halloween costumes over the last several years, sporting getups that "are more strip club than storybook." Stephanie Rosenbloom, "Good Girls Go Bad, for a Day," *New York Times,* October 19, 2006.

9. Kathleen Wereszynski, "Girl Culture Begets Backlash," FoxNews.com, April 22, 2004, accessed at www.foxnews.com/story/0,2933,117822,00.html.

10. "Sex Sells: Marketing and 'Age Compression'" (CBC broadcast, January 9, 2005), accessed June 20, 2006, at www.cbc.ca/consumers/market/files/money/sexy/marketing.html.

11. Nicole Maestri, "Today's Dolls Too Provocative, Says Survey of Moms," Reuters, September 25, 2006.

12. Kirsten Powers, "Ho', Ho', Ho': Dolls to Make You Cry," *New York Post,* December 14, 2006.

13. Beth Teitell, "Toddler 'Tude: Pimpfants Pushes Tyke-Trash Style," *Boston Herald,* May 3, 2006.

14. Katherine Snow Smith, "Underdressed," *St. Petersburg (FL) Times*

online, June 11, 2005, accessed at www.sptimes.com/2005/06/11/news_pf/Floridian/Underdressed.shtml.

15. Aviva Ariel, "Too Sexy for My Clothes," *Ms.* online, May 12, 2005, accessed June 20, 2006, at www.msmagazine.com/radar/2005-05-12-ariel.asp.

16. Valli Herman, "Lingerie Moves Further into the Light of Day," *Los Angeles Times,* October 17, 2005.

17. Anitha Reddy, "Little Women: Retailers' Efforts to Court Teens and 'Tweens' Include Lingerie Shops for the Junior-High Set," *Washington Post,* September 2, 2001.

18. Ramos, "For Adults Only?"

19. Ruby Mata-Viti, "Howzit Bra? Despite a Balking Older Generation, It Is Now Fashionable to See What Lies Beneath," *Honolulu Star-Bulletin,* August 29, 2002.

20. Pollet and Hurwitz, "Strip Till You Drop" (citations omitted).

21. Kristin Tillotson, "Liberation Gone Wild: Why Are Women Exploiting Themselves?" *Minneapolis–St. Paul Star Tribune,* December 18, 2005.

22. Betsy Hart, "The 'Whore Wars,'" *Jewish World Review,* June 18, 2002, accessed June 27, 2006, at www.jewishworldreview.com/cols/hart061802.asp; Laura Sessions Stepp, "Nothing to Wear: From the Classroom to the Mall, Girls' Fashions Are Long on Skin, Short on Modesty," *Washington Post,* June 3, 2002.

23. NBC4i.com (Columbus, OH), "Revealing Prom Gowns Horrify Parents," January 25, 2005, accessed at www.nbc4i.com/news/4128870/detail.html.

24. Ruth Ferla, "What Stylish Young Women Are Wearing: More," *New York Times,* June 8, 2004; Jean Patteson, "Modest Gain for Modesty: Latest Teen Fashions Are Far Less Revealing," *Orlando Sentinel,* July 19, 2004.

25. Meredith Goldstein, "After Many Seasons of Baring Skin, Fashion Finally Covers Up," *Boston Globe,* July 21, 2005; Joseph Montes, "Style: Schoolroom Chic," *Atlanta Journal-Constitution,* August 14, 2005.

26. Ellen Wulfhorst, "'Slutwear' Is So Last Year on New York Runways," Reuters, September 14, 2004.

27. Becky Yerak, "'Attitude' Clothing Making the Grade with Teens, Retailers," *Chicago Tribune,* August 31, 2005.

28. See http://f**kthemainstream.com/product.php?pid=320.

29. See www.bewild.com/sluttshirt.html, accessed June 20, 2006.

30. Laura Sessions Stepp, "Playboy's Bunny Hops into Teens' Closets," *Washington Post,* June 17, 2003.

31. Gloria Goodale, "Erotica Runs Rampant," *Christian Science Monitor,* February 1, 2002.

32. Valerie Seckler, "Sexuality's New Subtle Appeal," *Women's Wear Daily,* May 4, 2005.

33. English, "The Disappearing Tween Years."

34. *Reader's Digest,* "Are You Spending Too Much on Back-to-School Needs?" RD.com, accessed June 20, 2006, at www.rd.com/content/open Content.do?contentId=11181.

35. Ibid.

36. "Rock On: Teens Take Fashion Cues from Their Favorite Musical Artists," Cotton, Inc., accessed June 20, 2006, at www.cottoninc .com/lsmarticles/?articleID=162.

37. Ibid.; see also Martha Kleider, "Fighting Back: Teens Demand Modest Clothing," Concerned Women for America, January 9, 2003, accessed at www.cwfa.org/articledisplayasp?id=2995&department=CFI& categoryid=cfreport.

38. YM.com, "June Fashion News," June 2006, accessed at www .ym.com/jsp/style/latesttrends/jun0106.jsp.

39. "Fashion Shows: Jennifer Lopez," NewYorkMagazine.com, fall 2006, accessed June 20, 2006, at http://nymag.com/fashion/fashionshows/ designers/bios/jenniferlopez.

40. *Dateline* (NBC News television broadcast, June 15, 2006).

41. See www.hottopic.com/store/nodePage.asp?LS=0&RN=110, accessed June 20, 2006.

42. Robin Givhan, "Oops, Again and Again," *Washington Post,* June 23, 2006.

43. Maria Elena Fernandez, "Search for a New Doll—Too Freaky," *Los Angeles Times,* January 20, 2007.

44. Booth Moore, "Baby Glam," *Los Angeles Times,* June 24, 2006.

45. David Mehegan, " 'Opal' Aided by Marketing Firm That Targets Teens," *Boston Globe,* May 8, 2006.

46. Magazine Publishers of America, "Teen Market Profile," 2004, at 8, accessed at www.magazine.org/content/files/teenprofile04.pdf.

47. Ibid., at 9.

48. "Watchdog Group Slams 'Soft Porn' Paris Hilton TV Ad," Reuters, May 24, 2005.

49. "Sex Sells: Marketing and 'Age Compression' " (CBC broadcast,

January 9, 2005), accessed June 20, 2006, at www.cbc.ca/consumers/mar
ket/files/money/sexy/marketing.html.

50. Magazine Publishers of America, "Teen Market Profile," at 12.

51. John Reinan, "Hip-Hop Fashions Losing Ground to Preppy Look,"
Minneapolis–St. Paul Star Tribune, October 6, 2005.

52. Anne Morse, "'Field Guide' Bye-Bye," *National Review Online,*
December 1, 2003.

53. D. Parvaz, "Nudity, Sex Articles in Abercrombie & Fitch 'Magalog' Draw Fire," *Seattle Post-Intelligencer,* December 3, 2003.

54. Morse, "'Field Guide' Bye-Bye."

55. See www.abercrombie.com/anf/lifestyles/html/homepage.html#,
accessed June 27, 2006.

56. See www.abercrombie.com/webapp/wcs/stores/servlet/Product
Display?storeId=10051&catalogId=10901&parentCategoryId=12202&
childCatgroupId=12202&categoryId=12236&productId=1&langId=-1,
accessed June 27, 2006.

57. Theresa Howard, "Teen Fragrance's Titillating PR Push Could
Create a Stink," *USA Today,* September 10, 2003.

58. Ibid.

59. Sessions Stepp, "Playboy's Bunny Hops Into Teens' Closets."

60. Mehegan, "'Opal' aided by marketing firm that targets teens."

61. Rich Lipski, "Skimpy Underwear, Ample Commentary," *Washington Post,* October 5, 2005.

62. Stuart Elliott, "Pony Adds to Its Maverick Image," *New York
Times,* February 24, 2003.

63. Dr. Laura Schlessinger, "As Predicted, Bestiality Goes Mainstream," *Jewish World Review,* March 24, 2000.

64. Elliott, "Pony Adds to Its Maverick Image."

65. "Sex Sells" (CBC broadcast, January 9, 2005).

66. Robin Abcarian, "Letting It All Hang Out," *Los Angeles Times,*
July 4, 2006.

67. Pollet and Hurwitz, "Strip Till You Drop."

68. Booth Moore, "Greatest of Teese: Burlesque Queen and Fetishist
Has Become Fashion's 'It' Girl," *Los Angeles Times,* February 3, 2006.

69. Dennis Prager, "Why Young Women Are Exposing Themselves:
Part One," Townhall.com, February 17, 2004, accessed at www.townhall
.com/columnists/DennisPrager/2004/02/17/why_young_women_are
_exposing_themselves_part_one.

70. Pollet and Hurwitz, "Strip Till You Drop."

71. Patricia Dalton, "What's Wrong with This Outfit, Mom?" *Washington Post,* November 20, 2005.

72. Prabha Natarajan, "Rules, Fashion Collide in Offices," *Pacific Business News (Honolulu),* May 29, 2006.

73. For example, the advice on tops and blouses reads, "Make sure there is at least one inch of room between body and fabric and that it is long enough to conceal your midriff. Stomach, breasts, back and shoulders should be covered. Fabric should not be overly sheer and a bra should be worn (with no straps revealed)." Kate Lorenz, "Are You Too Sexy for Your Job?" CareerBuilder.com, accessed January 30, 2006, at www.careerbuilder. com/JobSeeker/careerbytes/CBArticle.aspx?articleID=467&path=_arti cle&cbRecursionCnt=1&cbsid=7a8aee55b17e4b5c8d1d9561550fb99a-204484618-TP-1.

74. Glick, P., Larsen, S., Johnson, C., and Branstiter, H. "Evaluations of Sexy Women in Low- and High-Status Jobs," *Psychology of Women Quarterly* 29, No. 4 (2005), pp. 389–395.

CHAPTER 8: PAYING THE PIPER

1. Ebrahim, S.H., McKenna, M.T., and Marks, J.S., "Sexual Behavior: Related Adverse Health Burden in the United States," *Sexually Transmitted Infections* 81, No. 1 (2005), pp. 38–40 at 38.

2. Centers for Disease Control, *Tracking the Hidden Epidemics 2000* (Washington, DC: 2000), at 1, accessed at www.cdc.gov/nchstp/dstd/ Stats_Trends/Trends2000.pdf.

3. Centers for Disease Control, *Trends in Reportable Sexually Transmitted Diseases in the United States, 2004,* accessed at www.cdc.gov/std/ stats/trends2004.htm.

4. Weinstock, H., Berman, S., and Cates Jr., W., "Sexually Transmitted Diseases Among American Youth: Incidence and Prevalence Estimates, 2000," *Perspectives on Sexual and Reproductive Health* 36, No. 1 (2004), pp. 6–10 at 8–9.

5. Rector, R.E., Johnson, K.A., Noyes, L.R., and Martin, S., *The Harmful Effects of Early Sexual Activity and Multiple Sexual Partners Among Women: A Book of Charts* (Washington, DC: Heritage Foundation, 2003), at 1. The report is based on analysis of the 1995 National Survey of Family Growth.

6. CDC, *Tracking the Hidden Epidemics 2000,* at 3.

7. Ibid.

8. Landy, D.J., and Turnbull, W., *Issues in Brief: Sexually Transmitted Diseases Hinder Development Efforts* (New York: Guttmacher Institute,

1997), accessed at www.guttmacher.org/pubs/ib_std.html; Blum, R.W., *Mothers' Influence on Teen Sex: Connections That Promote Postponing Sexual Intercourse* (Minneapolis: University of Minnesota Center for Adolescent Health and Development, 2002), at 4.

9. Centers for Disease Control, *STD Surveillance 2005, National Profile: Chlamydia,* accessed at www.cdc.gov/std/stats/chlamydia.htm. It should be noted that some of the increase may be due to better screening and more comprehensive reporting.

10. Weinstock, Berman, and Cates, "Sexually Transmitted Diseases Among American Youth," at 6.

11. CDC, *STD Surveillance 2005, National Profile: Chlamydia.*

12. CDC, *Tracking the Hidden Epidemics 2000,* at 4.

13. Kaiser Family Foundation, *It's Your (Sex) Life* (Menlo Park, CA: Kaiser Family Foundation, 2003 [updated June 2005]), at 18, accessed July 30, 2006, at www.kff.org/youthhivstds/upload/MTV_Think_IYSL_Booklet.pdf.

14. CDC, *STD Surveillance 2005, National Profile: Chlamydia.*

15. CDC, *Tracking the Hidden Epidemics 2000.*

16. Kaiser Family Foundation, *It's Your (Sex) Life,* at 19.

17. CDC, *Tracking the Hidden Epidemics 2000,* at 13.

18. Press release, "CDC's Advisory Committee Recommends Human Papillomavirus Virus Vaccination," June 29, 2006, accessed at www.cdc.gov/od/oc/media/pressrel/r060629.htm.

19. Ibid.

20. Ibid.

21. Ibid.

22. Tara Grassia, "HIV Positive Youth Reach Out to Peers," *Infectious Disease News,* December 2006, accessed at www.infectiousdiseasenews.com/200612/frameset.asp?article=hiv.asp.

23. Kaiser Family Foundation, *HIV/AIDS Policy Fact Sheet: Women and HIV/AIDS in the United States* (Menlo Park, CA: Kaiser Family Foundation, 2006), accessed at www.kff.org/hivaids/upload/6092-03.pdf.

24. Joyce Howard Price, "Black Teen Girls at Very High Risk for HIV Infection," *Washington Times,* July 11, 2004 (citing DiClemente, R.J., Wingood, G.M., Harrington, K.F., Lang, D.L., Davies, S.L., Hook III, E.W., Oh, M.K., Crosby, R.A., Hertzberg, V.S., Gordon, A.B., Hardin, J.W., Parker, S., and Robillard, A., "Efficacy of an HIV Prevention Intervention for African American Adolescent Girls," *Journal of the American Medical Association* 292, No. 2 [2004], pp. 171–179).

25. National Institute of Allergy and Infectious Diseases, *Workshop Summary: Scientific Evidence on Condom Effectiveness for Sexually Transmitted Disease (STD) Prevention*, July 20, 2001, at 13–14, accessed at www3.niaid.nih.gov/research/topics/STI/pdf/condomreport.pdf.

26. Centers for Disease Control, *STD Surveillance 2005: STD's in Adolescents and Young Adults*, accessed at www.cdc.gov/std/stats/adol.htm.

27. Kaiser Family Foundation, *It's Your (Sex) Life*, at 19.

28. Centers for Disease Control, *Trichomoniasis: CDC Fact Sheet*, accessed January 21, 2007, at www.cdc.gov/std/Trichomonas/STDFact -Trichomoniasis.htm#Common.

29. Ibid.

30. American Social Health Association, *Vaginitis/Trichomoniasis: Questions and Answers*, accessed January 21, 2007, at www.ashastd.org/ learn/learn_vag_trich.cfm.

31. Kaiser Family Foundation, *It's Your (Sex) Life*, at 20.

32. Ibid.

33. CDC, *STD Surveillance 2005: STD's in Adolescents and Young Adults*.

34. Ibid.

35. Trent, M., Millstein, S.G., and Ellen, J., "Gender-Based Differences in Fertility Beliefs and Knowledge Among Adolescents from High Sexually Transmitted Disease–Prevalence Communities," *Journal of Adolescent Health* 38, No. 3 (2006), pp. 282–287 at 283.

36. Thomas Lickona, PhD, "Sex, Love, and Character: A Talk to High School Students," 1998.

37. Trent, Millstein, and Ellen, "Gender-Based Differences in Fertility Beliefs and Knowledge," at 285.

38. Centers for Disease Control, *Fact Sheet for Public Health Personnel: Male Latex Condoms and Sexually Transmitted Diseases*, 2003, accessed at www.cdc.gov/nchstp/od/latex.htm.

39. Child Trends, *Facts at a Glance* (Publication 2005-02, March 2005), accessed at www.childtrends.org/files/Facts_2005.pdf.

40. Press release, "One-Third of Sexually Experienced Girls Have Been Pregnant," National Campaign to Prevent Teen Pregnancy, May 3, 2006, accessed at www.teenpregnancy.org/press/pdf/Science_Says_23_PR .pdf.

41. Centers for Disease Control, *Births: Final Data for 2003*, National Vital Statistics Report 54, No. 2 (2005), table 17, accessed at www.cdc .gov/nchs/data/nvsr/nvsr54/nvsr54_02.pdf.

42. Kirby, D., *No Easy Answers: Research Findings on Programs to Reduce Teen Pregnancy (Summary)* (Washington, DC: National Campaign to Prevent Teen Pregnancy, 1997), accessed at www.teenpregnancy.org/resources/data/report_summaries/no_easy_answers/sumpref.asp.

43. Abma, J.C., Martinez, G.M., Mosher, W.D., and Dawson, B.S., "Teenagers in the United States: Sexual Activity, Contraceptive Use and Childbearing, 2002," *Vital Health Statistics* 23, No. 24 (2004) (National Center for Health Statistics).

44. Medline Medical Encyclopedia, "Adolescent Pregnancy," accessed July 29, 2006, at www.nlm.nih.gov/medlineplus/ency/article/001516.htm.

45. Ibid.

46. Ibid.

47. Markovitz, B.P., Cook, R., Flick, L.H., and Leet, T.L., "Socioeconomic Factors and Adolescent Pregnancy Outcomes: Distinctions Between Neonatal and Post-Neonatal Deaths?" *BMC Public Health* No. 5 (2005).

48. Maynard, R.A., editor, *Kids Having Kids: A Robin Hood Foundation Special Report on the Cost of Adolescent Childbearing* (New York: Robin Hood Foundation, 1996), at 5.

49. Terry-Humen, E., Manlove, J., and Moore, K.A., *Playing Catch-Up: How Children Born to Teen Mothers Fare* (Washington, DC: National Campaign to Prevent Teen Pregnancy, 2005), at 3, accessed at www.teenpregnancy.org/works/pdf/PlayingCatchUp.pdf.

50. Press release, "Teen Birth Rates Continue Their Dramatic Decline," Child Trends, March 16, 2005.

51. Centers for Disease Control, *Abortion Surveillance—2002*, 54 (SS07) (2005), pp. 1–31, accessed July 27, 2006, at www.cdc.gov/mmwr/preview/mmwrhtml/ss5407a1.htm.

52. Ibid.

53. Ibid.

54. Rector, Johnson, Noyes, and Martin, *The Harmful Effects of Early Sexual Activity,* at 19 (citing the 1995 National Survey of Family Growth).

55. Ibid., at 2.

56. National Cancer Institute, *Fact Sheet: Abortion, Miscarriage and Breast Cancer Risk* (updated May 30, 2003), accessed July 29, 2006, at www.cancer.gov/cancertopics/factsheet/Risk/abortion-miscarriage.

57. Medical News Today, "Breast Cancer Link Real, Studies Flawed," December 31, 2005, accessed at www.medicalnewstoday.com/medicalnews.php?newsid=35551; see also Dr. James Howenstine, "Abortion

Causes Breast Cancer," December 26, 2003, accessed July 29, 2006, at www.newswithviews.com/Howenstine/james3.htm; Lickona, "Sex, Love, and Character."

58. See, for instance, Fergusson, D.M., Horwood, L.J., and Ridder, E.M., "Abortion in Young Women and Subsequent Mental Health," *Journal of Child Psychology and Psychiatry* 47, No. 1 (2006), pp. 16–24.

59. Schmiege, S., and Russo, N.F., "Depression and Unwanted First Pregnancy: Longitudinal Cohort Study," *British Medical Journal* 331 (2005), pp. 1303–1308, accessed at http://bmj.bmjjournals.com/cgi/reprint/331/7528/1303.

60. American Psychological Association, *Briefing Paper on the Impact of Abortion on Women,* 2005, accessed July 29, 2005, at http://web.archive.org/web/20050304001316/http://www.apa.org/ppo/issues/womenabortfacts.html.

61. Rector, Johnson, Noyes, and Martin, *The Harmful Effects of Early Sexual Activity,* at 2. The report is based on an analysis of the 1995 National Survey of Family Growth.

62. Hal Marcovitz, *Teens & Sex, The Gallup Youth Survey: Major Issues and Trends* (Broomhall, PA: Mason Crest, 2004), at 40.

63. Hofferth, S.L., Reid, L., and Mott, F.L., "The Effects of Early Childbearing on Schooling Over Time," *Family Planning Perspectives* 33, No. 6 (2001).

64. National Campaign to Prevent Teen Pregnancy, *Not Just Another Single Issue: Teen Pregnancy's Link to Other Critical Social Issues* (Washington, DC: National Campaign to Prevent Teen Pregnancy, 2002), accessed at www.teenpregnancy.org/resources/data/pdf/notjust.pdf.

65. Maynard, *Kids Having Kids,* at 13.

66. Ibid., at 12.

67. National Campaign to Prevent Teen Pregnancy, *Not Just Another Single Issue.*

68. Coard, S.I., Nitz, K., and Felice, M.E., "Repeat Pregnancy Among Urban Adolescents: Sociodemographic, Family, and Health Factors," *Journal of Adolescence* 35, No. 137 (2000), pp. 193–199; see also National Campaign to Prevent Teen Pregnancy, *National Teen Pregnancy and Birth Data: General Facts and Stats,* updated November 2006, accessed at www.teenpregnancy.org/resources/data/genlfact.asp.

69. National Campaign to Prevent Teen Pregnancy, *Not Just Another Single Issue.*

70. Population Research Bureau, *Nonmarital Births to Teenagers,*

1950–2001, accessed July 29, 2006, at www.prb.org/pdf/DecliningFertility AmongTeenagers2.pdf.

71. Only 13 percent of teen births were out of wedlock in the 1950s. Ibid. The figure climbed modestly to 15 percent in 1960. David Popenoe, "Teen Pregnancy: An American Dilemma," testimony before the House of Representatives, Committee on Small Business, Subcommittee on Empowerment (Washington, DC, July 16, 1998).

72. Maynard, *Kids Having Kids,* at 12.

73. Thomas Lickona, "The Neglected Heart," *American Educator,* summer 1994, pp. 34–39 at 34. For an enormously helpful, comprehensive discussion of the emotional repercussions of early uncommitted sex, also see Thomas Lickona, "How to Talk to Kids About Sex, Love and Character," in *Character Matters: How to Help Our Children Develop Good Judgment, Integrity, and Other Essential Virtues* (New York: Touchstone, 2004).

74. This is especially true when the sex occurs in the context of dating relationships. See Manning, W.D., Giordano, P.C., and Longmore, M.A., "Hooking Up: The Relationship Contexts of 'Nonrelationship' Sex," *Journal of Adolescent Research* 21, No. 5 (2006), pp. 459–483. The researchers found that "girls (76%) significantly more often than boys (57%) who had sex within dating relationships reported that having sex made them feel closer to their boyfriend or girlfriend." Ibid., at 472. Conversely, boys more often than girls—17 versus 7 percent— reported that sex made them feel less close. Ibid.

75. Ian Kerner, *Be Honest—You're Not That into Him Either: Raise Your Standards and Reach for the Love You Deserve* (New York: HarperCollins, 2005), at 25.

76. Gary Langer, "ABC News Poll: Sex Lives of American Teens," ABC News, May 19, 2006, accessed at http://abcnews.go.com/Primetime/Poll Vault/story?id=1981945&page=1. The report analyzes an ABC poll—conducted in summer 2004 but released in May 2006—of a thousand boys and girls between thirteen and seventeen. See ABC News Poll, "The Sex Life of American Teens: A Battle of Restraint vs. Impulse," May 18, 2006, accessed at http://abcnews.go.com/images/Primetime/959a2TeensandSex.pdf.

77. Albert, B., *With One Voice 2004: America's Adults and Teens Sound Off About Teen Pregnancy, An Annual National Survey* (Washington, DC: National Campaign to Prevent Teen Pregnancy, 2004), at 5.

78. *Seventeen* magazine and Sex, Etc., "2006 Hookup Survey," accessed

July 15, 2006, at www.seventeen.com/health/smarts/articles/0,,625884
_694391,00.html.

79. Ott, M.A., Millstein, S.G., Ofner, S., and Halpern-Fisher, B.L.,
"Greater Expectations: Adolescents' Positive Motivations for Sex," *Perspectives on Sexual and Reproductive Health* 38, No. 2 (2006), pp. 84–89
at 86.

80. See, for instance, Kempner, M.E., *Toward a Sexually Healthy
America: Abstinence-Only-Til-Marriage Programs That Try to Keep Our
Youth 'Scared Chaste'* (New York: Sexuality Information and Education
Council of America, 2001), accessed at www.siecus.org/pubs/tsha_scared
chaste.pdf.

81. Marcovitz, *Teens & Sex,* at 13.

82. ABC News Poll, "The Sex Life of American Teens: A Battle of
Restraint vs. Impulse," May 18, 2006.

83. See, for instance, Kowleski-Jones, L., and Mott, F.L., "Sex, Contraception and Childbearing Among High-Risk Youth: Do Different Factors Influence Males and Females?" *Family Planning Perspectives* 30, No. 4
(1998), pp. 163–169 (sampling adolescents from somewhat disadvantaged
backgrounds); see also DiClemente, R.J., Wingood, G.M., Crosby, R.A.,
Sionean, C., Brown, L.K., Rothbaum, B., Zimand, E., Cobb, B.K., Harrington, K., and Davies, S., "A Prospective Study of Psychological Distress
and Sexual Risk Behavior Among Black Adolescent Females," *Pediatrics*
108, No. 5 (2001), p. e85 (finding that psychologically distressed adolescent girls were more likely to have had unprotected vaginal sex and nonmonogamous sex partners).

84. Rector, R., Johnson, K., and Noyes, L., "Sexually Active Teenagers
Are More Likely to Be Depressed and to Attempt Suicide," Heritage Foundation Center for Data Analysis Report No. CDA03-04 (2003), accessed
at www.heritage.org/Research/Family/cda0304.cfm. The study controlled
for gender, race, age, and family income.

85. Hallfors, D.D., Waller, M.W., Bauer, D., Ford, C.A., and Halpern,
C.T., "Which Comes First in Adolescence—Sex and Drugs or Depression?" *American Journal of Preventive Medicine* 29, No. 3 (2005), pp.
163–170.

86. Ibid., at 167–168. Sexual experimentation has "greater depressive
consequences for girls than for boys." Ibid., at 169. Sexually active boys
are more than twice as likely to be depressed as those who are not active;
for girls, however, the sexually active are fully three times more likely to be

depressed than abstainers. Rector, Johnson, and Noyes, "Sexually Active Teenagers Are More Likely to Be Depressed."

87. Orr, D.P., Beiter, M., and Ingersoll, G., "Premature Sexual Activity as an Indicator of Psychosocial Risk," *Pediatrics* 87, No. 22 (1991), pp. 141–147.

88. Rector, Johnson, and Noyes, "Sexually Active Teenagers Are More Likely to Be Depressed." The study controlled for gender, race, age, and family income.

89. Ethier, K.A., Kershaw, T.S., Lewis, J.B., Milan, S., Niccolai, L.M., and Ickovics, J.R., "Self-Esteem, Emotional Distress and Sexual Behavior Among Adolescent Females: Inter-Relationships and Temporal Effects," *Journal of Adolescent Health* 38, No. 3 (2006), pp. 268–274 at 272.

90. Bearman, P.S., and Bruckner, H., "Promising the Future: Virginity Pledges and First Intercourse," *American Journal of Sociology* 106, No. 4 (January 2001), pp. 859–912 at 898. It's worth noting that one review of scientific literature found that 60 percent of the empirical tests of the relationship between self-esteem and teen sexual decision making discovered no statistically significant associations—and suggested that self-esteem should be examined as an outcome, rather than as a determinant, of sexual activity. Goodson, P., Buhi, E.R., and Dunsmore, S.C., "Self-Esteem and Adolescent Sexual Behaviors, Attitudes, and Intentions: A Systematic Review," *Journal of Adolescent Health* 38, No. 3 (2006), pp. 310–319.

91. ABC News, "Teen Girls Discuss Their Sex Lives," May 17, 2006, accessed at http://abcnews.go.com/Primetime/Health/story?id=1968984& page=1 (citing ABC News Poll, "The Sex Life of American Teens: A Battle of Restraint vs. Impulse," May 18, 2006).

92. Salts, C.J., Seismore, M.D., Lindholm, B.W., and Smith, T.A., "Attitudes Toward Marriage and Premarital Sexual Activity of College Freshmen," *Journal of Adolescence* 29, No. 116 (1994), pp. 775–779.

93. "The Lost Children of Rockdale County," produced by Rachel Dretzin Goodman and Barak Goodman, PBS *Frontline*, October 19, 1999.

94. Chesson, H.W., Blandford, J.M., Gift, T.L., Tao, G., and Irwin, K.L., "The Estimated Direct Medical Cost of Sexually Transmitted Diseases Among American Youth, 2000," *Perspectives on Sexual and Reproductive Health* 36, No. 1 (2004), pp. 11–19 at 15.

95. David D. Bellis, US General Accounting Office, "Abstinence Education Grants and Welfare Reform," presentation at Abstinence Educa-

tion Grants and Welfare Reform Conference, June 6, 1997, accessed at www.welfareacademy.org/conf/past/bellis2.shtml.

96. Saul Hoffman, *By the Numbers: The Public Costs of Teen Childbearing* (Washington, DC: National Campaign to Prevent Teen Pregnancy, 2006), at 27.

97. Ibid.

98. Ibid., at 3.

99. Ibid., at 13–14.

100. Ibid., at 14.

101. Ibid., at 16–17. This estimate doesn't include a variety of other costs, including those associated with the juvenile justice system.

102. Ibid., at 23.

103. Ibid., at 27.

104. Ibid.

105. Maynard, *Kids Having Kids*, at 19–20.

106. Levine, J.A., Pollack, H., and Comfort, M.E., "Academic and Behavioral Outcomes Among the Children of Young Mothers," *Journal of Marriage and Family* 63 (2001), pp. 355–369 at 367.

107. Hoffman, *By the Numbers*, at 17.

CHAPTER 9: DO-ME FEMINISTS AND DOOM-ME FEMINISM

1. Benoit Denizet-Lewis, "Friends, Friends with Benefits and the Benefits of the Local Mall," *New York Times Magazine*, May 30, 2004. Much of the discussion of early dating rituals comes from this piece, as well as from Leon Kass, "The End of Courtship," *The Public Interest* 126 (1997), pp. 39–63.

2. For a witty, thorough, informative, and politically incorrect look at feminism, read Carrie L. Lukas, *The Politically Incorrect Guide to Women, Sex and Feminism* (Washington, DC: Regnery, 2006).

3. Kate O'Beirne, *Women Who Make the World Worse* (New York: Sentinel, 1996), at 16 (citing Erika Bachiochi, ed., *The Cost of "Choice": Women Evaluate the Impact of Abortion* [New York: Encounter Books 2004] at 7).

4. Shaunti Feldhahn and Diane Glass, "Is the Modesty Movement Necessary?" *Atlanta Journal-Constitution*, April 15, 2005.

5. Tad Friend, "Yes," *Esquire*, February 1994.

6. Laura Sessions Stepp, "The Buddy System: Sex in High School and College: What's Love Got to Do with It?" *Washington Post*, January 19, 2003.

7. Laura Sessions Stepp, "Nothing to Wear: From the Classroom to

the Mall, Girls' Fashions Are Long on Skin, Short on Modesty," *Washington Post,* June 3, 2002.

8. Tamara Straus, "Lipstick Feministas," *Metro Santa Cruz,* November 29–December 6, 2000, accessed at www.metroactive.com/papers/cruz/11.29.00/feminism-0048.html.

9. Caryn James, "Beneath All That Black Lace Beats the Heart of a Bimbo . . ." *New York Times,* December 16, 1990.

10. Ibid.

11. Friend, "Yes."

12. Naomi Wolf, *Promiscuities* (New York: Ballantine Books, 1998) (paperback).

13. This approach was, of course, contrary to the theory underlying much of sexual harassment law, which sprang from an assertion that an inherent power imbalance existed in workplace affairs between male bosses and subordinate female employees.

14. Charles Taylor, review of *Our Monica, Ourselves: The Clinton Affair and the National Interest* by Lauren Gail Berlant, Salon.com, October 26, 2001, accessed at www.powells.com/review/2001_10_26.html.

15. See "Ask Amy," Feminist.com, www.feminist.com/askamy/sh/sh6.html.

16. WorldNetDaily, "NARAL Hosts 'Screw Abstinence Party,' " July 12, 2005, accessed at www.wnd.com/news/article.asp?ARTICLE_ID=45242.

17. Alex Kuczynski, "She's Got to Be a Macho Girl," *New York Times,* November 3, 2002.

18. Lisa Colangelo, "Sex and the Ciggie: Teen Girls Drawn to Smoking by Hot Cable Series," *New York Daily News,* August 10, 2006.

19. Wenn, "Lohan's Lifestyle Inspired by 'Sex and the City,' " Entertainment News Network, August 15, 2006, accessed at www.hollywood.com/news/detail/id/3543306.

20. Personal observation, Rubio's, Paseo Colorado, Pasadena, CA, April 7, 2006.

21. Personal observation, AMC Santa Anita 16, Arcadia, CA, May 26, 2006.

22. Liza Mundy, "Sex & Sensibility," *Washington Post Magazine,* July 16, 2000.

23. Liz Stevens, "Are Girls the New Sexual Aggressors?" *Fort Worth/Dallas Star-Telegram,* July 17, 2005.

24. Liza Mundy, "Sex & Sensibility," *Washington Post Magazine*, July 16, 2000.

25. Michael Fisher, Linda Lou, and Iona Patringenaru, "Youthful Sexuality Worries Adults," *(Inland Southern California) Press-Enterprise,* December 10, 2003, accessed at www.pe.com/localnews/inland/stories/PE_News_Local_sex10.a155d.html (citing Bill Troost, a teacher at North Mountain Middle School in San Jacinto, CA).

26. Emily Limbaugh, telephone interview, October 11, 2006.

27. Albert, B., *With One Voice 2004: America's Adults and Teens Sound Off About Teen Pregnancy, An Annual National Survey* (Washington, DC: National Campaign to Prevent Teen Pregnancy, 2004), at 35.

28. Kaiser Family Foundation and *Seventeen* magazine, SexSmarts Survey, "Gender Roles," December 2002, at 3, accessed at www.kff.org/entpartnerships/upload/Gender-Rolls-Summary.pdf.

29. Centers for Disease Control, *Youth Risk Behavior Surveillance—United States 2003,* May 21, 2004.

30. Susan Reimer, "Teen Girls Are as Pushy Sexually as Boys," *(Southern Oregon) Mail Tribune,* December 30, 2004.

31. Abma, J.C., Martinez, G.M., Mosher, W.D., and Dawson, B.S., "Teenagers in the United States: Sexual Activity, Contraceptive Use, and Childbearing, 2002," *National Center for Health Statistics* 23, No. 24.

32. Anderson, P., Arceneaux, E., Carter, D., Miller, A., and King, B., "Changes in the Telephone Calling Patterns of Adolescent Girls," *Journal of Adolescence* 30, No. 20 (1995), pp. 779–784.

33. Kaiser Family Foundation and *Seventeen* magazine, SexSmarts Survey, "Gender Roles," at 3.

34. Louanne Brizendine, *The Female Brain* (New York: Morgan Road Books, 2006), at 91.

35. Ibid., at 89.

36. Caitlin Flanagan, "Are You There God? It's Me, Monica," *Atlantic Monthly,* January–February 2006.

37. Anne Jarrell, "The Face of Teenage Sex Grows Younger," *New York Times,* April 2, 2000.

38. Personal interview, September 8, 2006.

39. Manning, W.D., Giordano, P.C., and Longmore, M.A., "Hooking Up: The Relationship Contexts of 'Nonerelationship' Sex," *Journal of Adolescent Research* 21, No. 5 (2006), pp. 459–483 at 460.

40. An interesting discussion of this dynamic among college women is found in a study commissioned by the Independent Women's Forum. See Glenn, N.D., and Marquardt, E., *Hooking Up, Hanging Out and Hoping*

for Mr. Right: College Women on Dating and Mating Today (New York: Institute for American Values, 2001).

41. Manning, Giordano, and Longmore, "Hooking Up," at 469.

42. Indeed, one study found that although a similar percentage of boys in dating and nondating sexual relationships were "monogamous" (46 versus 45 percent), fully 66 percent of girls in dating relationships believed those relationships were exclusive (compared with 50 percent of girls having sex in nondating sexual relationships). Manning, Giordano, and Longmore, "Hooking Up," at 476.

43. Steven E. Rhoads, *Taking Sex Differences Seriously* (San Francisco: Encounter Books, 2004), at 47.

44. Philip Elmer-DeWitt, "Now for the Truth About Americans and Sex," *Time,* October 17, 1994.

45. Brizendine, *The Female Brain,* at 89.

46. Anderson, E., "Sex Codes Among Inner City Youth," in *Sexuality, Poverty, and the Inner City,* edited by M. Smith (Menlo Park, CA: Kaiser Family Foundation, 1994), pp. 1–36 at 14.

47. For more on the hookup culture on college campuses, see Glenn and Marquardt, *Hooking Up, Hanging Out.*

48. Dr. Drew Pinsky, personal interview, October 8, 2006.

49. Dr. Drew Pinsky, personal interview, September 13, 2006.

50. Sessions Stepp, "The Buddy System." See also Manning, Giordano, and Longmore, "Hooking Up." Interestingly, statistical tests indicated that boys and girls reported at similar rates that they expected their sexual relationship to transfer into a dating relationship; however, the more open-ended relational histories conducted by the researchers found that girls were seeking relationships more than boys were. Ibid., at 474. Could this have been because girls provided the "right" feminist responses to more structured questions, and a less rigid format was more successful in eliciting their true feelings?

51. Dr. Drew Pinsky, personal interview, October 8, 2006.

52. Ian Kerner, *Be Honest—You're Not That into Him Either: Raise Your Standards and Reach for the Love You Deserve* (New York: Harper-Collins, 2005), at 37.

53. James Meikle, "Good Sex Really Is Mind-Blowing for Women," *Guardian,* June 21, 2005, accessed at www.guardian.co.uk/life/science/story/0,12996,1510817,00.html.

54. Kerner, *Be Honest—You're Not That into Him Either,* at 37.

55. Rhoads, *Taking Sex Differences Seriously,* at 51.

56. Ibid.

57. Dr. Drew Pinsky, personal interview, October 8, 2006.

58. See Sessions Stepp, "Nothing to Wear."

59. Sessions Stepp, "The Buddy System."

60. Sarah E. Hinlicky, "Subversive Virginity," *First Things* 88 (1998), pp. 14–16.

61. Marina Vataj, "Your Lays Are Numbered," *New York Post,* October 24, 2006.

62. Personal conversation, August 12, 2006.

63. Leon Kass, "The End of Courtship," *The Public Interest* 126 (1997), pp. 39–63.

64. Kerner, *Be Honest—You're Not That into Him Either,* at 31.

65. Melissa Healy, "Intimate Makeover," *Los Angeles Times,* March 13, 2006.

CHAPTER 10: FROM LIBERTY TO LICENTIOUSNESS

1. *Lawrence v. Texas,* 539 US 558, 574 (2003) (quoting *Planned Parenthood of Southeastern Pennsylvania v. Casey,* 505 US 833, 851 [1992]).

2. An observation attributed to philosopher Leo Strauss notes that "[t]he mystery of Western thought is how a term that originally meant the manliness of a man [virtue] came to mean the chastity of a woman." "Virtue," Wikipedia, accessed January 23, 2007 at http://en.wikipedia.org/wiki/Virtue.

3. Personal interview, Dr. Thomas Lickona, October 19, 2006.

4. This point was originally made by Professor Thomas West in a lecture to the Claremont Institute's Lincoln Fellows on August 12, 2006.

5. "The 411: Teens & Sex," Katie Couric, NBC *Today Show,* January 31, 2005, accessed at www.msnbc.msn.com/id/6872269.

6. Mark Morford, "My Totally Gay Boy Scout Leader," *San Francisco Chronicle,* May 11, 2005, accessed at www.sfgate.com/cgi-bin/article.cgi?file=/gate/archive/2005/05/11/notes051105.DTL.

7. Thomas G. West, *Vindicating the Founders* (Lanham, MD: Rowman & Littlefield, 1997), at 99–100.

8. *Board of Education of Kiryas Joel Village School v. Grumet,* 512 US 687, 703 (1994).

9. Editorial, "Multiple-Choice God," *Los Angeles Times,* September 17, 2006.

10. In contrast to the Founders, however, they view public religiosity as a threat, rather than as an aid, to maintaining a truly free society.

11. Associated Press, "U.S. Advises Parents to Preach Abstinence:

ACLU Accuses Web Site of Dictating Values," *Arizona Daily Star,* April 1, 2005.

12. Rod Dreher, Crunchy Cons blog, *National Review Online,* March 22, 2006.

13. Jeff Sharlet, "The Young & the Sexless," *Rolling Stone,* June 2005, accessed at www.rollingstone.com/news/story/7418688/the_young_the_sexless.

14. Jeff Sharlet, "Genuinely Innovative, Assuredly Radical," *The Revealer,* June 30, 2005, accessed at www.therevealer.org/archives/timely _002012.php.

15. *The West Wing:* The Midterms (NBC television broadcast, October 18, 2000).

16. Personal interview, March 16, 2006.

17. Susan Phinney, "An Issue of Rights and Thongs for Today's Teens," *Seattle Post-Intelligencer,* May 13, 2002.

18. Kate Brian, *The Virginity Club* (New York: Simon Pulse, 2004), at 295.

19. Ibid., at 296.

20. "The 411: Teens & Sex, Part 3: Choosing Abstinence," Katie Couric, NBC *Today Show,* January 31, 2005, accessed at www.msnbc.msn .com/id/6872486.

21. Carina Chocano, "Sitting in Judgment of Those Who Judge," *Los Angeles Times,* September 1, 2006.

22. Frank Rich, "The Plot Against Sex in America," *New York Times,* December 12, 2004.

23. Kay Hymowitz, "Parenting: The Lost Art," *American Educator,* spring 2001.

24. ABC 7 News, "Police: 'Cool Mom' Hosts Teen Parties with Alcohol, Sex," TheDenverChannel.com, January 20, 2005, accessed at www .thedenverchannel.com/news/4111231/detail.html.

25. Patricia Dalton, "What's Wrong with This Outfit, Mom?" *Washington Post,* November 20, 2005; see also CBC Marketplace, "Interview with an Expert: Shari Graydon on the Sexing Up of Pre-teens," January 9, 2005, accessed at www.cbc.ca/consumers/market/files/money/sexy/ graydon.html.

26. Freak dancing involves boys dancing behind female partners, grinding their hips against the girls' backsides as the girls gyrate against them.

27. Anne Jarrell, "The Face of Teenage Sex Grows Younger," *New York Times,* April 2, 2000.

28. Anna Bahney, "High School Heroes: Mom and Dad," *New York Times,* May 16, 2004.

29. See Blum, R.W., *Mothers' Influence on Teen Sex: Connections That Promote Postponing Sexual Intercourse* (Minneapolis: University of Minnesota Center for Adolescent Health and Development, 2002), at 11. ("[P]revious research has suggested that the influence of mothers outweighs that of fathers as it relates to the sexual behavior of their teenage sons and daughters.")

30. For more, read Kay Hymowitz, *Ready or Not: What Happens When We Treat Children as Small Adults* (San Francisco: Encounter Books, 2000).

31. "The Lost Children of Rockdale County," produced by Rachel Dretzin Goodman and Barak Goodman, PBS *Frontline,* October 19, 1999.

32. Ibid.

CHAPTER 11: STEMMING THE TIDE

1. *US Teenage Pregnancy Statistics: National and State Trends and Trends by Race and Ethnicity* (New York: Guttmacher Institute, 2006), at 2, accessed at http://guttmacher.org/pubs/2006/09/12/USTPstats.pdf.

2. Centers for Disease Control, *Births: Final Data for 2004,* National Vital Statistics Reports 55, No. 1 (2006), at 6, accessed at www.cdc.gov/nchs/data/nvsr/nvsr55/nvsr55_01.pdf. Rates for teens aged fifteen through seventeen between 1991 and 2004 fell a respectable 43 percent. Ibid.

3. Hal Marcovitz, *Teens & Sex, The Gallup Youth Survey: Major Issues and Trends* (Broomall, PA: Mason Crest, 2004), at 39–40.

4. Santelli, J.S., Abma, J., Ventura, S., Lindberg, L., Morrow, B., Anderson, J.E., Lyss, S., and Hamilton, B.E., "Can Changes in Sexual Behaviors Among High School Students Explain the Decline in Teen Pregnancy Rates in the 1990's?" *Journal of Adolescent Health* 32, No. 2 (2004), pp. 133–134 at 134.

5. Albert, B., *With One Voice 2004: America's Adults and Teens Sound Off About Teen Pregnancy, An Annual National Survey* (Washington, DC: National Campaign to Prevent Teen Pregnancy, 2004), at 8.

6. Ibid., at 5.

7. Kay Hymowitz, "It's Morning After in America," *City Journal,* spring 2004, accessed at www.city-journal.org/html/14_2_its_morning.html.

8. David Brooks, "Public Hedonism and Private Restraint," *New York Times,* April 17, 2005.

9. Bearman, P.S., and Bruckner, H., "Promising the Future: Virginity Pledges and First Intercourse," *American Journal of Sociology* 106, No. 4 (2001), pp. 859–912 at 900.

10. Kralewski, J., and Stevens-Simon, C., "Does Mothering a Doll Change Teens' Thoughts About Pregnancy?" *Pediatrics* 105, No. 3 (2000), pp. 1–5.

11. There is, in fact, some evidence that a risk-based approach may not be all that effective. See Rostosky, S.S., Regnerus, M.D., and Wright, M.L.C., "Coital Debut: The Role of Religiosity and Sex Attitudes in the Add Health Survey," *Journal of Sex Research* 40, No. 4 (2003), pp. 358–367 at 365. ("Fears of the negative consequences of pregnancy or sexually transmitted diseases did not significantly reduce the likelihood of coital debut for either boys or girls in this sample.")

12. Hoff, T., Greene, L., and Davis, J., *National Survey of Adolescents and Young Adults: Sexual Health Knowledge, Attitudes and Experiences* (Menlo Park, CA: Kaiser Family Foundation, 2003), at 16. Fully 17 percent of girls and 20 percent of boys aged fifteen through seventeen aren't aware that STDs are a possible consequence of oral sex. Ibid.

13. In fact, more girls—38 percent—say they're not having sex because it's against their religion or morals than report they're abstaining to avoid pregnancy or an STD (26 percent). Child Trends, *Facts at a Glance,* Publication 2005-02, March 2005, accessed at www.childtrends.org/Files/Facts _2005.pdf (citing 2002 National Survey for Family Growth).

14. Commission on Children at Risk, *Hardwired to Connect: The New Scientific Case for Authoritative Communities: Executive Summary* (2003), accessed at www.americanvalues.org/pdfs/hwexsumm.pdf.

15. Personal interview, October 19, 2006.

16. Personal interview, October 19, 2006.

17. Robert Lerner, "Can Abstinence Work? An Analysis of the Best Friends Program," *Adolescent and Family Health* 3, No. 4 (2004), pp. 185–192.

18. Personal interview, October 19, 2006.

CHAPTER 12: PROUDLY, A PRUDE

1. Sarah E. Hinlicky, "Subversive Virginity," *First Things* 88 (1998).

2. Rector, R.E., Pardue, M.G., and Martin, S., "What Do Parents Want Taught in Sex Education Programs?" *Heritage Foundation Backgrounder* 1722 (January 28, 2004) (citing Zogby International Poll, 2004, of a representative national sample of parents with children seventeen or younger).

3. In fact, 96 percent of parents with children seventeen or younger approve of their children being taught that abstinence from sexual activity is best for teens. Ibid.

4. Gardiner Harris, "Panel Unanimously Recommends Cervical Cancer Vaccine for Girls 11 and Up," *New York Times,* June 30, 2006.

5. Associated Press, "Parents Protest H.S. Sex Newspaper," March 31, 2007.

6. See, for instance, Michelle Malkin, "Standing Up to the 'Girls Gone Wild' Culture," speech to the Clare Booth Luce Institute's Conservative Leadership Seminar, July 26, 2004, accessed at www.michellemalkin.com/archives/000292.htm.

7. Fischer, P.M., Schwartz, M.P., Richards, J.W., Jr., Goldstein, A.O., and Rojas, T.H., "Brand Logo Recognition by Children Aged 3 to 6 Years: Mickey Mouse and Old Joe the Camel," *Journal of the American Medical Association* 266, No. 22 (1991), pp. 3145–3148.

8. Meg Meeker, *Epidemic: How Teen Sex Is Killing Our Kids* (Washington, DC: Regnery, 2002), at 13.

9. Olivia Mascheroni, "Let's Talk About Sex (And Love, If We Have Time), *Phillipian,* June 4, 2006.

10. Deborah M. Roffman, "What Does 'Boys Will Be Boys' Really Mean?" *Washington Post*, February 5, 2006.

11. Liberal Thinking, "Is Sex Intrinsically Good?" Daily Kos, May 26, 2006, accessed at www.dailykos.com/story/2006/5/27/0433/30648.

12. Carol Platt Liebau, "Separation of Sex and State," *Los Angeles Times,* December 11, 2005.

13. Liberal Thinking, "New Thoughts of Sex (with Poll)," Daily Kos, May 27, 2006, accessed at www.dailykos.com/story/2006/5/28/0242/66758.

14. See the extended discussion in the chapter on fashion.

15. BBC News, "Girl Power Goes Mainstream," January 17, 2002, accessed at http://news.bbc.co.uk/1/hi/uk/1765706.stm.

16. Karen Springen, "Gender Equality," *Newsweek,* April 27, 2006.

17. Associated Press, "More Teen Girls Trying Drugs Than Boys," February 10, 2006.

18. Caitlin Flanagan, "Are You There God? It's Me, Monica," *Atlantic Monthly,* January–February 2006.

19. Robert McElvaine, "'Hooking Up' Makes a Feminized World More Bound Than Ever by Men's Rules," *Los Angeles Times,* August 5, 2001.

20. A piece in the Virginia Tech student newspaper, authored by a

female student, actually mentioned that the comment *nice tits* could be used by men as a pickup line, and that some girls would take such an observation as a compliment. Ashley Puckett, "Winning Isn't Everything Unless You're Trying to Get Your Opponent in Bed," *Collegiate Times,* October 21, 2005, accessed at www.collegiatetimes .com/news/3/ARTICLE/5929/2005-10-21.html.

21. Joseph S. Nye, "The Power We Must Not Surrender," *New York Times,* January 3, 2000.

22. Scott Galupo, "US Pop Culture Seen as Plague," *Washington Times,* December 31, 2004.